Middle English Literature

Middle English Literature

A Cultural History

CHRISTOPHER CANNON

polity

First published in 2008 by Polity Press

Polity Press
65 Bridge Street
Cambridge CB2 1UR, UK

Polity Press
350 Main Street
Malden, MA 02148, USA

ISBN-13: 978-07456-2441-9
ISBN-13: 978-07456-2442-6 (pb)

A catalogue record for this book is available from the British Library.

Typeset in 11.25 on 13 pt Dante
by SNP Best-set Typesetter Ltd, Hong Kong
Printed and bound in Great Britain by MPG Books Ltd, Bodmin, Cornwall

For further information on Polity, visit our website: www.polity.co.uk

Contents

Illustrations

Abbreviations

EETS o. s.	Early English Text Society, Original Series
EETS e. s.	Early English Text Society, Extra Series
EETS s. s.	Early English Text Society, Supplementary Series
ELH	*English Literary History*
MWME	*A Manual of the Writings in Middle English*, 11 vols [to date], ed. J. B. Severs (vols 1–2), Albert E. Hartung (vols 3–10), Peter G. Beidler (vol. 11), New Haven: Connecticut Academy of Arts and Sciences, 1967–.
MS	manuscript
MED	*The Middle English Dictionary*, ed. Hans Kurath et al., Ann Arbor: University of Michigan, 1954–.
OED	*The Oxford English Dictionary*, 2nd edn, 20 vols, ed. J. A. Simpson and E. S. C. Weiner, Oxford: Clarendon Press, 1989 [1st edn 1888–1933].

A Note on Texts and Quotations

Throughout I have replaced obsolete letters with their modern equivalents. *Thorn* (þ) is replaced with *th*, *yogh* (3) is rendered as *gh*, *g*, *y* or *z* as modern spelling dictates. The letters *i/j* and *u/v* are normalized. Ampersands have been changed to *and*.

I have provided full translations for early Middle English texts (which, unless otherwise indicated, are my own) and marginal glosses for difficult vocabulary and syntax in later texts.

Although my general preference is for the critical and standard edition of a Middle English text, where such an edition is difficult to obtain I have often turned to more widely available editions; where later texts still employ a difficult Middle English (as in the case, say, of the poems of the *Gawain*-poet) I have turned to an edition that normalizes spelling according to the conventions described above.

All quotations from *The Canterbury Tales* are from Geoffrey Chaucer, *The Canterbury Tales*, ed. Jill Mann, London: Penguin, 2005. All quotations from *Troilus and Criseyde* are from Geoffrey Chaucer, *Troilus and Criseyde*, ed. Barry Windeatt, London: Penguin, 2003. All quotations from other poems by Chaucer are from *The Riverside Chaucer*, gen. ed. Larry D. Benson, Boston: Houghton Mifflin, 1987. Unless otherwise indicated, all quotations from *Piers Plowman* are taken from William Langland, *The Vision of Piers Plowman: A Complete Edition of the B-text*, ed. A. V. C. Schmidt, 2nd edn, London: J. M. Dent, 1995 (first pubd 1978). All quotations from the C-text are taken from William Langland, *Piers Plowman: An Edition of the C-text*, ed. Derek Pearsall, London: Edward Arnold, 1978, and marked as 'C' in the text.

Acknowledgements

It was a great comfort to have the extraordinary literary histories by Derek Pearsall and James Simpson always to hand as I was writing this book, but I was even more fortunate, when I had nearly finished it, to find both of these fine scholars willing to read all that I had written and offer many improving suggestions. James was also instrumental in helping me craft a proposal for this volume many years ago. I owe Jill Mann an enormous debt for agreeing, as ever, to read my work in its penultimate form, as ever, too, catching errors both minute and major, often understanding what I was trying to say better than I had as yet understood it myself. I owe thanks too to the anonymous reader commissioned by Polity Press for saving me from a number of errors and challenging me to rethink key points. For help with historical details and bibliography I owe particular thanks to Richard Beadle and Miri Rubin. For the brilliance of their thought as well as the quality of their friendship I also thank Sarah Kay and Nicolette Zeeman. I have often had cause to be grateful to Sarah McNamer for the attention she is willing to give my work, but I am particularly in her debt for rescuing the introduction to this book from a variety of confusions. A term of sabbatical leave from the Faculty of English in Cambridge and Girton College combined with another term funded by the Arts and Humanities Research Council's Research Leave Scheme allowed me to finish this project. Colleagues in both institutions (particularly Helen Cooper, Barry Windeatt, Sinead Garrigan-Mattar and Deana Rankin) graciously spared me during this time, even though it meant more work for them. Throughout the writing of this I often felt guided by – and, therefore, immensely grateful to – those many generations of Girton women whose vision and learning ensured that the college library was so deeply provisioned; Frances Gandy, the current librarian, and her staff were also unfailing in their generosity in the face of my voluminous demands on this collection. I would also like to thank my fine editors at Polity Press, Lynn Dunlop (who commissioned this book), Sally-Ann Spencer (who was patient while I spent four years writing something else) and Andrea Drugan (who, with unparalleled efficiency, good humour and tact has shepherded my manuscript into print). I am very grateful, too, to Caroline Richmond, whose keen eye smoothed out so many of the book's rough edges. I can only hope that Anne Piehl, my *consigliere*, and Simon Gaunt, my soul mate to the stars, know just how much and how often they have helped.

Introduction

The word 'culture' has extremely wide reference, and this history of Middle English literature relies on what are usually taken to be two very different definitions of the term. The first derives from the theories of Karl Marx (1818–83) and, in particular, his insistence that 'the economic structure of society' produced all other 'forms of social consciousness' and the 'intellectual life process in general'.[1] 'Culture' in this sense is all the 'legal, political, religious, aesthetic, or philosophic . . . forms' projected out of this economic foundation, so much 'superstructure', which, whatever importance may be attributed to it by individuals or society, is fully determined by – and only ever completely explained in terms of – this 'material' base.[2] The second theory of 'culture' I subscribe to in these pages seems the near inverse of this view, and it was articulated with particular clarity by a contemporary of Marx, the poet and critic Matthew Arnold (1822–88). For Arnold, 'culture' was not the product of an economic structure or even the whole of a society, but, rather, the creation of some unitary and magnificent 'individual' and his capacities of 'right reason'.[3] This 'culture' is neither basic nor material but, rather, the 'perfection' achieved by a truly unique person who, in his turn, has helped to perfect a larger world; it is 'an inward condition of the mind and spirit, not an outward set of circumstances' – to rephrase the view in Marxist terms – an element of the superstructure with sufficient productive power to alter the base.[4]

Since there is nothing obvious about how such diametrically opposed definitions may be either mutually illuminating or useful in a history of Middle English literature, I want to begin with a practical example that generates the necessary common ground. This example will also be useful for surveying some of the particular interpretative and methodological problems involved in relating literature to culture, however the latter term is defined. My text is a short love lyric by Chaucer, usually called *To Rosemounde* after the woman it addresses. It is a straightforward ballade (in eight-line stanzas, rhyming *ababbcbc*, of which the last line is a refrain), accomplished in every way, but perhaps most striking for the image of the lover with which its third stanza begins:

Nas never pyke* walwed* in galauntyne	*pike / rolled in, wrapped*
As I in love am walwed and ywounde,*	*wound up*
For which ful ofte I of myself devyne	
That I am trewe Tristam the secounde.	
My love may not refreyde* nor affounde,*	*grow cold / turn numb*
I brenne* ay in an amorous plesaunce.	*burn*
Do what you lyst,* I wyl your thral* be founde,	*you wish / servant*
Thogh ye to me ne do no daliaunce.	

(ll. 17–24)

The comparison of a lover to something as mundane and messy as a fish covered in sauce is imaginatively daring, but time has also rendered the image obscure, since few modern readers will know what Chaucer meant by 'galentyne'.[5] It is easy to find help in contemporaneous documents, however, and London, British Library, MS Harley 4016, a cookbook compiled around 1450, gives the following recipe for 'pike . . . in galentyne':

> Take browne brede, and stepe it in a quarte of vinegre, and a pece of wyne for a pike, and quarteren of pouder canell and drawe it thorgh a streynour skilfully thik, and cast it in a potte, and lete boyle; and cast there-to pouder peper, or ginger, or of clowes, and lete kele. And then take a pike, and seth him in good sauce, and take him up, and lete him kele a litul; and ley him in a boll for to cary him yn; and cast the sauce under him and above him, that he be al y-hidde in the sauce; and cary him whether ever thou wolt.[6]

> [*pece*: cup   *quarteren*: quart   *kele*: cool   *seth*: boil]

This would at first seem a happy association for the definition of 'culture' I cited from Marx, since it appears to return the poem at its most extravagantly literary (the point of its most unusual image) directly to its base: to place this recipe next to Chaucer's poem is to work back, along the chain of production, from one of the more striking poetic thoughts Chaucer ever had to the kind of food that would have inspired such thought because Chaucer ate it. Less happy for this association, however, is the date of this cookbook, since, at fifty years' remove, it cannot itself count as a witness to the methods of food production that inspired *To Rosemounde*. There is in fact a recipe for 'lampray in galentyne', very like the one I have just quoted for a 'pike', in a cookbook whose compilation almost certainly preceded *To Rosemounde*, the *Diversa Servicia* (c.1381).[7] And yet, even if this recipe makes it clear that the kind of 'galentyne' Chaucer imagines was certainly being produced by kitchens in his day, things remain untidy since the earliest evidence we have of the material practice in which we have sought to root Chaucer's image – that is, the saucing of a *pike* in a 'galentyne' – turns out to be that image. We could say that such untidiness is no more than a side-effect of the impoverished record of culinary practice in fourteenth-century England, but we must then also recognize that surviving recipes are part and parcel of that poverty, texts designed to guide preparation rather than descriptions of actual practice, no matter how faithfully followed at least one level removed from actual cooking in a kitchen. In fact, what the association of *To Rosemounde* and these cookbooks shows best of all is that literature is not only as close to the base as any recipe, but, for that very reason, there is no reason whatsoever that literature could not guide cooking practice – that someone accustomed to saucing only 'lampray in galentyne', as suggested in the *Diversa Servicia*, might wish to sauce a 'pike' in a 'galentyne' because he or she had read *To Rosemounde*.

The importance of such untidy relationships was in fact quickly evident to Marx himself and, not long after he made the stark distinction between superstructure and base that I quoted above, he recognized that ideas and imagination were necessarily a part of material production ('At the end of every labour process, a result emerges which had already been conceived by the worker at the beginning, hence had already existed ideally').[8] Marxist thinkers particularly concerned with literature have further troubled this distinction by noticing that language is fundamental to both superstructure and base, for it is, at once, the vehicle for all ideas and a form 'conditioned . . . by the social organization of the participants involved and . . . the immediate conditions of their interaction'.[9] It is therefore also a Marxist view that ideology 'may not be divorced from . . . material reality'.[10] This is also true, as Louis Althusser explained, because ideology, or the 'representation of the imaginary relationship of individuals to their real conditions of existence',[11] necessarily resides in concrete 'practices' and 'rituals', in the institutions, or, as he termed them, 'ideological apparatuses', such as the church, school, family, or laws which foster, preserve and inculcate such representations in the minds of individuals.[12] But, even as he explained this, Althusser also noted that the positing of superstructure and base was an important step in the description of their interpenetration, that the division of culture into 'levels' was, in fact, a 'great theoretical advantage' in Marxist analysis.[13] On the one hand, such division makes it possible to discern and describe the various ways that our abstract imaginings are *in fact* rooted in the real conditions of our existence (all those ways that the base does in fact produce the superstructure), while, on the other hand, such division also makes it possible to notice the way that our imaginings may alter concrete conditions (all of the ways that there is a 'reciprocal action of the superstructure' on the base).[14]

We may identify the superstructure and base of a culture, in other words, not only to keep these levels apart, but to describe their rich, uneven and constant intermixture *as* a culture. And if we begin again with the image of the 'pike in galentyne' in *To Rosemounde*, looking now not for the base that produced its imagery but, rather, for the variety of cultural transactions in which that image participated, what we quickly discover is not only the possibility that literary representation could have preceded certain techniques of cookery (as above), but the surprisingly literary form that medieval cookery sometimes took. This is particularly obvious in the menus that survive from this period,[15] where courses are often said to have concluded with a *sotelte* [subtlety], often further identified only by the name of an animal, 'aquila' [eagle], say, or a 'lebarde' [leopard].[16] To look at a variety of such descriptions is to realize that these were a kind of sculpture in which cooked food as well as the parts of animals discarded during cooking (feathers, skin or hair, say) were reassembled in the form of some animal not commonly eaten (a leopard or eagle, say), or simply reassembled to present what had now been cooked as if it were still alive. Where the figure was human, as such subtleties often were, dyed or painted sugar was used as the basic material,[17] and, as in the menu for the feast celebrating the installation of John Stafford as Archbishop of Canterbury in 1443, such figures were often presented as a kind of meaningful tableau:

> A sotelte. Seint Andrew, sitting on an hie Auter of a-state, with bemes of golde; afore him knelyng, the Bisshoppe in pontificalibus; his Croser kneling behinde him, coped.[18]
>
> [*hie*: high   *Auter*: altar   *a-state*: state   *pontificalibus*: bishop's ceremonial dress   *croser*: bearer of bishop's staff   *coped*: dressed ceremonially]

Because we know about them from menus, it is fair to assume that these figures were not only a part of actual meals, but that, in their less elaborate forms, they were eaten. And yet such figures are also well described as *allegorical*, since, as in such literature, they represent one thing by means of another. We might therefore wish to say that the *sotelte* is an instance in which medieval cookery borrows from the literary or visual arts, as if the poetic capacity to represent, say, a lover as a 'pike in galentyne' (in this sense a technique of the superstructure) had filtered down to kitchens. And yet, this very image must then count as an instance of reciprocity in such relationships, since, in the light of these *soteltes*, it is possible to see that a 'pike in galentyne' is also a figurative foodstuff, for it transforms a cooked pike, on a plate, into a fish once again 'swimming' about in liquid ('cast the sauce under him and above him, that he be al y-hidde in the sauce; and cary him whether ever thou wolt'). When Chaucer imagines himself as such a fish, also swimming about in this sauce, he is not only creating an image out of something he might have eaten, but adapting a kind of figuration *already* native to cookery to a particular poetic purpose.

A Marxist cultural history worthy of the name is therefore dedicated to the discovery and careful description of this sort of complex transaction, and, that being the case, it is also true that where such transactions involve movements in which the superstructure actually and verifiably alters the base (where, say, a poem can be shown to have really changed practice) the Arnoldian model of culture has emerged as the truth that *Marxist* analysis has discovered. Such a theoretical convergence and examples that prove it true have not featured very largely in cultural criticism of late, nor have they been much noticed in literary history on the whole, but they did once have a spokesman in Raymond Williams, whose largest contribution to the Marxist study of literature was probably the long-term insistence that human creativity necessarily played a key part in historical change. Williams sometimes made this point by discovering the Arnoldian claim in Marx's own writing, noticing, in particular, all of the times and all of the ways in which Marx's theories were predicated on the human capacity for (as Marx himself put it) 'creating something that has never yet existed'.[19] But Williams also insisted that Marxist cultural history necessarily described not only all those ways in which 'art reflects its society', but also all those ways in which 'art creates, by new perceptions and responses, elements which the society, as such, is not able to realize'.[20] Rather than identify 'base' or 'superstructure', Williams preferred to regard culture as a 'totality' comprised of activities and processes,[21] and, rather than attempting to establish the priority of 'political, economic, and "social" arrangements' over 'literature, art, science, and philosophy', he preferred to insist on the 'genuine parity' of these elements, seeking above all to describe the 'patterns' and 'relationships between these patterns', the 'unexpected identities and correspondences' as well as 'discontinuities' that assemble these disparate 'elements' that comprised 'a whole way of life'.[22]

A book focused on a literature, as this one is, can only hope to keep the complexity of this whole in mind, since so many of these processes, so much of the way of medieval life, extended far beyond the precincts of literary writing. But the structure of what follows is meant to give some emphasis to each one of the various relationships that may obtain between literature and a larger culture. Chapters 1 and 2 form a kind of balanced and oppositional pair, the first describing many of the ways in which Middle English literature was fundamentally shaped by techniques of material production or 'technology', the second offering as detailed an account as possible of all the ways in which Middle English literature was sufficiently 'insurgent' to have brought about real social or political change. Chapters 3 and 4 tread the middle ground between these two extremes, showing, first, in a chapter on 'statecraft', how the political and the literary can overlap and converge, and, second, in a chapter on 'place', how certain sorts of writing were embedded in social circumstances and institutions. The book concludes by describing the complex process by which Middle English literature actually pulled free from the 'jurisdiction' of other areas of culture, actively working to define itself as an autonomous practice, thereby giving us the notion of 'literature' that we still use today. Although chapter 5 describes this emergence rather than its consequences, sustained attention to this momentous change makes clear why Middle English writing must be one of the places we look if we wish to understand why cultural study of this kind is needed: for one of the more distinctive and lasting contributions of Middle English literature is the idea (as distinct from the reality) that 'art' is a separate and independent cultural sphere.

This book is not in itself revolutionary, and my highest aspiration has been to tell a different sort of story. My chapter titles represent the boldest departure from more traditional literary history, and I have hoped that these categories might themselves disrupt customary connections, while also allowing the less familiar works of Middle English literature to jostle the more familiar, and, in these new circumstances, to show the latter in a new light. Because I want this book to be useful to those who are also reading Middle English according to the traditional syllabus, however, I have used more standard terms as sub-titles within individual chapters. For this same reason, I have tried to cite what I take to be certain classics of scholarship in the field (criticism that, while old, offers insights that seem to me undimmed) while attempting, in so far as I was able, to cite and make use of the most innovative recent scholarship.

If this book does make a contribution to Middle English scholarship, I hope it will be to underscore the need for other, more thorough, revaluations of the literature of this period by way of demanding theories of culture. To my mind, such revaluations will go the furthest towards satisfying what Elizabeth Salter so memorably defined as the goal of any student of this period: 'we should . . . wish . . . to extend . . . rather than limit the number of medieval English poems which may be expected to interest and move us', and we may do this best by refusing to allow for any 'safe area', by actively resisting our own literary tastes 'as they have been shaped by post-Renaissance poetry', relying, instead, on our 'imaginative curiosity', always making a 'conscious effort . . . to widen more our reach'.[23] Many historical and analytical methods would count as such an effort, but I believe that cultural study is uniquely effective in the activity of such widening.

1

Technology

During a visit to the Gallery of Machines at the Great Exhibition of 1900 in Paris, the historian Henry Adams was alarmed by the quiet force of the dynamo that confronted him, its 'huge wheel, revolving within an arm's-length at some vertiginous speed, and barely murmuring'.[1] Although he was aware that the dynamo seemed so powerful because he could not understand it, the mystery of this 'silent and infinite force' (361) was not nearly so worrying to Adams as its novelty, that here was something that really defeated the historian's capacity to 'arrange sequences . . . of cause and effect' (362–3), a 'sudden irruption of forces totally new' (363). Turning for comfort to what he took to be a more explicable sort of force, Adams found himself equally struck in France by the quiet power of the Virgin Mary: in this omnipresent symbol, he felt, was an energy whose operations he could track but whose effects were no less impressive than those of the dynamo ('All the steam in the world could not, like the Virgin, build Chartres') (368). Although he did not press the point, Adams meant the stark contrast to express an overwhelming anxiety about the post-medieval world and its technological direction; he was worried that humankind had finally unleashed forces it could not control, that in the place of building in the name of human warmth and feeling, growth and accomplishment occurred at the behest of machines. And yet, a history of the Virgin that was less techno-phobic might have realized that there was no difference between the turning of a turbine that generates electricity and the lifting of heavy stones that make a cathedral, that the force Adams perceived in the dynamo and identified with the Virgin (those mechanical and architectural innovations which made cathedral-building possible) was, *mutatis mutandis*, also technological – a deployment of mechanical power that made building possible in so far as it magnified human strength and reach.[2]

Although the profusion of machines, and their increasing sophistication, in the last two centuries makes us think of our own period as the age of technology, the Middle Ages in the West can be described as 'the first industrial revolution', the place and moment in which machines were first put to wide and systematic use.[3] The stirrup, which greatly increased the power of mounted warriors, and the heavy plough with coulter, share and mould-board (the better to turn heavy earth), were brought into wide application in early eighth-century France.[4] At roughly the same period the horseshoe was introduced and a harness for a team of horses (vastly stronger than the oxen which had been used until that point), and the 'three-field system' of crop rotation (considerably more productive than simple autumn and winter plantings) transformed agricultural production (and increased yields by 50 per cent).[5] The Utrecht Psalter, produced near Rheims some time between 816 and 834, contains an illumination that shows the use of a mechanical crank (a device for transforming reciprocal motion – pedalling, pulling and pushing – into continuous rotary motion).[6] Evidence of a water-powered mill for the manufacture of cloth in 983 in Tuscany counts as the first use of water power for something other than grinding grain and involved the 'first useful application of the cam' (a notched or eccentrically shaped wheel which converts circular to alternating or intermittent motion).[7] At the end of the twelfth century windmills were coming into use in Normandy and England.[8] The spinning wheel appears in Germany in 1280.[9] There is a mechanical clock in Dunstable Priory in 1283.[10] The printing press employing moveable metal type is invented by Gutenberg in the 1440s and arrives in Britain in 1475.[11]

None of these transformative devices, however, can be classed as an invention of the medieval West. The heavy plough was already in limited use in the Po Valley of Italy in the first century AD;[12] windmills were simply an adaptation of the ancient technology of the watermill; the mechanical clock was long preceded by the water clock;[13] the cam was known in ancient Greece;[14] the stirrup was known in India in the second century AD,[15] the crank was in use in China in AD 31,[16] and books were being printed in China in the ninth century.[17] What in fact distinguished the European Middle Ages from the rest of the world was the eagerness with which it embraced devices and structures that had the capacity to bend natural forces to human use, and how, having happened upon such capacities, medieval culture elaborated itself by creating more and more opportunities for their widespread diffusion. A figure often cited in histories to prove this point, and certainly impressive enough in its own right, is that although the watermill was known in ancient times it is almost never referred to until 1086, when *Domesday Book* (the great survey of land and possessions commissioned by William the Conqueror) counts 5624 mills in some 3000 different English communities.[18]

The novelty that rendered the West so substantially different from the rest of the world, and which still accounts for the importance of technology in its culture, Lynn White has argued, is a particular, and defining, attitude toward human labour. Where the application of brute force had acquired extremely negative connotations in Greco-Roman antiquity, when much physical labour was performed by slaves, early medieval Christianity revalued such work – as, indeed, it revalued servitude – as a positive spiritual pursuit.[19] The transformation is well marked in the *Regula Monachorum* (*c.*530–40), the widely influential monastic rule written by Benedict of Nursia (d. 547), where manual labour is placed at the centre of piety and a fully Christian life ('Idleness is the enemy of the soul. The brethren, therefore, must be occupied at stated hours in manual labour' [Otiositas inimica est animae; et ideo certis temporibus occupari debent fratres in labore manuum]), and labour was also equated with the act of worship in the general category that included both, the *opus dei* ('work of God').[20] This valuation was given more systematic articulation by the Benedictine monk Theophilus, who, in the *De Diversis Artibus* (1122–3), claimed that all mechanical devices (from kilns to blast furnaces) and crafts of all kinds (from painting to glass-making) flowed from 'the power and the guidance of the Holy Spirit' [magisterio et auctoritate Spiritus sancti].[21] The notion that labour was a particularly Christian virtue is also captured neatly in a pictorial tradition that represents the virtue of temperance in a figure whose capacities for measurement and regulation are represented by the mechanical devices ranged round her: in an illustration of 1450 she is shown with a clock on her head, a bit and bridle in her mouth, holding eyeglasses and reins, with her feet resting on a windmill (fig. 1).[22] The aspirational nature of the machine in such a culture is best captured in a story about a Benedictine monk from the period just before 1066, told by William of Malmesbury (1080–1142) in his *Gesta Regum Anglorum*:

> [Æthelmær] was a good scholar, advanced in years by now, though in his first youth he had taken a terrible risk: by some art, I know not what, he had fixed wings to his hands and feet, hoping to fly like Daedalus, whose fable he took to be true. Catching the breeze from the top of a tower, he flew for the space of a stade and more; but with the violence of the wind and the eddies, and at the same time his consciousness of the temerity of his attempt, he faltered and fell, and ever thereafter he was an invalid and his legs were crippled. He himself used to give as a reason for his fall that he forgot to fit a tail on his hinder parts.
>
> [Is erat litteris. . . . bene imbutus, aeuo maturus, immanem audatiam prima iuuentute conatus: nam pennas manibus et pedibus haud scio qua

Fig. 1 Bodleian Library, University of Oxford, MS Laud 570, fol. 16r., showing Temperance, with a clock on her head, a bit and bridle in her teeth, reins in her right hand, eyeglasses in her left hand, resting her feet, which wear spurs, on a windmill. Reproduced by permission of the Bodleian Library, Oxford.

> innexuerat arte, ut Dedali more uolaret, fabulam pro uero amplexus, collectaque e summo turris aura spatio stadii et plus uolauit. Sed uenti et turbinis uiolentia, simul et temerarii facti conscientia, tremulus cecidit, perpetuo post haec debilis et crura effractus. Ipse ferebat causam ruinae quod caudam in posteriori parte oblitus fuerit.][23]

Æthelmær's 'art' has no direct relation to the more successful modern devices for mechanical flight, but even more visibly than for the Virgin and the dynamo, the continuity in hope and method is clear: non-human power is used to augment labour so that a person may wildly transcend his physical limitations.

This embrace of technology is not without its paradoxes, for what begins as a valuing of labour in religious life becomes, in the end, an embrace of a wide variety of labour-*saving* devices. And yet this makes the medieval Western embrace of technology an ideology entirely worthy of the name, ideas about that world that not only determined the way it was perceived, but which are themselves powerful enough to substitute themselves for (and therefore even conceal) the actions they promote and produce. We might also seek deeper material causes for particular technological innovations (the general pressures of population growth and settlement which led to the improvement of the plough, the particular necessities of warfare which made the stirrup so valuable for the military advantage it gave), but, in describing the machines themselves, we have gone far enough to understand the various ways that Middle English writing might be shaped by technology. For while it is too much to say that Middle English writing was a product of the ideology I have described, the kinds of writing we have, the subjects it treated, and, most of all, the quantity that has survived were all deeply affected by the Western fascination with technology.

Romance

It is, fittingly, the kind of writing we tend to call romance that would have been impossible were it not for the infatuation with technology that led medieval Western culture to embrace the stirrup. Such writing has been described as the 'self-portrayal of feudal knighthood with its mores and ideals', and technological innovation sits at the root of any such representation because it created the fundamental social role that was so portrayed (the mounted warrior, *chevalier* – from French *cheval* for horse – or knight).[24] Until recently 'feudalism' was understood to be a fairly rigid social and political system wholly organized around knighthood: certain favoured subjects of a king or overlord were given the right to farm and live on a particular tract of land in exchange for services rendered 'in respect' of that land, and the most important of these services were military, either defending or assisting in the campaigns undertaken by that king or overlord.[25] More recent scholarship has shown, however, that feudalism 'was a pretty fugitive affair', with enormous variation over time and, from very early on, the possibility that a feudal tenant might be 'allowed to pay' his overlord rather than to provide him with knight service.[26] It is also clear that the relationship between concrete or 'real' versions of feudalism and literature make it wrong, particularly early on, to describe the latter as a 'self-portrayal': in many cases it is clear that literary accounts of feudalism actually preceded the social structures they purport to describe.[27] On the other hand, the development of a sizeable body of literature in order to celebrate the activities of mounted combat was an important social change and is itself one consequence of the transformative power of the stirrup.

The stirrup also thoroughly revolutionized warfare because it made it possible for a rider to brace himself as he attacked, 'delivering the blow not with his muscles but with the combined weight of himself and his charging stallion'.[28] The diffusion of this technology took some time, and while the stirrup began to be used in France in the eighth century, the mounted, braced lance was not employed widely in combat until the eleventh century,[29] but it is in this period that a celebratory literature first began to emerge. One of the earliest such works is the French *Song of Roland*, a text that also plays a significant part in the cultural history of England since, as legend has it, one of the soldiers of William the Conqueror, Taillefer, sang the *Song* to inspire the Norman troops on the eve of their campaign against the English in 1066.[30] This poem's celebration of heroism and sacrifice in battle is an exemplary instance of the *chanson de geste*, and William's success at Hastings ensured that this poem became a part of English history (the oldest surviving manuscript of the *Roland* is Oxford, Bodleian Library, MS Digby 23), but it is also a text celebrating exactly the sort of mounted combat which produced that success ('Here is how a knight, armed and astride a good horse, ought to show his worth' [Itel valor deit aveir chevaler / Ki armes portet e en bon cheval set]),[31] for it is not too much to say that the Norman Conquest was made possible by the stirrup.[32] The records make clear that the Anglo-Saxons had the stirrup, and their soldiers certainly made use of horses: William of Jumièges writes that, when Harold Godwineson heard that William of Normandy had landed with a fighting force near Hastings in 1066, having 'gathered innumerable English forces' [contracta Anglorum innumera multitudine], he hastened to the coast by 'riding through the night' [tota nocte equitans].[33] But these facts are themselves a way of illustrating that technology is not so much a particular innovation as the willingness to exploit it, for when the Anglo-Saxons encountered the invading force of William the Conqueror, as the Bayeux Tapestry dramatically illustrates (fig. 2), they 'drew themselves up in very close order . . . abandoning the aid of horses' [protinus equorum ope relicta cuncti pedites constitere densius conglobati].[34]

This decision was certainly not the only factor in the defeat of the Anglo-Saxon force – Harold and his troops had just seen off a Norse invasion at Stamford Bridge in the North – but, even through its partisan attempt to emphasize the losses suffered on the Norman side, the *Anglo-Saxon*

Fig. 2 Bayeux Tapestry, showing Anglo-Saxon soldiers standing before William the Conqueror's mounted soldiers. Reproduced by permission of the City of Bayeux.

Chronicle makes clear that the mounted Norman force simply mowed down most of the Anglo-Saxon soldiers, including their leaders, right up to the king himself:

> Tha com Wyllelm eorl of Normandige into Pefnesea on scype Michaeles mæsse æfen . . . This wearth tha Harolde cynge gecydd, and he gaderade tha mycelne here, and com him togenes æt thære haran apuldran, and Wyllelm him com ongean on unwær ær his folc gefylced wære. Ac se kyng theah him swithe heardlice withfeaht mid tham mannum the him gelæsten woldon, and thær wearth micel wæl geslægen on ægthre healfe. Thære wearth ofslægen Harold kyng, and Leofwine eorl his brothor, and Gyrth eorl his brothor, and fela godra manna.
>
> [Then duke William sailed from Normandy into Pevensey, on the eve of Michaelmas . . . When king Harold was informed of this, he gathered together a great host, and came to oppose him at the grey apple-tree, and William came upon him unexpectedly before his army was set in order. Nevertheless the king fought against him most resolutely with those men who wished to stand by him, and there was great slaughter on both sides. King Harold was slain, and Leofwine, his brother, and earl Gurth, his brother, and many good men.][35]

Another consequence of this battle was the end of the kind of English writing that I have just quoted, a significant manifestation as well as record of the unusually rich vernacular culture in Anglo-Saxon England (on the

Continent, chronicles of this sort were almost always written in Latin): the Norman Conquest was so overwhelming and complete that the wholesale change in rulership resulted in a wholesale change in culture. In fact, William's all-conquering knights constituted the first wave of an entire French-speaking aristocracy which was systematically installed in England, not only as overlords of the land, but in all important positions of authority in the cathedrals and monasteries, the primary site of Anglo-Saxon learning. It was in these institutions that the various versions of the *Anglo-Saxon Chronicle* were written, and most of them simply break off just before or during (and, in one case, right in the middle of) their record for 1066.[36] The *Chronicle* kept at Worcester Cathedral (from which I have just quoted) continues until 1079 (an English bishop, Wulfstan, remained in Worcester until 1095),[37] and one version (now lost) was continued until at least 1121, at which point it was borrowed by the abbey at Peterborough (which seems to have lost its own copy in a catastrophic fire of 1116); Peterborough monks then continued this version of the *Chronicle* until 1154. This last sequence of events can be seen as a surprising local resilience in the face of a broader transformation, and it is also the story of how the nearly complete demise of Anglo-Saxon literary culture necessitated the rebirth of English writing in what were, at first, very fragile forms. In language, and very often in outlook, the entries in the *Peterborough Chronicle* for the years after 1121 can be understood as the birth of Middle English writing.[38]

The most important way in which this new writing bore the impress of the cultural changes brought about by the Norman Conquest was, however, in the central role it had in developing the ideology that came to govern knighthood, an 'ideal' in so far as it placed the knight at the centre of the whole social world, and a set of 'mores' or ethics as it everywhere equated the knight and his acts of military service with 'the good'. 'Romance' is the term usually given to the texts that most fully articulate this ideology, although the term itself is complicated because *roman*, the French word from which 'romance' is derived, was at first applied to long narratives of all kinds (and, consequently, for some time in English, to any such narrative originating in French).[39] Moreover, as I have already suggested, the idealization of knighthood was also a central function of the texts we still refer to as *chansons de geste*. A mechanical division can be made if one looks only to the verse form of such texts in French, since *chansons de geste* were written in *laisses* or 10-line strophes joined by assonance in their last syllable, while romances were written in octosyllabic, rhyming couplets. The distinction can also be avoided if we speak not of 'romances' and *chansons de geste*, but of 'chivalric literature', and include in the category all those poems that celebrate an aristocratic world in which mounted combat was socially determinate.[40] On the other hand, certain distinctions of subject and emphasis are also possible, since *chansons de geste* tend to focus on exemplary action (the *geste*) and to envision the mounted soldier as an embodiment of the qualities and destiny of large armies and peoples,[41] while romances tend to narrow their focus, projecting the identity of a whole class onto a particular individual, developing their ethics by way of that knight's successes and failures. *Chansons de geste* also tend to describe clashes of large massed force, while romances tend to reduce the social and political world to two combatants:[42]

> Ains que la joie fust remese,
> Vint, d'ire plus ardans que brese,
> Li chevaliers a si grant bruit
> Com s'i cachast un cherf du ruit.
> Et maintenant k'il s'entrevirent,
> S'entrevinrent et sanlant firent
> Qu'il s'entrehaïssent de mort.
> Chascuns ot lanche roide et fort,
> Si s'entredonnent mout grans cos,
> Qu'andeus les escus de lors cols
> Perchent et li hauberc deslichent;
> Lor lances froissent et esclicent,
> Et li tronchon volent en haut.

> [Before their joy had subsided the knight arrived, more blazing with rage than live coals, and making as great a din as if he were hunting a rutting stag. And the moment they saw each other they rushed together, both seemingly full of mortal hatred. They each had a stout, strong lance; and they exchange such hard blows that both of the shields at their necks are pierced, the hauberks are rent, the lances shatter and shiver, and the splinters from them fly aloft.][43]

This passage is taken from Chrétien de Troyes's *Yvain*, or 'The Knight with the Lion' (*c*.1177), and this and the clutch of other romances written by Chrétien are both influential and exemplary in the emergence of this particular literary mode. At stake, in this battle, between Yvain and (as we later learn) Esclados is no more really than the 'shame' (honte, l. 587) which accrued to Yvain's cousin Calogrenant when he was defeated by this knight on an earlier occasion. *Yvain* also makes clear how the narrowing of focus from armies to individuals tends to bring with it an emphasis on 'love' (romance in the modern sense, 'the private relationship par excellence between two human beings').[44] Such love tends not only to follow from combat (as the successful knight's reward), but to draw its consequences back into the private sphere (rather than conquering kingdoms, a knight in romance conquers hearts). Thus, when Yvain succeeds in this combat, he finds himself 'in love' with Laudine, the 'lady' of the late Esclados. In the private sphere also, Yvain's success in wooing Laudine, as well as a variety of other ladies, yields further proof of his particular excellence *as* a 'knight', that he is – within the particular grid of others this romance sets him against – the 'more worthy' (miex vaille, l. 1696).

Chronology is also complicated in describing the emergence of romance in English, not least because that emergence occurs after the Norman Conquest, when England was increasingly a part of French literary culture: in the century when Chrétien was active, much of England's literature was written in French (or Anglo-Norman, as this dialect is usually termed), and the central matter of a great deal of this romance concerned the legends of the 'British' king Arthur and his knights (including Yvain). Matters are further complicated by the generic progress of this material in England. It first appears at the heart of Geoffrey of Monmouth's *Historia Regum Britanniae* (*c.*1138), a fiction whose wit lies partly in its very form which adopts the Latin prose customary in chronicles, and silts historical, or near-historical, kings and events in among a great variety of invented incident. Geoffrey's narrative then passes quickly into an Anglo-Norman translation that employs the octosyllabic couplets that were the common form of romance (this is Wace's *Roman de Brut* [*c.*1155]). Arthur and his story first appear in English in the *Brut* (*c.*1200) of Laȝamon, where heroic action is routinely set in the context of a group identity and dynastic politics, and, as in *chanson de geste*, the key issue is not individual action but the conquest of peoples:

> Arthur igrap his sweord riht   and he smat aenne Sexise cniht
> That that sweord that wes swa god   aet than tothen atstod.
> And he smat enne other   that wes thas cnihtes brother,
> That his halm and his haefd   halden to grunde.
> Thene thridde dunt he sone yaf   and enne cniht atwa claef.
> Tha weoren Bruttes   swithe ibalded,
> And leiden o than Saexen   laeyen swithe stronge
> Mid heore speren longe   and mid sweoreden swithe stronge
> Sexes ther uullen   and faeie-sih makeden,
> Bi hundred bi hundred   haelden to than grunde;
> Bi thusund and bi thusend   ther feollen aevere in thene grund.

[Arthur grasped his sword firmly and struck a Saxon warrior so that the sword, an excellent one, lodged in the teeth. And he struck another who was the warrior's brother, so that his helmet and his head fell to the ground. Instantly he delivered a third blow and cut a warrior in half. Then the Britons were greatly heartened, and inflicted very fierce strokes upon the Saxons with their long spears and their stout swords. Saxons fell there, met their doom, sank in their hundreds to the ground; thousands upon thousands without cease fell to earth there.][45]

Matters are further complicated in Lagamon's case because he chooses to celebrate the British victory over a Saxon enemy in an alliterative metre that recalls the style generally employed by Anglo-Saxon poets. But this sequence of changes is itself a measure of just how many sorts of literary strategies, techniques and styles may be used to think through the same sort of social life (and the above evidence is itself a way of showing that romance and *chanson de geste* – and even chronicle – may be understood as 'alternative narratives' for one another, each mode called into being by aspects of chivalry the other leaves out).[46]

The blow dealt to English writing in general by the Norman Conquest is, again, a factor in the uneven diffusion of genre, and while Lagamon follows the standard pattern for cultural exchange ('virtually every Anglo-Norman romance had a Middle English descendent'),[47] his translation is early in the process, and the birth of romance in English has to wait for another century (an English translation of *Yvain* did not come until 1325–50).[48] The first English text that we might wish to categorize as a romance is *King Horn* (*c.*1240), but because the verse form of this text, as well as of many of the other earliest English romances, is so irregular (often more reliably consistent in the number of stresses than the number of syllables per line), the new category of 'popular romance' is often created for it and other early productions, usually thought to have been corrupted by the oral delivery for which they were designed, and the casual recording that was, for that same reason, their lot. Such popularity for writings about the exploits of an aristocratic class is itself strong evidence for a dramatic change in social norms, a manifestation of the improved 'standard of living' throughout Europe in the later Middle Ages, the spreading of the surplus made possible by those technologies of husbandry I have described, and the burgeoning of a middle class of 'skilled artisans and merchants' with the interest and leisure time to care about such idealizations.[49] As *King Horn* makes abundantly clear, neither an increased distance from the place and time in which romance first arose nor these changed patterns of reception and dissemination had any effect whatsoever on the rarefied world *of* romance, where there is only ever (really) one class, and hardly ever an event worth mentioning that does not take place among the aristocracy:

> The king com into halle
> Among his knightes alle.
> Forth he clupede* Athelbrus,   *called*

That was stiward of his hus.*	house
. . .	
'Horn thu underfonge*	take charge of
And tech him of harpe and songe'.	
Athelbrus gan lere*	teach
Horn and his y-fere.*	companions
Horn in herte laghte*	comprehended
All that he him taghte.	
In the curt* and ute	court
And elles all abute.[50]	

Particularly when compared to the kinds of actions in Lagamon in which a 'king' might engage, such a scene is also useful for showing how, in romance, chivalry appeared less as a mode of warfare and more as a governing ethics, a system (though never a 'code', for it is only in parody that anyone ever tries to set out the subtle and endlessly negotiated norms of chivalric life) often described as 'courtesy' or 'courtliness' (courtoisie in French texts), or sometimes simply 'knighthood' or 'worship' in English,[51] a sense, almost always both delicate and complex, that certain sorts of behaviour are appropriate in court and others are not. Romance can often be said to be 'about' this ethic, and in this sense even a text written in the thirteenth century, such as King Horn, is a kind of meditation on the place such an ethic defined, what is here (as generally) called 'the curt'. Such a court – in structure an especially lavish and elaborated household (or, as here, 'hus') – was also made possible by the technologies used to exploit a horse's strength, but in this case it was not the stirrup but the 'wide application of the heavy plough' and the development of the harness (which allowed horses to pull such ploughs).[52] Each of these developments occurs first in the eighth century, but diffusion is again surprisingly slow, and it was not until William the Conqueror brought it that the horse-drawn plough was known in England, and it was only at the end of the twelfth century that the technology was widespread here.[53] When added to the three-field system of crop rotation, these new methods of husbandry produced an ever-increasing surplus and wealth,[54] most quietly visible in this passage of Horn as Athelbrus has gathered round him a band of loyal followers ('his knights'), which, along with an administrative machinery that bespeaks its size ('a stiward'), constitutes the household as a kind of institution.[55] There is no single origin for the ethic associated with such a house, but it is clear from the insistent balance of warfare and good manners between warriors that one of the crucial functions of the ideology celebrated in such texts (if not, often, of those texts themselves) was to redirect the energies of a class of persons each capable of killing one another toward thoughts and endeavours which would give their life together some order.[56] The process of sublimation involved (the rendering of hard social facts as an admirable beauty) is also neatly on view in this passage from *Horn* – which in this sense is almost an allegory of the rise of the genre of romance – as Horn and his 'y-fere' [knights one and all] come into this court and every possible martial activity is converted to 'songe'.

This scene in *Horn* also shows how the ideology of romance delicately shadowed the kinds of expansion that its technological and social bases made possible, for, where more heroic versions of conquest (such as that by Lagamon) might not only stage confrontations between enemy hosts but were also deeply interested in the disasters that might ensue (as Lagamon says, 'thus is this eitlond igon from honde to hond' [thus is this island passed from hand to hand], l. 1033), romance almost always concerns itself with various kinds of social absorption, often by representing its ethics as so compelling that anyone who confronts the court inevitably becomes a part of it. This is markedly true of the next surviving Middle English romance, *Floris and Blancheflour* (c.1250), where an Emir who is prepared to put Floris to death melts when he is told of the 'grete love' (1047) that led Floris to search for Blancheflour.[57] The basic manoeuvre appears in a more standard form in *Havelok the Dane* (c.1280), the other thirteenth-century English romance that survives:

> The Englishe men bigunne falle
> O knees and greten* swithe sore*   *wept / bitterly*
> And saiden, . . .
> . . .   'We haven misdo* mikel*   *done wrong / greatly*
> That* we again you have be fikel,*   *in that / disloyal*
> For Englond aughte forto been
> Youres and we youre men'.
>
> . . .
>
> Quoth Havelok, 'Whan* that ye it wite,*   *since / know*
> Nu* wile* ich that ye doune sitte'.[58]   *now / want*

As Fredric Jameson has emphasized, the link between these texts and what we know of the cultures from which they arose is well described as 'unconscious' since, without much altering the political scenery and bases from which it emerged, romance provides an 'imaginary resolution' to the problem of the implacable 'enemy', a process repeatedly realized in romance – almost *as* romance – in which 'the antagonist ceases to be a villain' and 'becomes one more knight among others'.[59]

The moment in which such thinking can be said to have definitively passed into English is hard to mark, since our early evidence is so frail, but one solid object that marks the epoch is Edinburgh, National Library of

Scotland, MS 19.2.1, the 'Auchinleck' manuscript, compiled *c.*1330–40 and
containing among its forty-four texts a kind of conspectus of the important kinds of English poetry at that moment (saint's life, religious debate,
a chronicle, and poems of religious instruction), and, along with these,
eighteen romances, which in their very number, as well as their achieved
variety, measure the consequence of the genre in English at this point.[60] In
addition to *Floris and Blancheflour* and *Horn Child* (*c.*1330), a version of the
Horn story, this volume contains tales of knightly exploits and conquest in
the East (*Kyng Alisaunder* [*c.*1300], *Richard Coeur de Lion* [*c.*1300]), pseudo-
histories of knights native to some region of England (*Guy of Warwick*
[*c.*1300] and *Bevis of Hampton* [*c.*1300]), magical stories of redemption and
transformation (*Sir Orfeo* [*c.*1330] and *Lay le Freine* [*c.*1330]), another version
of the story of Arthur (*Arthur and Merlin* [*c.*1300]), and an English version of
the Tristan legend (*Tristrem* [*c.*1300]). It also offers helpful documentation
of the central role romance was to play in Middle English literature as such,
for while it is probably not true that Geoffrey Chaucer held the Auchinleck
manuscript 'in his hands',[61] as was once claimed, Chaucer certainly read
something like this collection of texts, as he makes clear in his Tale of Sir
Thopas (1392–5), where he names many of them:

> Men speken of romances of pris,*   *excellent*
> Of Horn child and of Ipotis,
>   Of Beves and Sire Gy,
> Of Sire Libeaux and Pleindamour
> But Sire Thopas, he bereth the flour*   *is the best*
>   Of real* chivalry!   *regal, kingly*
>
>   (VII. 897–902)

Sir Thopas is one of two tales set within the larger fiction of *The Canter-*
bury Tales assigned to the narrator of the whole of the *Tales* (the other is
The Tale of Melibee).[62] It is less a romance than a burlesque of romance
style, a conglomeration of all the clichés and stylistic excesses to which the
genre had grown prone, here in particular, a carelessness in descriptive
detail (Thopas, for example, lacks both sword and spurs) as well as metre
(especially in the tendency for the last line of the tail-rhyme stanza – two
four-stress lines followed by a three-stress line rhyming *aabccb* – 'to drop
off from the main stanza like a mortified limb').[63] The whole of the poem
is therefore a delicious joke presenting 'Chaucer' as the one Canterbury
pilgrim incapable of telling a tale, but it has also been described as ungrate-
ful in its mockery, since the 'plain and easy verse style in romance narrative'
formed the 'tap-root of Chaucer's poetry' (as one critic put it, Sir Thopas
'has the effect not just of biting the hand that fed but of snapping it off at
the wrist').[64] There is, to be sure, a certain affection in the very exuberance

of the send-up (which itself quietly acknowledges a deep familiarity), and the stanza I have just quoted still offers a surprisingly full documentation of Chaucer's reading in romance (*Horn Child*, *Bevis of Hampton* and *Guy of Warwick* are all extant romances). Romance was certainly a genre Chaucer took seriously elsewhere (although they each ring consequential changes on the genre, The Knight's Tale [*c.*1387], The Squire's Tale [*c.*1392–5], The Wife of Bath's Tale [1392–5], and The Franklin's Tale [1392–5] can all be so categorized), but perhaps the most concrete measure of its significance is the extent to which the language of romance (and, in particular, a newly elaborate vocabulary for describing the nuances and complexities of human feeling)[65] as well as its narrative techniques (in particular, the capacity to project a psychology and an ethics into dramatic events) were spreading into Middle English writing of all kinds. This is particularly clear in Chaucer's earliest poems, especially the *Book of the Duchess* (1369), where this language and these techniques are deployed in the even more inward genre of dream vision. But perhaps the best evidence of this generality is offered by John Gower's *Confessio Amantis* (*c.*1390–3), for this monumental allegory, structured by the Seven Deadly Sins (each of which is accorded a book), and unfolding as a lengthy version of the sacrament of confession, generally envisions the 'pointz of schrifte' [confession],[66] not only in those octosyllabic couplets that romance normalized as a part of English verse, but in the most resolutely chivalric terms:

> And thus ful many a worthi knyht
> And many a lusti* lady bothe   *pleasing, fine*
> Have be fulofte* sythe* wrothe.   *very many / times*
> So that an yhe* is as a thief   *eye*
> To love, and doth ful* gret meschief;   *very*
> And also for his oghne* part   *own*
> Fulofte thilke* firy Dart   *this very*
> Of love, which that evere brenneth,
> Thurgh him into the herte renneth.
>   (1.316–24)

As it happens, the confessor in this poem is himself just such a 'worthy knight'. Amans, as his name implies, is a man preparing himself spiritually 'to love', and if the 'firy darts' in this confessional frame, as in many of the exemplary narratives that fill it, tend to draw more on the ethical than on the martial aspects of chivalric literature, the *Confessio Amantis* is a poem that, in just the manner of such imagery, *relies* on the defining techniques of Middle English romance even as it directs them toward entirely different purposes.[67]

At this high-water mark in its prospects, Middle English romance acquired an increasingly acute sense that the social system it idealized 'contained many inner contradictions which . . . made it unstable', and although, once detected, these contradictions can be seen in every romance, early and late, it is in this later moment that Middle English busies itself particularly with their exposure.[68] The contradiction follows from that absorption of the 'enemy' so basic to romance, which I described above, for the realization such absorption always makes possible is that the 'knight' who is the enemy is so characterized only because he is a 'mirror image' of the good knight, 'evil' only in so far as his conduct lies outside the court at that particular moment,[69] with the result that his very absorption to the court may serve as an acknowledgement that there is a certain 'evil' inside it. This observation is fundamental to *Sir Gawain and the Green Knight* (*c.*1390), a romance that also shows the general importance of this genre as it is absorbed to a newly burgeoning alliterative tradition.[70] It is possible to see Gawain's fault as small, an error in courtesy to his host, when he fails to honour his pledge to exchange all his daily winnings[71] after having received the 'girdel' (l. 1829) of 'grene sylke' (l. 1832) from his host's wife. It is also possible to overlook Gawain's moment of real cowardice for it comes so early and is so little emphasized: although he finally accepts the Green Knight's challenge, he is nevertheless a significant member of the whole of Arthur's court as it 'dares for drede' (cowers in fear, l. 315), and does nothing when the Green Knight first offers his challenge ('If he hem stowned upon fyrst [stunned them at first] stiller were thanne / Alle the heredmen [courtiers] in halle, the hygh and the lowe, ll. 301–2).[72] Nor is Gawain at all equivocal himself about this 'untruth' at the poem's end:

'Lo! lorde,' quoth the leude,* and the lace hondeled,*	*man* *took hold of*
'This is the bende* of this blame I bere in my nek,	*band*
This is the lathe* and the losse that I laght* have	*injury / suffered*
Of couardise and covetyse that I haf caght* thare;	*acquired*
This is the token* of untrawthe that I am tan* inne	*sign / taken*
And I mot nedez* hit were* wyle I may last;	*must / wear*
For mon may hyden his harme, but unhap* ne may hit*	*[cannot] unfasten* *it*
For ther* hit onez is tachched*	*wherever / fastened*
twynne* wil hit never'.	*go away*

(ll. 2505–12)

And when 'kyng' and 'alle the court . . . comfortes' (l. 2513) Gawain, there also follows a general acknowledgement of the extent to which Gawain's behaviour implicates the whole of the court, for Arthur insists that all of his knights should wear such a girdle because it 'was acorded [suited] the renoun of the Rounde Table' (l. 2519), as if one of the functions of this narrative is that the irremediable 'untrawthe' that has been discovered within Gawain must rightly be acknowledged as a fundamental fact discovered about the whole of Arthurian chivalry ('for . . . twynne wil hit never').

In time, therefore, romances served to critique chivalry's ethics as much as to celebrate it, and we might even imagine that this counted as an important part of their social function – a way of sufficiently demystifying an ideology for its contradictions and difficulties to come clear. *Sir Gawain* offers one of the more gentle critiques of this kind, but a much more bracing sort is found in those stories about the court of Arthur which focus on the sequence of disasters that unwind the ethics binding the court, as knight is set against knight, and the 'death of Arthur', or *Morte Arthur*, as these texts are usually called, becomes equivalent to civil war. The alliterative *Morte Arthur* (*c.*1400) draws on Wace and Lagamon, but it throws its energies so fully into the heroic and bloody side of this story ('There chaped [escaped] never no child [knight], cheftain ne other, / But choppes them down in the chase; it charges [matters] but little!')[73] that it is no longer comfortably described as a 'romance', although the story becomes so tragic in this instance only because of the intensity of its investigation of the problem the evil knight poses for chivalric societies.[74] In the version of the Arthurian story this figure is not only a knight of Arthur's court, but his nephew, Mordred, and the form his wickedness takes, when he is entrusted with the kingdom during Arthur's campaigns on the Continent, amounts to a kind of insistence that he *is* (or ought to be) Arthur:

'Sir, thy warden is wicked	and wild of his deedes,	
For he wandreth* has wrought	senn thou	*trouble*
away passed.		
He has castels encroched*	and crownd himselven,	*captured*
Caught in all the rentes*	of the Round Table	*revenue*
He devised* the rewm*	and delt as him likes.	*divided / realm*
. . .		
But yet a word witterly,*	thou wot* not the	*certainly / know*
worst!		
He has wedded Waynor	and her his wife holdes,	
And wonnes* in the wild boundes*	of the	*dwells / borders*
west marches,		
And has wrought her with child	as witness telles!	

(ll. 3523–7 and 3549–52)

Another version of the story, usually called the stanzaic *Morte Arthur* (*c*.1400) because it is written in four-stress lines, grouped in eight-line stanzas (rhyming *abababab*), represents a wholly different tradition: its main source is the French *La Mort le Roi Artu* (*c*.1230–5), which focuses on the adulterous relationship between Lancelot and Guenevere and describes how this one irregular intimacy throws almost every relationship in the court into question. The stanzaic *Morte Arthur* was itself a source and inspiration for Thomas Malory's prose *Morte Darthur* (1468–70), a compendious retelling of the whole Arthurian story which concludes with a particularly moving account of this destruction. Malory's touch is at times so light – often to be found in the way he adjusts the language or structure of the French sources on which he draws so heavily – that the vigour of his scepticism has often eluded criticism.[75] Certain passages do serve, however, to summarize both the tenor and the nature of his doubts about chivalric ethics, and perhaps the best of these is the threnody offered by Lancelot's brother Hector after Lancelot's death, a kind of prose poem on the theme of the knight whose very goodness, in chivalric terms, places him at odds with himself:

> A, Launcelot! . . . there thou lyest, that thou were never matched of erthely knyghtes hande. And thou were the curtest knyght that ever bare shelde! And thou were the truest frende to thy lovar that ever bestrade hors, and thou were the trewest lover, of a synful man, that ever loved woman, and thou were the kindest man that ever strake wyth swerde. And thou were the godelyest persone that ever cam emonge prees of knyghtes, and thou was the meekest man and the jentyllest that ever ete in halle emonge ladyes, and thou were the sternest knyght to thy mortal foo that ever put spere in the reeste.[76]
>
> [*curtest*: most courteous   *bestrade*: rode   *strake*: struck   *godelyest*: most handsome   *jentyllest*: most well-mannered]

It helps in reading this to know that the 'shelde' Launcelot most recently bore set him against his king, as indeed did the 'truth' he bore to his 'lovar' (who was, of course, that king's wife), and that he was 'good', lately, 'emonge prees of knyghtes' because he did not *mean* to kill the knight, Gareth, who loved him most in the world ('in very trouth sir Launcelot saw [him] nat', 684). But the point here and throughout this intense narrative is not that Launcelot is more wrong than Hector will admit, but that right and wrong are so fully entwined that Launcelot cannot, finally, escape calumny.[77] The delicate precision with which Malory registers the extent to which Arthur's court harbours the very evil it proposes to fight is most clear, however, in a famous sentence which describes how Mordred, already run through on Arthur's lance, delivers the fatal blow:

> And whan sir Mordred felte that he had hys dethys wounde he threste hymselff with the myght that he had upp to the burre of kyng Arthurs speare, and ryght so he smote hys fadir, kynge Arthure, with hys swerde holdynge in both hys hondys, uppon the syde of the hede, that the swerde perced the helmet and the tay of the brayne. (3: 1247)

[*burre*: ring   *tay*: outer membrane]

That a knight should kill his king is as nothing to the fact that a son should kill 'hys fadir', Malory notes, and, in gently recording the biological fact at precisely the moment when it is most transgressed, what Malory also makes clear is that the father (and all he stood for, in fact) begot the very calamity to which he has fallen victim.

As Mordred's wound would suggest, the stirrup and the horse occupy a crucial place in this critique of the ideology of chivalry, but in the fifteenth century the technological innovation that becomes of most importance to Middle English romance is paper. There was, again, nothing new about this substance at this moment: it was invented in China, known throughout Islam after 756, and manufactured in quantity as early as 1276 in Europe (in Italy).[78] It seems to have been known in England in the intervening centuries, but it was rare until about 1450, at which point at least 20 per cent of manuscripts employ it (rising to 50 per cent by the end of the century).[79] Since paper was much easier and much cheaper to produce than animal skin (or 'vellum'), the material used for book production up until this point, this move to paper responded to a considerable growth in literacy and leisure time. The shift to prose visible in Malory is another response to this widening, for it reflects a shift from writing, where court performance kept it in close touch with the related genre of song (as is evident in *Horn*), to private reading, where the interest of plot could take precedence over verbal show. Many verse romances of the fourteenth century also exist in fifteenth-century prose versions (an *Ipomedon* in tail-rhyme [*c.*1390] yields an *Ipomedon* in prose [*c.*1460], the Auchinleck *Arthur and Merlin* in octosyllabic couplets yields a prose *Merlin* [*c.*1450], and the events in the story of Horn are adapted as *King Ponthus and the Fair Sidone*),[80] and, as many of the verse romances I have already mentioned were also recopied alongside these new prose texts to meet the ever-increasing demand, the fifteenth century became the 'great age of *fourteenth-century* romance'.[81] In this period, when England had generally descended into civil war (in the constantly shifting affinities of lords and knights usually described as the 'Wars of the Roses'), a great number of the prose romances concerned themselves with chivalric disaster in the manner of the *Morte* (the *Siege of Troy* [*c*.1450], the *Siege of Thebes* [*c*.1450], the *Pseudo-Turpin Chronicle* [*c*.1450], the *Life of Alexander* [*c*.1430], *Valentine and Orson* [*c*.1502]).[82] Since the roots of romance involve a sublimation that can sweep all difficulties away, it is no surprise that this period also produced new romances of the most standard kind, poems (in this sense, stylistically anachronistic too) such as *Partonope of Blois* (*c*.1440), *Generydes* (*c*.1440), and *The Squyr of Lowe Degre* (*c*.1500) that celebrated chivalry whole-heartedly. In their broader cultural context such celebrations must seem to have 'an air of obsolescence' and 'nostalgia' about them, but in this they also testify to the resilience of romance's sublimations, its capacity, even in the face of the most concrete contradictions, to insist that chivalric life, courtliness and courtesy were achievable and unmitigated goods.[83]

Confession

Since writing is a physical production requiring mechanical devices (pen and ink or stylus and tablet) and systematic structural invention (the devising of alphabets and grammars), it too may be understood as a technology. Indeed, at its root, *techné* meant not only 'craft' but 'art', and *technology* was therefore a term that originally gathered together under a single heading all knowledge about the creation of objects from the stirrup to the poem.[84] It is in this broader sense that Michel Foucault coined the influential phrase 'technology of the self', although to understand this phrase we must also understand 'the self' as akin to an object, a body and the individualized shape it acquires through certain activities, a set of boundaries between that body and the larger world, as those boundaries are defined by certain ways of thinking. Given what I have so far said about such writing, romance certainly participated in such definitions,[85] but, for Foucault, romance was only one part of a much larger process in all of the Christian West whereby 'taking care of oneself became linked to constant writing activity'.[86] The watershed for such activity was the 'writing' [has litteras] in which Augustine (d. 430) made his 'confessions' [confessiones], so that 'those who know me and those who do not' [qui me noverunt, et non me noverunt] might 'learn about' his 'inner self' [volunt ergo audire . . . quid ipse intus sim], where 'they cannot penetrate with eye or ear or mind' [quo nec oculum nec aurem nec mentem, possunt intendere].[87] Such a self is ephemeral by definition, but it also comes into being through the act of confession and the writing connected to it; it is, in this sense, like the results of the other technologies I have described, an object that human activity *produces*.[88]

Augustine of Hippo (354–430) was an extraordinarily influential figure, but the model of his *Confessions* gained new force, and this technology of the self was much more extensively elaborated throughout Western culture in the provisions of the Fourth Lateran Council, called by Pope Innocent III in 1215. The seventy decrees issued by the council constituted a broad attempt to reform various aspects of the church, but the twenty-first of these most closely touched, and therefore transformed, the lives of every Christian:

> All the faithful of either sex, after they have reached the age of discernment, should individually confess all their sins in a faithful manner to their own priest at least once a year, and let them take care to do what they can to perform the penance imposed on them.
>
> [Omnis utriusque sexus fidelis, postquam ad annos discretionis pervenerit, omnia sua solus peccata confiteatur fideliter, saltem semel in anno proprio sacerdoti.][89]

Although such mandated confession was oral, its immediate effect was to produce a variety of written instructions for the procedures of confession. The earliest of these in English writing was the lengthy section on 'schrift' [confession] in *Ancrene Wisse* (1215–24), an elegantly phrased and metaphorically rich prose rule for the daily life of a group of women anchorites (such people tried to remove themselves from all worldly distractions and lived in solitude).[90] The timeliness of this rule along with its quality quickly ensured a broad circulation,[91] and the rule itself is particularly clear to emphasize that its description of confession 'limpeth to alle men iliche' [pertains to all people alike][92] and, also, that confession is nothing if not hard work, what Foucault characterized as an 'immense labor':[93]

> Schrift schal beo wreiful, bitter mid sorhe, ihal, naket, ofte imaket, hihful, eadmod, scheomeful, dredful ant hopeful, wis, soth, ant willes, ahne ant studeuest, bithoht bivore longe.
>
> [Confession must be accusatory, bitter with sorrow, complete, naked, made often, speedy, humble, full of shame, full of fear, full of hope, wise, true and willing, one's own and steadfast, thought about long before.] (1: 115 / 141)

This technology of the self answers then to the same valuations that caused the West to embrace with equal fervour the stirrup, the crank, the windmill and the clock – inventions of other cultures but never widely exploited there – born in the reflexive connection Christianity made between physical difficulty and great reward. But *Ancrene Wisse* also makes clear that the self that emerges by means of this technology and through such hard labour has a specific and determinate shape:

> Ah to hir ahne schrift-feader, other to sum lif-hali mon, yef ha mei him habben, culle al the pot ut: ther speowe ut al thet wunder, ther with fule wordes thet fulthe efter thet hit is tuki al to wundre, swa thet ha drede thet ha hurte his earen thet hercneth hire sunnen.

> [Let her pour all the pot out to her own father confessor, or to some man of holy life, if she can get him – spew out there all the outrageous facts, there with foul words, ill-treat that filth quite outrageously, in accordance with what it is, so that she is afraid of hurting the ears of the person listening to her sins.] (1: 130/158–9)

The metaphor at work here is, at root, a continuation of the Augustinian notion that the self is defined, above all, by having an inside that something can come 'ut' [out] of, but it is typical of *Ancrene Wisse* to equate the self with an object as familiar and homely as a 'pot', and, as it extends this metaphor, it shows how a self understood in these terms gains the nearly concrete shape of a made object.[94] *Ancrene Wisse* insists on this materiality by forging a surprisingly literal connection between the shape its own words assume in any book in which they are printed and this self, for its eight 'leasse bokes' [smaller books] are themselves divided into 'inre' [inner] and 'uttre' [outer] rules, the former pertaining to the self lodged within the body, the latter with the daily devotions and care of that body, with the inner rule (books 2–7) lodged within the outer rule (books 1 and 8), which, therefore, surrounds it as if it were a kind of skin.

Another technique of this technology is a process of inversion whereby confession pretends to *reveal* the very thing it creates, as if the need to confess something preceded the moment before confession was demanded. Augustine says that his '*conscience* makes confession' [confitetur conscientia mea],[95] and *Ancrene Wisse* claims that it is 'inwit' or 'conscience' that is constantly 'furculiende hire seoluen with the fur of sunne' [blackening itself with the fire of sin] (1: 116/142), but Nietzsche observed long ago that such a 'sting of conscience' may be understood as an 'internalization' of a demand, a response to a set of prior constraints (rather than the outpouring it pretends to be), a movement from a list of rules (of the kind *Ancrene Wisse* offers) to the idea that a certain guilt or sin has accrued to a person for having disobeyed them.[96] This technique defines a text which coins a new English word to refer to this 'sting', the prose *Ayenbite of Inwyt* (c.1340) by 'Dan Michel' – 'ayenbite' means the 'again-bite' or 'remorse' – an important confessional manual in the fourteenth century ('This boc

is ywrite uor englisse men, thet hi wyte hou hi ssolle ham-zelve ssriue'
[This book is written for English men, so that they know how they ought
to confess themselves]).[97] Following exactly the structure that Nietzsche
predicts, the *Ayenbite* spends a large proportion of its pages setting out rules
for proper Christian conduct (the Ten Commandments, the Articles of the
Creed), following this with a detailed description of the internalized forms
of these rules, or the Seven Deadly Sins and all their manifestations. The
extent to which rules are themselves a key instrument in the production of
the sinful self is revealed best in the *Pricke of Conscience* (*c.*1350), yet another
text named by the process of this inversion. This text also illustrates the
growing importance of this genre, for, despite the arduousness of the
labour it demands, it survives in more manuscripts (115) than any other
Middle English text (there are, by way of comparison, only eighty-two
surviving manuscripts which contain the whole of *The Canterbury Tales*,
or a significant proportion of them),[98] and these forms are diverse enough
in 'geographical distribution and dialectical diversity' to suggest that there
were many more.[99] The text focuses less on rules than on the difficulty of
life in an unstable world, and it spends the bulk of its lines dwelling on the
four last things (death, judgement, heaven and hell) in order to frighten
people into behaving well, as it makes clear early on:

Yf thai rede or here, til the hende*	*end*
The maters that er thar-in contende,	
And undirstand tham al and trow*	*believe [them]*
Parchaunce thair hertes than sal bow,	
Thurgh drede* that thai sal consayve* thar by,	*fear / conceive*
To wirk gude werkes and fle foli	
. . .	
To make tham tham-self first knaw*	*know*
And fra syn and vanytese* tham draw	*vanities*
And for to stir tham til right drede,	
When thai this tretisce here or rede,	
That sal prikke thair conscience with-yn,	
And of that drede may a lofe* bygyn.[100]	*love*

The difference in subject executes the defining reversal, for the 'maters' of
this poem are still understood to produce the 'drede' that in turn produces
the self ('make tham tham-self first knaw'), a 'conscience with-yn' born in
the 'prikke' administered by this very writing.

Yet another technique of this important technology was narrative itself,
and Robert Mannyng of Bourn's *Handlyng Synne* (*c.*1303) is a text virtually
organized around this technique. *Handlyng Synne* also sets out rules (the

Ten Commandments), describes their internalization (the Seven Deadly Sins), and spends a considerable number of lines on the twelve 'points' and graces of 'shrift'. The overall structure and much of the content of *Handlyng Synne* is dictated by its source, the Anglo-Norman *Manuel des pechiez (c.*1260), but this text is already unusual in using exemplary stories to elaborate doctrinal points.[101] Mannyng adds seven more such stories,[102] some of them clearly drawn from local legend, but almost all of them scabrously sensational, as, for example, the story of the husband and wife who committed sacrilege by having sex near a church and, as a result, are permanently stuck together:

O nyght thyr was, he knewe hys wyff	
Of flesshely dede, as fyl* here lyff	*happened*
And god was nat payd* ne wlde* hyt noght,	*pleased /wanted*
So nygh* the cherche swyche dede were wrog ht.	*near*
They myghte no more be broghte asondre*	*asunder*
Than dog and bych that men on wonder.	
Bytydde* a shame they gun to crye	*befell*
That wndyr fyl* on here folye.[103]	*was directed [toward]*

To couch a rule in a homely narrative of this kind, however lurid its details, does more than exemplify doctrine, however: it makes it an active part of the daily world into which a Christian reader is meant to take it.[104] To the very extent that it is sensational, such a narrative is far removed from the kinds of experiences such a reader has probably ever encountered, and yet what the doctrine carried in the narrative gains from narrative's structure – its location in time ('o nyght') and space ('so nygh the cherche'), and above all its sequence, so powerfully imitative of lived 'lyff' – is the insistence that this is how things actually are. This subtle but powerful process is abetted in Mannyng's case by the kinds of stories he is willing to tell, as well as his own extraordinary capacity to shape a story so as to make the abstract concrete. In the example I have just quoted, husband and wife each become a kind of emblem of sin for the other (stuck together by virtue of the sinful act that constitutes that attachment), but Mannyng's skills in this area are nowhere in better evidence than when he turns his narrative powers to the larger issue I have been addressing in this section, the carving out of an 'inner' space in the body as the repository of all that constitutes the self by the technology of confession:

Of a womman y herde ones spelle,*	*talk*
That alle here synnes wlde nat telle.	
Thys womman had do* a synful dede:	*done*

Here shamede to telle hyt for drede.
On o day grace was here gyve
That she thoghte she wlde be shryve.*   *confessed*
Thys woman come unto a frere,
And, preyd hym, here lyffe to here.
As she sat here shryfte ynne,
She thoghte uppon thys yche* synne,   *every*
The frere comforted here weyl,
Boldely to sey everydeyl;*   *everything*
Hys cumforte made here ryght bolde,
So that she furth the synne tolde,
That she hadde longe forhole,
Thurgh cunseyl* of the devyl stole.*   *counsel* / *[in a] fixed place*
But at that yche breyde*   *very moment*
That she furth that synne seyde,
Come fleyng out of here mouthe a blak,*   *black [thing]*
Ryght as she the wrd* spak.   *word*
The frere sagh hyt apertly*   *clearly*
And thanked god of hys mercy.

(ll. 11, 853–74)

This story is not original to Mannyng, but he gives it characteristic immediacy. Where in the *Manuel* we simply know that 'there was' such a 'foolish woman' ['fole femme . . . esteit'], Mannyng insists that he has himself 'herde' the story. Where the *Manuel* says that there is also a woman with 'deble' [devil] inside her, in Mannyng's hand what comes flying out of the woman's mouth is not this 'devil' but a tangible object, '*a blak*', or blackness, an object that we also learn the friar actually sees as it emerges from the woman's insides.

The 'self' as we now know it is often said to have emerged in the Renaissance (Foucault, in fact, tended to focus on the eighteenth century), but there is a serious claim for marking this emergence at the moment when confession has exceeded its religious brief and is no longer illustrated by, but fully absorbed to, the processes of narrative. John Gower's *Confessio Amantis*, which I have already mentioned, marks an epoch in its capacity to involve romance in this programme (and, as will be seen, marries these to even broader political purposes),[105] but the texts that really mark the crucial transition are the most self-dramatizing of the prologues to *The Canterbury Tales*. The characteristics of all the pilgrims joined together for the journey to Canterbury are largely drawn from the social stereotypes that had long been traditional in the genre of 'estates satire' (an anatomy of social ills, profession by profession), but Chaucer has a great variety of his own techniques for working up such traditions into the 'extraordinarily vivid *impression*' of the 'existence' of 'individuals', and this is nowhere more true than in the lengthiest of the prologues to the tales, those of the Wife of Bath, the Pardoner and the Canon's Yeoman.[106] Each of these texts generates its individualizing, confessional account from the traditional but 'specialized discourses' of medieval misogyny or anti-feminism (the Wife of Bath), penance (the Pardoner), and alchemy (the Canon's Yeoman).[107] Only the Pardoner places himself at all obviously in the literature of confession, but all of these texts posit (or create) a 'self' in the manner of the texts I have been describing, beginning, in each case, with the distance between that self's hidden reality and the perceptions of an outer world. The Wife of Bath, for example, is everywhere clear that her success in marriage relies on a studious programme of concealment and falsehood:

> Lordinges, right thus, as ye han understonde,
> Bar* I stifly mine olde housbondes on honde*   *[bar . . . on honde =]*
>   *accused*
>
> That thus they seiden in hir dronkenesse;
> And al was fals, but that I took witnesse
> On Janekyn and on my nece also.
> O Lord, the peine I dide hem and the wo,
> Ful giltelees, by Goddes swete pine!*   *pain*
> For as an hors I koude bite and whine.*   *whinny*
> I koude pleine* and I was in the gilt,   *complain*
> Or elles often time I hadde been spilt.*   *ruined*
> Whoso that first to mille comth, first grint;*   *grinds*
> I pleined first, so was oure werre* ystint.*   *war / ended*
> They were ful glad t'excusen hem ful blive*   *very quickly*
> Of thing of which they nevere agilte*   *were never guilty*
>   hir live.*   *in their lives*
>
>   (III.379–92)

Of the three confessional Canterbury pilgrims, the Wife of Bath executes the most deft of these reversals, for her general point is not that she is a liar (though she clearly lies), but that the discourse of misogyny – to which her husbands so generally subscribe – forces her into the impossible position of always having different views than those ascribed to her. It is part of Chaucer's brilliance as a technician of such reversals that he creates the Wife of Bath as a back-formation from the discourse of misogyny (he puts its very language in the Wife of Bath's mouth so that she can say what she is not, a fact always marked by the phrase 'thou seyst' which peppers a large section of her self-portrait),[108] but it is inherent to the discourse of misogyny that the Wife can portray herself as a sovereign individual simply by declaring that such a rigorous and popular set of fantasies about women and their nature is a lie:

Thou seyst also that it displeseth me	
But if* that thow wolt preise my beautee,	*if not*
And but thow poure* alwey upon my face,	*gaze*
And clepe* me 'faire dame' in every place,	*call*
And but thow make a feeste on thilke day	
That I was born, and make me fressh and gay,	
And but thow do to my norice* honour,	*nurse*
And to my chamberere* withinne my bour,*	*chambermaid / room*
And to my fadres folk and his allies;*	*kinsfolk*
Thus seystow, olde barel-ful of lies!*	*lees, dregs [punning on 'lies']*
(III.293–302)	

Some have found the Wife of Bath's thorough dependency on the texts and interpretative techniques of misogyny to severely damage the kind of self she can claim ('she remains confined within the prison house of masculine language'),[109] although others have admired the extent to which she uses this male discourse to fashion an extraordinarily exuberant self-hood (she 'renovates the patriarchal hermeneutic to accommodate the feminine').[110]

The strongest evidence that the Wife may be meant to fall somewhere in between these two extremes is offered by her tale itself, which, like the tales of the other confessional pilgrims, seems to extend the disclosures of the Prologue, in a different key. The two texts end on a similar note, with the Prologue describing how her fifth husband's decision to abandon his misogyny (he gives her control of 'hous and lond' [III.814] and burns the collection of misogynist texts) allows her to be 'trewe' (III.825) to him at last, while the tale, an Arthurian romance in which a knight, who has been sentenced, after raping a woman, to discover 'what thing is it that wommen moost desiren' (III.905), discovers that 'wommen desiren to have sovereintee / As wel over hir housbonde as hir love' (III.1038–9). One might emphasize the way that The Wife of Bath's Tale is also caught in the masculine prison-house of anti-feminism (once the wife in the tale has achieved sovereignty we are told she also 'obeyed' her husband 'in every thing / That mighte do him plesance or liking', III.1255–6), but the knight's capitulation in this romance goes an extraordinary step further in a moment when he is shown to live by his new understanding of women, to yield, not because he has to, but *willingly* because he knows that such yielding is the best (rather than the prudent) course:

My lady and my love, and wif so deere,
I putte me in youre wise governaunce.*   *control*
Cheseth yourself which may be moost plesaunce,*   *pleasure*
And moost honour to yow and me also.
I do no fors* the wheither of the two,   *do not care*
For as yow liketh, it suffiseth* me.   *satisfies*

(III.1230–5)

That this is as much a wistful fantasy of the Wife's as it is part of a romance in its own right is a fact underscored by the observation that this husband and wife 'live unto hir lives ende / In parfit joye' (III.1257–8) at the conclusion of this tale, for of her own improved marriage the Wife can only say that 'we hadden nevere debaat' (III.821). In placing this wish just beyond the Wife's extraordinarily energetic self-disclosures ('Now dame . . . / This is a long preamble of a tale!', III.830–1), this tale and its relation to its prologue continue to elaborate the Wife's selfhood according to the technology I have been describing – insisting that her 'self' is that which confession cannot quite capture because it is, finally, and irreducibly, that which cannot be fully present in the external world.

Printing

Although the widespread use of printing in the making of books is sometimes described as a 'revolution' that swept away all older modes of production, it is a surprisingly conservative technology.[111] In fact, we must speak of the 'widespread use' of printing rather than its invention, however often we may hear that Gutenberg 'invented printing' in the 1440s or that the Gutenberg Bible is the 'first printed book' (c.1455), for neither statement is close to the truth.[112] The technique of 'xylography', or block printing, was in use from the end of the fourteenth century in the West (although most often for the reproduction of images rather than words), and it was clearly employed in China before 868 (the date of the oldest book printed in this manner which survives).[113] Gutenberg *perfected* the use of moveable type in printing, for printing with moveable type fashioned from clay was in use in China as early as 1041.[114] Like many early printers, Gutenberg was a goldsmith by trade, and his innovation was 'technically . . . an advanced achievement in metallurgy', the separate casting of letters which could then be repeatedly reassembled in 'founts' or page-like moulds.[115] What most marks the conservatism of printing as a technology, however, is the way that it tended to use new means to achieve the oldest ends: the earliest printed books so carefully mimicked handwritten manuscripts that they even reproduced the abbreviations scribes had employed to save time and space when writing on vellum, and the type-faces fashioned for these books were actually modelled on the handwriting of particular scribes.[116] Nor is printing a more orderly way of making books, since it also allows for the kind of variation in copies that so dogs scribal production, and it therefore puts multiple versions of texts in wide circulation.[117] Moreover, as the discovery of a manuscript copy of Malory's *Morte Darthur* in 1934 confirmed, a printer such as William Caxton (*c*.1415–1492), who had produced, in 1485, the only text of the *Morte* available before this discovery, could intervene very heavily in the texts that came into his hands. Caxton had not only altered innumerable small details of diction, but he had completely transformed the narrative structure of the work (dividing it into twenty-one 'books', and then subdividing these books into 506 separate chapters, also adding a table of contents that describes – and therefore shapes – the contents of each book and chapter).[118]

William Caxton was, however, the earliest printer of English texts and, although he printed that text in Bruges (where he learned his trade), the first English book printed in any form was his own translation of Raoul Lefèvre's *Le Recueil des histoires de Troyes* (1475–6).[119] Caxton set up a press in Westminster in late 1475 or early 1476 – the first English book printed in England has proved difficult to determine, but if it was not an extant edition of the *Sarum Hours*, then it was very likely a quarto edition of *The Canterbury Tales*.[120] The advent of printing did not end the hand-copying of books, and, at least initially, Caxton even sold such books in his shop.[121] But the transformation produced by this technology was also dramatic, and before his death, in 1492, Caxton had printed over a hundred books, the more popular of them in multiple editions (three alone, for instance, of the *Dicts and Sayings of the Philosophers*).[122] Indeed, although Caxton began his professional life as a 'mercer', or cloth merchant, it has been said that he changed his wares rather than his trade when he became a printer,[123] for he not only produced an astonishing number of books, he created a whole new market.

For this last reason, he and his books were as much effects of the transformation brought about by print as their determinate cause, since, in order to satisfy the demand he had fostered, he was also driven to create more and more printable texts, not only by commissioning translations and new writings, but by translating twenty-two different works himself.[124] In the prologues that often precede such translations Caxton habitually insists that he is an amateur, and that printing is only something that he 'happens' to do when he has nothing else 'in hande':

After dyverse werkes made translated and achieved, havyng noo werke in hande, I sittyng in my studye, where as laye many dyverse paunflettis and bookys, happened that to my hande came a lytyl booke in frenshe, whiche late was translated oute of latyn by some noble clerke of fraunce.[125]

[*dyverse*: many and various   *paunflettis*: pamphlets]

Caxton wrote at such speed that the style of his translations is almost universally uninspired (he tended to leave a French word unchanged, even if this meant introducing a new word into English), but this did not mean that his goals were only mercenary (the creation of more product), or that he lacked ambition for his writings or himself as a writer, for he clearly chose the texts he printed and translated in order to raise the status of English as a literary language. It is no accident that the 'lytyl booke' Caxton says that he stumbled over in his study is the central monument of medieval Latinity, Virgil's *Aeneid* (published as Caxton's *Eneydos* in 1490), or that he makes particularly clear that it is meant, not for a 'rude uplondyssh man' [an uneducated country-dweller] but, rather, for 'a clerke and a noble gentylman'.[126] As part of this same programme Caxton not only printed a great deal of Chaucer's writing, from *Anelida and Arcite* in 1477 to *Troilus and Criseyde* in 1484, his translation of Boethius' *Consolation of Philosophy* (1478) and two editions of *The Canterbury Tales* (in 1478 and 1483), he also introduced the last of these with the claim that Chaucer was England's first 'laureate' poet because he had so substantially made English 'faire':

To fore alle other we ought to gyve a synguler laude unto that noble and grete philosopher Gefferey chaucer the whiche for his ornate wrytyng in our tongue may wel have the name of a laureate poete, for . . . he by hys labour enbelysshyd, ornated, and made faire our englisshe.[127]

[*to fore alle*: above all   *laude*: praise   *enbelysshyd*: embellished   *ornated*: ornamented]

We are right to hear Caxton's self-interest speaking under such historical claims, and these are even more nakedly revealed when he says that what is 'good and vertuous' in the *Tales* will 'prouffyte unto the helthe of our sowles' (in precisely the proportion he could convince an audience that this was true, the profits of his printing trade would increase).[128] But the eye fixed keenly on the bottom line is an eye attuned toward every sort of value (what sells is often what is extraordinarily good), and Caxton was also clearly a very good reader of texts, as not only their very popularity proved. His audacious intervention in the text of Malory's *Morte Darthur*, for example, tended to make it into much more of the 'hoole book' (3:

1260) that Malory said he had striven for than Malory's own divisions gave it,[129] and it could be argued that few readers since Caxton have understood Malory's complex ethical vision as clearly as Caxton does in his prologue:

> For herein may be seen noble chyvalrye, curtosye, humanyté, frendly-nesse, hardynesse, love, frendshyp, cowardyse, murder, hate, vertue, and synne. (94)

Where, as I suggested above, modern criticism is quick to see the *Morte* as typically idealizing, Caxton was one of the first to see just how fully (and movingly) Malory's narrative took in the odd admixture of good and bad that constituted chivalric culture ('humanyte' *and* 'hate'), the brittleness that was its defining condition as an ideology.

But everywhere shackled to the need to please, even the most sensitive literary sensibility will tend to narrow the range of available writings, and it could also be said that one of the more important effects of printing, for all the flood of books and texts it put into readers' hands, was to reduce variation and choice. A printer's intentions and the forces of the market wholly aside, the 'mechanical reproduction' of the work of art becomes, as Walter Benjamin observed, a very important aspect of that work, and simply having so many copies of the same work in circulation tends to homogenize taste, ensuring that 'the critical and the receptive attitudes of the public coincide', that 'the conventional is uncritically enjoyed, and the truly new is criticized with aversion'.[130] The kinds of books Caxton printed were very largely chivalric, and on the whole of a much more anodyne sort than Malory's *Morte Darthur*, in fact they are a roll-call of the kind of texts that would simply reinforce the long-established preferences and views of the 'noble gentlemen' who would have had the means to purchase them (*The Game of Chess* [1475], *Jason* [1475–6 and 1477], *The Book of Courtesy* [1477–8], *The Siege of Jerusalem* [1481], *The Knight of the Tower* [1484], *The Order of Chivalry* [1484], *Charles the Great* [1485], *Blanchardin and Eglantine* [1489], *Four Sons of Aymon* [1489], Christine de Pisan's *Feats of Arms* [1489/90?]). Caxton also favoured established and uncontroversial poets such as Chaucer or John Gower (he prints the *Confessio Amantis* in 1483), but, equally tellingly, he avoided the much more uncertain and challenging politics of *Piers Plowman*, which the manuscript record shows to have been just as popular as these others (fifty manuscripts of its three versions survive).[131] It has been suggested that one of the most important contributions of printing was the 'preservative power' of simply putting so many copies of individual writings in circulation.[132] The fragmentary record of early Middle English offers indirect confirmation of any such view (we have very few English romances from the thirteenth century, for example, even though this is a period when we know such texts were widely enjoyed). But it could also be said that a technology which harnessed the energies of popularity so fully was inevitably impoverishing, creating a kind of narrow pass for taste, if not for texts, making it less likely that the early and the unusual would be read at all after the fifteenth century, as indeed turned out to be the case for much Middle English literature, until a truly historical scholarship began to edit, reprint and reclaim this work – but not until the eighteenth and nineteenth centuries.[133]

2

Insurgency

At the end of May in 1381 a group of men, first in Essex, but slowly gathering followers from many other counties in the south and east of England, angered by generally heavy taxation, and particularly incensed by a recent poll tax as well as the increasingly insistent pattern of enforcement accompanying it, rebelled. Beginning with local attacks on officials and minor and major vandalism of local properties, the rebels gathered in number and force until, as one chronicle estimates, 60,000 of them marched on London on 12 June. The king and his court immediately fled to the Tower of London. On 13 June the rebels rampaged through the city, burning and pillaging important buildings, and throwing open the Fleet prison. When the king went to negotiate with some of these people at Mile End on 14 June, another group of them stormed the Tower in his absence and seized and then beheaded Simon Sudbury, the Archbishop of Canterbury, and Robert Hales, the king's treasurer, afterwards carrying their severed heads through the city on pikes. Once the king agreed to fix rents to a certain value and end vileinage (that is, the subjection of farm workers to a feudal lord in exchange for land rights) the rebels finally began to disperse. But, with the immediate danger averted, Richard reneged on his promise, and sent agents to scour the countryside for the now vulnerable rebels. Most of the leaders were soon caught and killed (often by being drawn, quartered and hanged).[1]

This was neither the first nor the last rebellion against royal authority in English history, but the particularly threatening nature of 'the rising' of 1381 (as it is now customary to describe it) was marked by the way the chronicler Thomas Walsingham – and as a consequence most historians ever after – described the rebels as *rustici* or 'peasants'.[2] In fact, the rebels came from all segments of medieval society ('peasants, poor priests, artisans, and wealthy townsmen alike'), and this rebellion was also unprecedented in trying to advance, not the self-interest of disgruntled aristocrats (as had happened in 1246–8 and would happen again in 1414 and 1450), but a broad and self-conscious populism.[3] This was most clear in the sermon on the subject of the equality of all men and women given on Blackheath on 12 June by John Ball, one of the rebel leaders. Although the number is as much a measure of his alarm as anything, the chronicler Thomas Walsingham estimated that Ball preached to 200,000 people, and that his text was the traditional, but incendiary, tag

Whan Adam dalf* and Eve span*	*dug / spun*
Wo* was thanne a gentilman?[4]	*Who*

This rising also produced a series of equally incendiary documents, described as *litterae* or 'letters' by Walsingham and Henry Knighton, the two chroniclers who preserve them.[5] Two of these are also attributed to John Ball, but the one that most clearly articulates the rebels' revolutionary social vision is written in the voice of 'Johon Schep':

> Johon Schep, som tyme Seynte Marie prest of York, and now of Colchestre, greteth wel Johan Nameles, and Johan the Mullere, and Johon Cartere, and biddeth hem that thei bee war of gyle in borugh, and stondeth togidre in Godes name, and biddeth Peres Ploughman go to his werk, and chastise wel Hobbe the Robbere, and taketh with yow Johan Trewman, and alle hiis felawes, and no mo, and loke schappe you to on heued, and no mo.
>
>> Johan the Mullere hath ygrounde smal, smal, smal;
>> The Kynges sone of hevene schal paye for al.
>> Be war or ye be wo;
>> Knoweth your freende fro your foo;
>> Haveth ynow, and seith 'Hoo';
>> And do wel and bettre, and fleth synne,
> And seketh pees, and hold you therinne;
> And so biddeth Johan Trewman and alle his felawes.[6]

[*borugh*: town   *loke schappe you to on heued*: unite yourselves [as a group or band]   *ygrounde*: ground   *Kynges sone of hevene*: the son of the king of heaven   *ynow*: enough]

This text, part address, part poem, was almost certainly not a 'letter' as we now think of such a document; it probably circulated as a *schedula*, or large bill, posted on a wall or door for all to read, since this was the most common vehicle for public protest of this kind in the decades around 1381.[7] What particular social or political ills prompted such an outcry is less clear, for the need for action is as indiscriminate as it is urgent ('Be war or ye be wo', 'do wel and bettre'), and that need is extended to the whole of a rural community by the series of personifications that also equate people with the things that they do ('Peres the Ploughman', 'Hobbe the Robbere', 'Johon Cartere'). Such personifications may be politically powerful, but they are also fundamentally poetic in origin, and this fact alone can stand for – just as it demonstrates – what an important part *literary* technique had to play in these dramatic events.

The rebellion had many causes, but it was, most simply, a dramatic but localized symptom of a number of very large problems that beset the whole English polity in the second half of the fourteenth century. First, there was a severe labour shortage as a direct consequence of the Black Death in 1348–50 (which may have killed one-third of the population), a shortage that had led directly to what Karl Marx later understood as one of the earliest laws regulating labour, the repressive Ordinance of Labourers (23 Edward III, 1349), which established a maximum wage (but no minimum) and stipulated that all landless men should work.[8] Second, the long war England was waging against France was going very badly (particularly in the period 1369–81), and aside from the blow such failure dealt to national feeling, the king and parliament had begun to seek funds to finance these foreign adventures through a number of 'poll taxes' whose burden fell on the whole of the male population (so on the lower and middle strata as much as the aristocrats and merchants who had paid the lion's share of taxes up until this point).[9] A third, and much more general, cause was the increasing sclerosis of the institutional church, widely perceived to be financially corrupt, as these problems appeared with unusual urgency, analysed by a rigorous theology, at the end of the fourteenth century in the writings of the Oxford theologian John Wyclif, and his followers, often called the 'Lollards'. The concerns of this movement were many, and it argued, above all, for the primacy of scripture – 'Lollardy was essentially a creed of the book'.[10] But, following on from this, Lollards also found much of the apparatus and authority of the church to be illegitimate (since none of it is mentioned anywhere in scripture), and they therefore urged the 'disendowment' of all the wealth that had accumulated in (and also *as*) the Christian church's ever-growing institutional apparatus. The Lollards firmly endorsed secular authority as that which might curb the institutional church, but it was an easy step from the idea that the current forms of religious authority were largely illegitimate to the notion that secular authority ought to play an active role in disendowment and, from there, to the notion that wealth so seized should be distributed in an egalitarian way – that secular rulers, in particular, through their legitimate authority, had 'a responsibility to ease the oppressions of the poor'.[11]

The rebel letter I quoted above may also be understood as an especially moving and urgent abstraction of this ideology – in the name of the 'Kynges sone of hevene' it urges a 'doing' that will transform a world full of 'gyle' and 'wo' into a world in which all who 'do' shall have 'enough'

– and, whether we call it a poem or a 'letter', because it clearly emerged before the rising (as Walsingham makes clear), it counts as an unusually *effective* mobilization of literary technique, a work of Middle English that had a demonstrable effect on the culture from which it also emerged. Writing with such a distinction is, I think, helpfully described as 'insurgent', and it is with such writing, as well as with the literary techniques and trends that enabled it, that this chapter is particularly concerned. The idea that Middle English literature may be 'political' in any 'revolutionary' sense – that it might 'dissent' from a current regime or 'protest' against it – has been described as 'unhistorical' and 'anachronistic', an over-reading of poetry that is only ever concerned with 'the inadequacy of human conduct' and which sits squarely within a culture in which 'the general principle of authority as such was never in question'.[12] Such a view is a strong reaction to the excavation, in the 1960s and 1970s, of a body of 'Middle English poems of protest' by Rossell Hope Robbins,[13] and, on closer inspection, what is most at stake in this argument is whether fourteenth-century 'protest' could have borne any relation to protest 'now' ('a modern protester in the Western world is protected by the legally enforced tolerance of the system he is angry with; the peasants of 1381 were staking their lives').[14] This not only sets the bar for literature's effectiveness in an odd place, it sets it so high as to exclude a text such as *Piers Plowman*, whose political role may have been wholly unintended, but which, as the language of 'Scheps's' letter itself proves ('and biddeth Peres Ploughman go to his werk'), was significant.[15] This older debate may therefore serve to clarify my concern here, which is not with literature of any particular political stripe (that focuses on the plight of the poor, say), but, rather, with any text that sought or brought about (or, in its elaboration of a technique, helped some later text bring about) cultural change.

Complaint

Complaint is not always easy to distinguish from satire, but I will understand it here as more descriptive than accusatory, its passions focused on elucidating the depths or extremity of a problem rather than attacking its cause. The importance of this mode in the Middle Ages is well illustrated by one of the earliest Middle English complaints we have, four terrifically pessimistic lines, casually jotted on the flyleaf of a thirteenth-century manuscript (and attributed there, as much proverbial wisdom was, to 'Aluredus [Alfred] king'):

Ald* man witles*	*old / witless*
Yung man recheles*	*reckless*
Wyman* ssameles*	*woman / shameless*
Betere ham were lifles.*[16]	*lifeless*

Such declarations may always be consoling to those who perceive their own situation to be equally grim, but in the Middle Ages such sentiments were very much rooted in the view that the whole of the world was in its 'old age', that all the centuries after Christ were part of the general state of decay that would endure until Christ's second coming.[17] There was, accordingly, a whole tradition of poems like the one I have just quoted, devoted not to detailing the problems of a particular time or place, but to describing just how general problems of every kind were. Such poems often consisted of no more than an enumeration of such 'abuses', and, while these problems varied in nature, in a very fertile tradition (derived from a Latin poem which dictated their catalogue) the number of such abuses customarily numbered twelve.[18] As in the example I have already quoted, the art of such poems lay very much in their pith, the extent to which the *whole* world could be declared bad in a short space, as can again be seen even in a more expansive version of this theme from early in the fifteenth century:

Geft* is Domesman*, and gyle is chapman;*	*bribery / lord / merchant*
Lordys ben owtyn* law, and chylderen ben withowtyn awe;	*outside*
Wyth* is trechery, and love is lecherye;	*wisdom [wit]*
And pley turnyt* to vylanye, and holyday* to glotonye.	*turns / holy day*
Eld* man is scornyng, wyse man in lesyng,*	*old / lying*
Ryche man in levyng,* and pore man in losyng;	*gaining*
Sly men ben blynd, and kenred* is onkynd;*	*family / unkind*
The ded is owtyn* of mynd, for he may fynd noo frond.*[19]	*out / friend*

It can seem that the 'ultimate objective' of such poetry is 'correction',[20] either personal or general, but the repetitiveness of the tradition – the frequency with which it catalogued such complete disaster – and the extent to which it understood the abuses it described to be irremediable (this is just how things 'are'), argues against any such view. The appeal and value of such poetry must have derived from its stridency and severity, the extent to which it evoked the *need* for amendment, the vividness with which, in evoking a general presumption of sinfulness so fundamental to Christian doctrine, it tended to bring about repentance.

The power they derive from their generality also makes such poems sur-prisingly weightless, condemning no particular action or person since they so roundly condemn everything; but they therefore also have a tendency to direct their indictments towards some present. The poem above does exactly this in its last lines: five Latin tags focusing on abuses in the church follow the lines I have quoted (e.g. 'clerus errat' [clergy do wrong]), and these criticisms are then given real immediacy by the poem's last line ('*Now* men levyn good thewis [qualities]'). The resulting combination of vague-ness and specificity also defines one of the earliest Middle English complaints in this 'abuses' tradition, a poem usually called the *First Worcester Fragment* (*c*.1100) because it was discovered only in the nineteenth century in the binding of a book in Worcester Cathedral Library (some time after 1250 the parchment on which it was written was used to stiffen a book's covers).[21] This poem catalogues only a few abuses, and it spends a large proportion of its lines enumerating the great achievements of the past, particularly in the areas of English learning (Bede, Ælfric and Alcuin are mentioned) and Christian piety (five of its twenty-three lines list some of the more famous of the Anglo-Saxon saints), the better to insist upon the depths of the disaster constituted by the destruction of these achievements:

Nu is theo leore forleten,   and thet folc is forloren.
Nu beoth othre leoden   theo læreth ure folc,
And feole of then lortheines losiæth   and thet folc forth mid.

[Now that teaching is forsaken, and the folk are lost.
Now there is another people which teaches our folk,
And many of our teachers are damned, and our folk with them.][22]

Because these repeated 'now's seem to root the catalogued abuses in a par-ticular moment, and because that moment seems to be one largely charac-terized by a decline in 'English' learning (as well as the date conventionally assigned to it), modern scholars have always assumed that the poem refers to 1066, and that the loss it laments is the richness of Old English literary culture, as it was destroyed in and after the Norman Conquest. This is prob-ably what such a poem (and its 'nows') would have meant to any medieval reader who encountered it in a post-1066 present.[23] And yet the 'now' to which the poem carefully dates itself is much earlier than this moment, for the latest event it refers to is the death of the saint Alphege (in 1012), and many of the saints it remembers are seventh-century figures. In fact, the 'now' of the poem covers the period of the Viking invasions that not only wrought enormous destruction on Anglo-Saxon culture between 793 and 1012, but which often involved a systematic attack on the monasteries, the primary sites of Anglo-Saxon teaching (in the very first of these raids the Vikings sacked the monastery at Lindisfarne with its rich library).[24] That this poem's 'now' is so easily misunderstood – that it *could* be so easily misunderstood as soon as its dating mechanisms were themselves dated – is a decisive illustration of the way the odd combination of generality and urgency that allows 'abuses' poems to insist on the omnipresence of disaster also allowed any such poem to specify any number of the various moments in which it might have been read.

Specificity in complaint is therefore, paradoxically, another strategy for insisting on the generality of abuse. This is particularly clear in the poem usually called the *Song of the Husbandman* (c.1300), in which a ploughman is overheard making great 'mon' (moan) about the corruption of the 'hayward', 'bailiff' and 'woodkeeper' who regulate him, the high taxes extorted by the 'master beadle', and the ruin he faces having sold his seed and cattle to pay what he owes 'to the king'. The abuses the poem describes are authenticated by the first person who describes them ('Thus I kippe and cacche cares ful colde', 61) as well as the detail with which they are rendered: here, it seems, for many passages of the poem, we have particular problems, of a particular place and time, even if the general issue (the exploitation of those who work the land by those who own it) is common enough.[25] But specificity of this degree is also transformed back into generalization by the poem's pessimism,[26] for the 'husbandman' is also keen to insist that, *despite* his complaint, his lot will never improve (for the world is governed by such abuses):

> Thus we carpeth for the kyng, and carieth ful colde,
> And weneth fore kevere, and ever buth a-cast.
> Whose hath eny god, hopeth he nouht to holde,
> Bote evere the levest we leoseth alast.
>
> [Thus we complain to the king and are troubled very much, and hope to recover and are always cast down. Whoever has anything, does not expect to keep it, but the most precious thing we have, we lose in the end.][27]

As this manoeuvre demonstrates, the 'abuses' tradition is not only the articulation of a pessimistic world view, but a set of techniques for making such pessimism urgent. Those techniques are most evident, too, in the kind of complaint usually characterized as a 'punctuation' poem, where a combination of lineation and carefully placed full stops becomes a way of insisting that trouble underlies any possible optimism. If one reads such a poem line by line, it describes a world in which all is well; but if one reads it in sentences (ending each clause at the full stop in the middle of each line), it describes a world in a state of collapse:

Nowe the lawe is ledde by clere conscience.
Full seld.* Covetise hath dominacioun.   *very seldom*
In every place. Right hath residence.
Neyther in towne ne feld. Similacion.*   *dissimulation*
There is truly in euery cas. Consolacioun.
The pore peple no tyme hase. But right.
Men may fynd day ne nyght. Adulacioun.
Nowe reigneth treuth in every. mannys sight.[28]

What this last poem also shows is that, despite a motivating worldliness in the 'abuses' tradition – the governing sense that such poems are describing real problems that beset real people – their interest and energy is formal and reside in the strategies they can marshal for making the most common Christian assumptions about human sinfulness striking.

We must suspect that even such generalizing forms frequently absorbed (and therefore, almost silently, expressed) real grievances and frustrations – that they provide the cover of generality for more urgent notions and feelings – but poems in the 'abuses' tradition also show very clearly how literary technique and the force of repetition can render the urgent anodyne; this, in turn, helps make clear how the anodyne might itself be an insurgent technique. This is generally the case with *Jack Upland* (*c*.1400), a text that renders its complaint the more insistent by a rigorous formal astringency, eschewing verse for prose, and, after a short introduction, resolving itself into a series of sixty-five hectoring, largely unanswerable questions, rained down upon the head of a nameless 'friar' ('Frere, whi hate ye that the Gospel schulde be prechid to the trewe undirstondinge of holi doctouris, and ye clepen it the newe doctrine in sclaundringe of Crist?').[29] Such questions might be described as rhetorical, and the text makes other sops to art. For example, the whole of its critique is entered as a 'moan' (as is common in complaint poetry), and the figure who moans is himself a personification of every man (any 'jack' from the country, or 'upland'):

> To veri God and to alle trewe in Crist, I, Jacke Uplond, make my moone,
> that Anticrist and hise disciples, bi coloure of holynes, wasten and dis-
> ceiven Cristis Chirche by many fals signes. (1–3)
>
> [*moone*: complaint [moan]   *bi coloure*: under the guise of]

But the text lodges a series of very particular criticisms ('Antecrist . . . hath suspendid prestis fro her office and govun hem greete wagis of posses-siouns and dignytees agens Cristis lawe', 44–6), and they are insistent, even furious, expressive and truly demanding, not as any function of this text and its technique – of ways in which it may be designed to persuade or move

– but, rather, as a function of Lollardy, an ideology both clearly articulated as well as socially active prior to this text. The main audience for any such expression would of course be only those who already shared such views, but *Jack Upland* is also important to our understanding of the methods and modes of insurgent literature, because it produced the result it most explicitly demands. Jack concludes by asking quite specifically that this friar 'geve Jack an answere' (333), and such a response was then written. *Friar Daw's Reply* (c.1400) is not a prose text, but an alliterative poem, and it is as generally anti-Lollard as *Jack* is Lollard ('But sith that wickide worme – Wiclyf be his name – Began to sowe the seed of cisme [schism] in the erthe'),[30] but it also explicitly and systematically rebuts *Jack Upland*, often point for point:

> Thou seist that we prechen fallace* and fables   *fallacy*
> And not Goddis Gospel to good undirstondinge,
> And we ben more holdun* therto than to alle other reulis.   *obligated*
>
> (ll. 601–3)

That the *Reply* was in turn answered by another, angry alliterative poem in the voice of Jack Upland ('Dawe, thou laborist fast to lede thi-self to helle')[31] is a further illustration that one of the most important consequences of demanding and urgent writings is *more* writing.

But complaint need not produce a result to move itself out of the general 'abuses' tradition, nor do we need to know that it produced particular results to note the techniques such writing employs to move complaint into action. A particularly good, if subtle, instance of such movement is *The Insurrection and Earthquake* (1382), a poem that fully inhabits the traditional territory of the 'abuses' genre ('But nou this wrecched worldes wele [wealth] / Maketh us live in sunne [sin] and care'),[32] but which also manages to insist, in this broad context, on the urgency of the present moment. It achieves this immediacy, in the main, by rooting all of the world's wretchedness in three horrifying events of 1381, the rebel uprising, an outbreak of the plague (a periodic occurrence after the initial outbreaks of 1348–9) and an earthquake:[33]

> The Rysing of the comuynes* in londe,   *commons*
> The Pestilens,* and the eorthe-quake –   *pestilence*
> Theose threo thinges, I understonde,
> Beo-tokenes the grete vengaunce and wrake*   *retribution*
> That schulde falle for synnes sake,
> As this Clerkes conne* de-clare.   *know to*
> Nou may we chese to leve or take,
> For warynng have we to ben ware.
>
> (ll. 57–64)

The specifics necessarily change the relationship of such poetic description to the world's wretchedness by changing the relationship of the addressed audience to that description. While the *First Worcester Fragment* makes clear how the temporal adverb 'now' can locate a poem in any time at all, the 'now' in these lines definitively places this poem in a specific time because of all the other temporal details it provides; that immediacy also gives real force to the poem's demand that 'we' take these warnings most seriously (correction is 'now' a real possibility). Such a poem can also help us to see how the rebel letters not only employ such techniques, but rely on the ambiguity inherent in them, and a particularly good example in this respect is the first of the two letters written in the voice of 'John Ball':

> John Balle, seynte Marye prist, gretes wele alle maner men and byddes hem in the name of the Trinite, Fadur, and Sone, and Holy Gost, stonde manlyche togedyr in trewthe, and helpez trewthe and trewthe schal helpe yowe.

Now regnith pride in pris,*	*as most excellent*
And covetys is hold* wys,*	*thought / wise*
And leccherye withouten shame,	
And glotonye withouten blame.	
Envye regnith with tresone	
And slouthe is take in grete sesone*.	*in its prime*
God do bote,* for nowe is tyme. Amen.[34]	*help us*

The poem that concludes this letter fits squarely into the 'abuses' tradition I have been describing, and this poem can also be seen to use the word 'now' in the most general way, to give a general indictment immediacy. But as Rossell Hope Robbins observed some time ago, the phrase 'nowe is tyme' in this poem exerts a different order of pressure, simply because of the moment in which it was used: with the actions of the rebellion itself at its back, even such a general 'now' can turn 'criticism' into 'subversion', and at such a juncture the vague problems named (which consist of six of the Seven 'Deadly Sins' – omitting 'wrath') necessarily absorb the rebellion's motivating abuses, turning this little allegory into a real 'call for action' and insisting that remedy can only come from doing *something* in the current moment ('for *nowe* is tyme').[35] Knowing something of the moment into which this letter issued makes it possible to see just how deftly it shakes an inert tradition into consequence – to see how the simple omission of a particular recommendation (now is the time for *what?*) becomes a way of insisting that the only way to contribute to the world's problems is to do nothing (it is, in this sense, also no accident that the last sin condemned in the poem's list is 'sloth').

The techniques of this rebel letter are also important for suggesting just how subtle the most effective forms of insurgency may be, and even how that insurgency might be effective in direct proportion to its subtlety. In fact, the most subtle calls for action in Middle English dress themselves as nothing of the sort, but appear, instead, as the most straightforward descriptions of things as they are, a 'realism' so accurate that it is finally 'critical', a view so clear (or a view of something so neglected) that it is itself a strong indictment.[36] What passes for 'reality' in literature is always the product of culturally determined conventions, of course,[37] and, in the literature of complaint, 'realism' inheres less in the vividness or detail of a representation than in an increased insistence (of a kind we have already begun to see) that whatever is being described is well and truly happening. One of the earlier examples of such realism in Middle English is the alliterative poem usually called *The Simonie* (c.1325). This poem's complaint fits broadly into the abuses-of-the-world tradition, though, like *The Insurrection and Earthquake*, it brings its general pessimism into the current moment by referring to particular disasters, to the bad harvests which caused famine in 1315–17 and the insurgencies of 1321–2.[38] It also makes liberal use of the word 'now' (e.g. ll. 124, 262, 266, 361), and what it points to by this means is not only the tendency of church officials to perform their spiritual duties for money ('simonie' in the technical sense), but a whole officialdom 'turned up-so-doun' (l. 259), largely by covetousness (so payment of every sort ends up in the wrong place), but also by widespread corruption and general impropriety among all the orders of society, including knights (ll. 259–70), justices, sheriffs and mayors (ll. 289–342), and merchants and craftsmen (ll. 355–66). In all such description, change is demanded, not by any call to arms, but by an 'appealing vividness',[39] a remarkably simple insistence that we 'look' at what is happening 'now' in a 'religion' gone wholly 'amiss':

And thise abbotes and priours don agein* here rihtes;	*violate*
Hii riden wid hauk and hound, and contrefeten* knihtes.	*imitate*
Hii sholde leve swich pride, and ben religious.	
And nu* is pride maister in everich*ordred hous;	*now / every*
I-wis,*	*certainly*
Religioun is evele* i-holde* and fareth the more a-mis.	*badly / observed*
For if there come to an abbey to pore men or thre,	
And aske of hem helpe *par seinte charité**	*for the sake of charity*
Unnethe* wole any don his ernde*	*with difficulty / bidding*
other yong or old,	

> But late* him coure* ther al day in hunger   *let / cower*
>   and in cold,
>   And sterve,*   *die*
> Loke what love ther is to God, whom
>   theih seien that hii serve!

(ll. 121–32)

The critique here lies less in the particular abuse (that abbots and priors go hunting when they should not) than in the shocking juxtaposition of pleasure-taking prelates and a poverty so crushing that it kills. Covetousness of the kind that is elsewhere decried in the poem can create poverty (the parson who 'taketh al that he may' even makes 'the churche pore', 79), but the stanzas I have just quoted are the more powerful because they do not connect any such cause with these effects, leaving the conclusion to be drawn *as* the appalled reaction of any reader.

The most powerful and sustained examples of such a careful redirecting of the techniques of literary representation towards a political claim – for that is what critical realism does – are to be found in our period in *Piers Plowman* (B-text, c.1378), a poem which *The Simonie* not incidentally influenced in content and technique.[40] Poverty and need are frequently recurring issues in the wide-ranging allegory of this poem and all its versions,[41] and Langland not only tends to regard the relief of the poor as the acme of Christian virtue ('Ac [but] if ye riche have ruthe [pity], and rewarde wel the poore . . . Crist of his curteisie shal conforte yow at the laste', 14.145–7), he sometimes sees the poor themselves as uniquely ennobled by their poverty ('For ther that Poverte passeth pees folweth after', 14.303). Some have discerned 'an imaginative withdrawal from the field of material production' in such idealization,[42] but this is hardly the case in the vivid account of poor people that Langland inserts in the last revision of his poem, the C-text (*c.*1387).[43] The key passage occurs in the list of those to whom the pardon, sent from Truth to Piers Plowman, will apply:

> Woet* no man, as y wene,* who is worthy to have;   *knows / I believe*
> Ac* that most neden aren oure neyhebores, and*   *but / if*
>   we nyme* gode hede,   *take*
> As prisones in puttes* and pore folk in cotes,*   *pits / cottages*
> Charged* with childrene and chief lordes rente;   *burdened*
> That they with spynnyng may spare,* spenen* hit   *save / spend*
>   on hous-huyre,
> Bothe in mylke and in mele, to make
>   with papelotes*   *porridge*

To aglotye* with here gurles* that   *fill the stomachs of / children*
   greden* aftur fode.   *cry out*
And hemsulve also soffre muche hunger,
And wo in wynter-tymes, and wakynge on nyhtes
To rise to the reule* to rokke the cradle,   *space between bed and wall*
Bothe to carde* and to kembe, to   *comb [wool, to prepare for spinning]*
   cloute* and to wasche,   *patch clothes*
And to rybbe* and to rele,* rusches   *scrape [flax] / wind [yarn]*
   to pylie,*   *peel*
That reuthe* is to rede or in ryme shewe   *piteous*
The wo of this women that wonyeth* in cotes.*   *dwell / hovels*

                          (C 9.70–83)

Such views could be seen as yet another of Langland's many attempts to explain exactly who may be 'worthy to have'. It follows lines in which 'beggares and biddares' are excluded from Truth's 'bulle' (C 9.61), and Latin authority is cited (in the form of the schoolroom text the *Distichs of Cato*) for the view that 'you should consider to whom you may give' ('Cui des, videto', C 9.69). The general issue of need is also much complicated by the lines, just after those I have just quoted, which introduce the category of 'lunatyk lollares' (C 9.107), or the witless poor ('barfoot and bredless', C 9.121), who never beg, and who are therefore the only poor people expressly named as worthy of charity ('Suche manere men, Matheu us techeth, / We sholde have hem to house and helpe hem when they come', C 9.124–5).[44] But the conflict and qualifications are also typical of Langland's thoughts on poverty, and equally typical is the trenchant realism of the complaint lodged between these argumentative extremes – as Muscatine observed, 'again and again, Langland's sense of the present reality rends the curtain of allegory'[45] – so, set in the midst of this tortured and (implicitly) contradictory attempt to reason the need of various sorts of poor people, the claim of 'pore folk in cotes' is simply and emphatically lodged. The *real* complaint here inheres entirely in the detail with which the unremitting arduousness (the veritable 'prison') of such lives is evoked, and, while charity to such persons is never expressly demanded, an implacable claim is carried in the proximity and immediacy also attributed to such destitution ('that most neden aren oure neyhebores'). This realism is all the subtler in Langland for his tendency to avoid blaming the institutional church, the rich and omnipresent institution charged with the charity that might alleviate such suffering.[46] But the appearance of 'Piers

Ploughman' in two of the rebel letters (one of those attributed to John Ball, quoted above, as well as a letter attributed to 'Jack Carter') suggests what a 'radical reader' could do with Langland's realism.[47] And it is clear that growing Lollard demands for the 'disendowment' or the dispossession of the church for the benefit of 'alle pore menne and beggers which mowe nat travaylle for her sustenaunce' (as a Lollard 'bill' circulating in the early fifteenth century put it) tended to employ Langlandian language.[48] In other words, although Langland never got near anything like Lollard views, the 'Lollards had Langlandian sympathies' in some part because Langland's own skills as a poet often produced an implicit urgency that trumped his more overt political restraint.[49]

These effects are also visible in a more traditional form in a poem usually called *Pierce the Ploughman's Crede* (c.1393), one of a number of texts in what is sometimes called the '*Piers Plowman* tradition' (because the texts that constitute it so fully absorb Langland's techniques as well as so many of his views). It is the *Crede* in particular, though, that employs critical realism to describe its central figure, 'Peres . . . the pore man, the plowe-man':[50]

Men myghte reken* ich a* ryb so reufull* they weren.	*count / every / piteous*
His wiif walked him with with a longe gode,*	*stick [for driving cattle]*
In a cutted* cote cutted full heyghe,*	*cut / very short*
Wrapped in a wynwe schete* to weren* hire fro weders,	*winding sheet* / *protect*
Barfote on the bare iis* that the blod folwede.	*ice*
And at the londes ende laye a littell crom-bolle,*	*scrap-bowl*
And thereone lay a litell childe lapped* in cloutes,*	*folded / rags*
And tweyne* of tweie yeres olde opon a-nother syde.	*two*

(ll. 432–9)

The speaker of this poem encounters Piers after having sought to learn the Creed from various corrupt friars, and this hostility to friars may also derive from Langland (in passus 2 of *Piers Plowman* 'Lyere' is dressed as a friar and allowed to roam freely [2.230–4], and in passus 20 the friars are the first in the procession of those following the Antichrist [20.58]). The *Crede* shows how corruption has infected every mendicant order (and the poem very deftly has each of the four orders of friars impugn the others), but for this Piers (as clearly for Langland) the friars are, above all, monumentally disappointing. Because their commitment to patient poverty gives them the best chance to live a good Christian life, they defile Christian ideals all the more as they so persistently fail in their attempts:

> But for falshed of freers y fele in my soule,
> Seyinge* the synfull liif that sorweth myn herte,   *seeing*
> How thei ben clothed in cloth that clennest*   *cleanest*
>   scheweth.*   *appears*
>
> (ll. 688–90)

The poem's emphatic embrace of Lollardy is a distinct departure from Langland ('Wytnesse on Wycliff that warned hem with trewth', l. 528), and so, finally, is the direction of its critical realism, for, if both the techniques and the subject of the passage I have quoted above could be said to come straight out of the C-text, this poet turns the implicit complaint in such realism in a wholly Lollard direction: for this Piers is poor (as Langland's Piers never is). In the face of the extensive criticism of the avariciousness of friars ('When bernes [barns] ben full . . . Thanne comen . . . a lymitour [friar] . . . and loke that he leve non house that somewhat he ne lacche [get]', ll. 595–8), this manoeuvre transfers all the ethical authority that accrues to the figure of Piers in *Piers Plowman* to poverty and poor people.

A very similar set of complaints, but in a very different register of realism, can also be found in the 'mystery plays', that cycle of dramas, put on in some towns and cities in the later Middle Ages, enacting scenes from the Old and New Testament.[51] It has been suggested that the very form of these plays, in which a wide variety of people participated as both actors and dramaturges, had a certain Lollard charge: they implicitly challenged the authority of the institutional church, enacting the Lollard ideal of a 'priesthood of all believers', simply by allowing non-clerics to enact and interpret the Bible.[52] That the surviving manuscripts of the plays post-date the most vigorous persecution of the Lollards (and that the plays were still performed until 1570) suggests just how subtle this Lollardy was, but this is less surprising when the texts are examined closely, for their effectiveness as drama often lies in the various modes they simultaneously inhabit, on their ability to muffle urgency in both comedy and pathos. Thus, the two mid-fifteenth-century texts usually called the 'First' and 'Second Shepherds' Plays' in the 'Towneley' manuscript[53] are not usually seen as complaints, but, in the first of them, the character called the First Shepherd begins with verses that fit right into the general 'abuses' tradition:

> Thus this warld, as I say,   farys* on ylk* syde,   *goes / each*
> For after oure play   com sorows unryde.*[54]   *hard*

This shepherd goes on to root these general problems in more specific ills such as plague (l. 26) and an overly heavy burden of taxation ('Fermes [rents] thyk ar comyng', l. 30), but the sense of real urgency that begins to emerge around these issues – the depths of the poverty behind the general 'sorows' – is also precisely and completely covered by the drama's comedy: for when the First Shepherd insists that he has the right to drive his sheep through the Second Shepherd's pasture ('I wyll pasture my fe [flock] / Where so ever lykys [pleases] me', ll. 107–8), what becomes both ridiculously and pathetically clear is that he actually has no sheep to drive ('Yey, bot tell me, good', a Third Shepherd demands, 'where ar youre shepe, lo?', l. 135). The argument over 'nothyng' (l. 31) was doubtless a source of merriment to any audience, but it also gives penury a vivid theatrical referent (what the Third Shepherd would gesture towards is the absence that constitutes all the First Shepherd 'has'). These complaints lodge themselves in just a few of the details scripture provides around the birth of Jesus ('And there were in the same country shepherds watching and keeping the night watches over their flock. And behold an angel of the Lord stood by them', Luke 2: 8–9), but as the angel in the play insists that this birth will 'slake' the shepherds' 'sorowe' (l. 299), it translates that poverty into yet another key (now neither comic nor tragic, but sublime), for the shepherds are to find their saviour 'betwix two bestys' (l. 304).

The Second Shepherds' Play, also in the 'Towneley' manuscript, is an alternative drama on the same theme (probably by the same playwright), elaborating all of these techniques of complaint, but broadening their comedy. Here, the First Shepherd offers even greater detail about the various kinds of exploitation shepherds endure, not only heavy taxation[55] but 'purveance' (l. 33), the setting of prices at an artificially low level by royal officials, and a seigneurial system in which men of greater status or 'mantenance' (l. 35) were in a position to appropriate the poor man's 'plogh' (l. 38).[56] In the central action of the play 'Mak' steals a sheep from these shepherds and, when they come looking for it, he hides it in a cradle. This also sublimes poverty, for even if the ruse is also a madcap reworking of Jesus as the 'lamb of God', who appears at the play's end, in what staging would insist was the very same crib,[57] Mak makes absolutely clear that his actions are as desperate as they are bizarre; he steals because he has nothing to eat:

> Therfor
> Full sore am I and yll,*   *ill*
> If I stande stone styll;
> I ete not an nedyll
> Thys moneth* and more.   *month*
>   (ll. 230–4)

The point is proved when the shepherds come looking for their sheep and find no food whatsoever in Mak's home ('I can fynde no flesh / Hard nor nesh [soft], / Salt nor fresh, / Bot two tome [empty] platers', ll. 544–7). Mak is found out, but his punishment is nominal, and the play has already withdrawn any sense that he ought to be punished by allowing him to redescribe his activity as 'borow[ing]' (l. 295), a loan he is himself certain that he will make good as soon as he is able ('eft-whyte when I may', l. 294).

This gentle, ethical inversion whereby the crime of the poor man becomes as moving as it is understandable also governs a whole category of insurgent narratives usually grouped together as 'outlaw tales'.[58] These texts are complaints in stance much more than form (they articulate a space, 'outside' the culture from which its problems can be decried), but it is no accident that they have been said to emerge as a 'by-product of the agrarian social struggle' that culminated in the rising of 1381,[59] or that the first mention of the 'Robin Hood' with which so many of these tales are associated occurs in the B-text of *Piers Plowman* (Sloth says that he 'kan [knows] rymes of Robyn Hood and Randolf Erl of Chestre', 5.396). These narratives are related to those romance plots in which a knight is precipitated into a series of adventures – and, usually, a sequence of conquests – by his disenfranchisement (the earliest English romances, *King Horn* and *Havelok the Dane*, are, in this loose sense, 'outlaw tales').[60] But *The Tale of Gamelyn* (*c*.1350) is the oldest English narrative usually described in this way not least because, while the disenfranchisement is reversed in the usual way ('Thus wan [won] Gamelyn his lond and his leede [tenants]'),[61] Gamelyn founds a kind of alternative society in the intervening period ('He moste needes walke in woode that may not walke in toune', l. 672), and it is from these fringes that he emerges to root out official corruption ('The justice and the sherreve [sheriff] bothe honged hie / To waiven [swing] with ropes and with the winde drie', ll. 879–80).[62] In fact, the stories of Robin Hood, like *Gamelyn*, do not champion the poor or the needy (Robin Hood and Little John are themselves usually described as 'yeoman'), but, rather, they hold up a 'funhouse mirror' to officialdom, showing the corruption in many ranks of society (but chiefly in its most authoritative figures), standing just outside normal social boundaries (and therefore, often, in forests).[63] *A Gest of Robyn Hood* (*c*.1500), for example, one of the most substantial medieval versions of these exploits, has Robin Hood draw up a code for his men that emphasizes probity above all ('But loke ye do no husbonde [bondsman] harme / That tilleth with his ploughe', ll. 51–2), and which also insists that they protect men of every class (each 'gode yeman', 'knyght' and 'squyer').[64] In fact, later in this narrative it is a knight who finds himself in need ('My godes [goods] beth sette and solde', l. 212), after he has signed over his land to an abbot in order to ransom his son's life:

> The abbot sware a full grete othe,
> 'By God that dyed on a tree,
> Get the londe where thou may,
> For thou getest none of me.'
>   (ll. 437–40)

In the earliest tale of Robin Hood that survives, *Robin Hood and the Monk* (*c.*1450), we find a more typical criticism of corrupt clergy (although the poem is unusually savage in allowing Little John to cut off a monk's head because he has – rightly as it happens – imprisoned Robin Hood for theft),[65] but, as in all stories of this kind, its more insurgent accomplishment is to legitimate an alternative to official culture, not least by showing that alternative's effectiveness. This demonstration may therefore occur in the most light-hearted register, as it does in *Robin Hood and the Potter*, where the Sheriff of Nottingham is lured to the forest by Robin Hood's surprisingly feeble disguise as a potter ('And all that say [saw] hem sell / Seyde he had be no potter long')[66] and is only punished modestly (stripped of his horse and goods), but whose punishable sin seems to be his admiration for the outlawry that victimizes him ('"Y had lever nar [rather than have] a hundred ponde", seyde the screffe . . . "That the fals outelawe stod be me"', ll. 223–5). Since the bulk of this literature is very late (with most ballads, however long they may have endured in oral traditions, surviving only in sixteenth-century copies), medieval texts can be said to have produced the talismanic figure of 'Robin Hood' himself, a constant point of purchase on officialdom who (in the stories he seems, still, endlessly to generate) is always capable of reifying the outside of a given culture, just by standing there.[67]

Middle English complaint may be said to issue finally in such a figure, but it may be said to culminate, slightly before this, in the most effective such poem in Middle English, the poem written in the early 1460s usually called *A Trade Policy*. Although the poem speaks on behalf of tradesmen, 'spynners, carders, wevers' and other skilled workers in the cloth trade,[68] and what is at issue is a fair price for 'oure Englysshe commodyteis' (l. 52), the poem makes these issues more urgent by couching them as problems of the poor:

> For and* ye knew the sorow and hevyness   *if*
> Of the pore pepyll levyng in dystress,

How thei be oppressyd in all maner of thyng,
In yevyng* theym to mych weythe* into the   *giving / weight*
   spynnyng.
For ix li,* I wene, they schall take xii.   *li[bri] (pounds)*
This is very trewth, as y know my-selff;
Theyre wages be batyd,* theyre weyte ys encresyd;   *lessened*
Thus the spynners and carders avaylys* be all seasyd.* *profits / ended*
                                    (ll. 97–104)

These views are actually adapted from the *Libelle of English Polycye* (1436), a standard work of propaganda urging favourable terms for trade, directed towards the King's Council, and doubtless written at the behest of one of its lords (perhaps the Duke of Gloucester).[69] *A Trade Policy* is most remarkable, however, for having produced the result it sought, for the very corrective 'ordynaunce' (l. 77) it demands – the provision that 'wyrkfolk be payd in good mone' (l. 94) – was passed by Parliament in 1463 and 1464.[70]

Satire

Satire is a species of writing sometimes subsumed in complaint, but I identify it here as that poetry which throws the weight of its indictment not on problems (as 'complaint' does) but on perpetrators; its considerable energies are directed, then, not toward vividly describing suffering, but in laying responsibility for a social or political ill firmly at someone's door. The modes are certainly not always separated in practice (we have already seen how a complaint such as *The Simonie* also blames the problems it so vividly evokes on knights, justices, sheriffs, mayors, merchants and craftsmen), but they are separated often enough to warrant independent discussion. The different sorts of attention these poems give to problems also governs much more than their subject matter. Where complaint tends towards pathos, satire tends to mock. Despite its tendency toward vitriol, moreover, satire also tends to be much more conservative than complaint, much more governed by convention (that which has proved safe in the past), and much more likely to focus on the less controversial (it might seem worthwhile to write a satire *On the Follies of Fashion*, for example, but hardly necessary to complain about them).[71] Satire is, then, a genre whose characteristic power is to contain or redirect an insurgent impulse into less effective forms.

Both this general pattern and the techniques involved in the manoeuvre are particularly clear in two of the oldest satires we have in English (they survive alongside a rich collection of lyrics in British Library, MS

Harley 2253).[72] *Satire on the Retinues of the Great* (1307) is typical in a ruth-
less exuberance which is carried, on the one hand, in the poem's verse
form (richly alliterative lines, in four-line mono-rhymed stanzas) but, also,
in accusations so wildly trivial that they actually make 'what lies behind
this invective . . . difficult to discern'.[73] The poem indicts retinues as such
('whil god wes on erthe', it says, he had 'no grom to go by ys syde'),[74] but
in most of its stanzas it decries – as if in the voice of 'the great' themselves
– the inadequacy of the servants currently available:

The rybaudz* a-ryseth er the day rewe.*	*rascal / dawns*
He shrapeth* on is shabbes* ant draweth huem	*scrapes / scabs*
to dewe	
Sene is* on is browe ant on is eye-brewe,	*it is visible*
That he louseth* a losynger*, and	*delouses / liar*
shoyeth* a shrewe.	*shoes*

(ll. 21–4)

In the other of these poems, *Satire on the Consistory Courts* (1307), the
progress of a case of fornication before the diocesan courts is described in
the voice of the accused, but, again, the sense of outrage is much clearer
than any particular deficiency in the court, and 'what precisely is at issue is
again unclear'.[75] The more intricate stanza form used in this poem impels
its description with even more energy (lines alliterate but are also linked
by an entwined sequence of tail-rhyme and short-couplets with the elaborate rhyme scheme *aabccbddbeebffgggf*), and that energy is matched by the
poem's vivid evocation of the passions that courtroom procedure has to
organize (the woman the poem's speaker has had sex with but refused to
marry enters and 'biginneth to shryke, and scremeth').[76] But, if interest in
these passions operates like a complaint, this poem is most interested in
blaming the court for every problem:

At chirche ant thourh cheping,* ase dogge	*market*
y am dryve,	
That me were levere of lyve* then so for	*[out] of life*
te lyve,*	*to live in this way*
To care* of al my kynne.	*to the sorrow*
Atte constorie heo kenneth* us care,	*teach*
Ant whissheth us evele and worse to fare.	
A pruest proud as a po*	*peacock*
Seththe* weddeth us bo;	*later*
Wyde* heo* worcheth* us wo	*greatly / they / do*
For wymmene* ware.*	*of women / the goods [i.e. genitals]*

(ll. 82–90)

The poem's speaker is beaten as punishment for fornication with the woman he is now forced to marry, but he never denies his own guilt, and the poem is clear both here and throughout that it is the court officials who are *really* behaving badly (here it is the 'proud' priest who is the problem).

Satire, particularly of the more vitriolic kind, succeeds only by virtue of a kind of built-in ineffectuality whereby confusion about aims actually contributes to the poem's affect (a bluster that seems to authenticate the speaker's rage or frustration), but which ensures, in direct proportion to this passion, that the poem's criticism will miss its target. It is worth leaping to the end of the tradition to underscore this point, because it was brought to such perfection by John Skelton (*c.*1460–1529) in another extraordinarily exuberant satire, *Collyn Clout* (1521–2). This poem begins with a sense of its own inadequacy ('What can it avayle . . . To ryme or to rayle?')[77] and then a long list of the kind of things the voice of satire might say ('His heed is so fat / He wottyth never what / Ne whereof he speketh', ll. 16–18) is undercut by the insistence that such attacks will have no effect, even if correct:

> And yf that he hytte
> The nayle on the hede
> It standeth in no stede.*   *does no good*
>   (ll. 33–5)

Skelton also screens himself behind a persona ('My name is Collyn Cloute', l. 49), derides his own 'ryme' as 'ragged, / tattered and jagged' (ll. 53–4) (that is, the trimeter lines that rhyme both irregularly and at length on a single syllable), and tends to present any criticism in the voice of others ('Laye men say', l. 75). Skelton was a courtier (a tutor to that Prince Henry who later ruled as Henry VIII), and the poem's pointed indictment of church corruption was certainly given a freer rein by all these forms of self-protection:

> Ye are so puffed with pryde,
> That no many may abyde
> Your hygh and lordely lokes.
> Ye caste up then your bokes
> And vertue is forgotten,
> For then ye wyll be wroken*   *avenged*
> Of every lyght quarell
> And call a lorde a javell.*   *rascal, rogue*
>   (ll. 593–600)

But since the 'ye' here and throughout this poem also seems, in a variety of particulars, to have been Thomas Wolsey, cardinal and Archbishop of York, member of Henry VIII's Privy Council and his principal minister, such screens were a vital way of ensuring that none of this mud really stuck. In this sense, for Skelton – but, perhaps, always – satire is a literary mode that is urgent only in so far as it deliberately steps on its own toes.

The most common method Middle English writers used to contain their criticism was to direct it at whole segments of society, drawing in this way on an established tradition of 'estates satire', a genre in which the details of such attacks were themselves slightly dulled by convention and reuse. In fact, poems of this kind can be found as early as the tenth century in Latin and the twelfth century in French, although the technique is only first taken up in English in the fourteenth century by the author of *The Simonie*.[78] 'Estate' in this formulation can be equivalent to 'class', but it usually anatomizes society in sufficient detail to be more equivalent to 'profession'; 'estates satire' tends to identify the wrongs of a whole society by attacking the deficiencies characteristic of particular lines of work.

The General Prologue to *The Canterbury Tales* is the most famous instance of the genre, and it is characteristic, too, of this mode of satire in so thoroughly containing every criticism it vividly lodges. In fact, the figures of each estate are themselves so vivid that for a long time the poem was thought to evoke real people,[79] even though the poem's narrator insists that his subject is a social scheme (the 'condicioun' and 'degree' of 'ech' pilgrim):

> But nathelees, whil I have time and space,
> Er* that I ferther in this tale pace,*   *before / proceed*
> Me thinketh it* acordant to resoun   *it seems*
> To telle yow al the condicioun
> Of ech of hem, so as it semed me,
> And whiche they weren and of what degree,*   *rank*
> And eek* in what array* that they were inne;   *also / clothing*
> And at a knight than wol I first biginne.
>
> (I.35–42)

The twenty or so portraits that follow these lines name each of the pilgrims who are to make their way to Canterbury by means of their roles or daily labours, and it is also in keeping with the tradition of estates satire that some of these figures represent ideals (the Knight, the Plowman, the Clerk and the Parson in particular), the more to point up the failures of those other pilgrims who pervert their roles to a greater or lesser extent. But, even when Chaucer's criticism is most severe, he tends to dull it by his systematic 'omission of the victim' of any particular chicanery,[80] and, more generally, by a 'consistent removal of the possibility of moral judgment', in large part through 'the presentation of class failings as if they were personal idiosyncrasies':[81] it is not 'monks' who dress themselves richly and love 'fat swan' (I.206) best of all, according to The General Prologue, but 'a Monk' (I.165). The emphasis on the 'free-floating individual' where social criticism might be 'too explicitly threatening' is typical of Chaucer,[82] but he is also adapting the stock of traits and techniques of presentation with which estates satire provided him to a much more complicated structural purpose (to provide differentiated story-tellers for *The Canterbury Tales*). This redirection is possible because of the capaciousness of estates satire itself, where its tendency to balance blame with praise, as well as its very breadth, ensured that it was one of the most unthreatening modes of social criticism available.

This capacity for balance could also work in the other direction, and one of the earliest surviving instances of estates satire in Middle English, *Winner and Waster* (1352–70), exploits the genre's capacity to look at all sides in order to make room for a most unusual set of thoughts. The poem's scene is set as its narrator falls asleep on 'ane hill' next to a hawthorn and dreams of two armies drawn up in ranks.[83] The first, we will eventually learn, gathers together the prosperous estates of society, beginning with the pope and a group of lawyers, who are the forces of 'Winner':

That hede es of holy kirke	I hope* he be there	*believe*
Alle ferse to the fighte	with the folke that he ledis.*	*leads*
Another banere es upbrayde*	with a bende* of grene	*unfurled / band*
With three hedis white-herede	with howes* one lofte,	*coifs*
Croked* full craftily	and kembid in the nekke.	*curled*
Thies are ledis* of this londe	that schold	*men*
oure lawes yeme*		*care for*
That thynken* to dele* this daye		*intend / fight*
with dynttis* full many.		*blows*

(ll. 147–53)

The narrator then describes four groups of 'folk' under banners which identify them as the four orders of friars, and these are followed by a group of merchants. 'Waster's' army is sketched in only vaguely at first, but its name alone seems to ensure that it will contain the villains of the piece, so it comes as some surprise when it emerges that this army is comprised of noblemen, 'bolde sqwyeres of blode' (l. 194). In fact, the poem is insurgent, not as it criticizes any particular segment of society, but as its generosity

accommodates the most extraordinary ethics. While the body of the poem
consists of an exchange in which Winner and Waster each stand before a
king and accuse each other of doing the most harm, the poem then sets
out the logic of capitalism as a resolving compromise, pointing out that
getting depends on spending, that without 'waste' – in the economic sense
that is the only one here admitted – no one 'wins':

The more [Wastour] wastis thi wele* the better	*wealth*
the Wynner likes.	
And wayte* to me, thou Wynnere, if thou wilt	*attend carefully*
wele chefe,*	*prosper*
When I wende* appon werre*	*go / campaign*
my wyes* to lede.	*men*

(ll. 495–7)

Such a conclusion may have been a careful way of deflecting criticism from
the reigning king, Edward III, since what is certainly at issue in *Winner
and Waster* is the cost of the war Edward had been waging in France all
through the period 1350–70, and the poem arrives at a conclusion in which
it is unnecessary to point a finger (its last lines have been, in this sense,
conveniently, lost). But the poem is also bolder than would really suit such
a stratagem of containment, for there could have been nothing prudent
about observing in such a context that scarcity of any kind is good for
Winner (he hopes 'aftir an harde yere' for the 'poure' [ll. 370–4]), nor, if
the poem is really a covert defence of aristocratic consumption, would it
be helpful to point out that the magnificence of rank and social degree are
something money can buy (as Waster puts it, 'if my peple ben prode me
payes alle the better' [l. 433]). It might be too much to say that the author
of *Winner and Waster* discovered in estates satire a way to give corruption
its own voice, but the poem is extraordinary, nonetheless, for its advocacy
of that covetousness which the church, as well as most medieval thinkers
and poets, roundly condemned.

This ethics remains an isolated production, but, formally, *Winner and
Waster* may have influenced *Piers Plowman*, with which it shares a general
provenance (both poems are written in Western dialects but show influence and knowledge of London). Langland certainly draws on estates satire
in the first two visions of *Piers* (passus 1–7), sometimes allegorizing professions ('Knyghthode', 'Clergie', Pro. 116), sometimes giving allegorized
sins ('Symonie', 2.63) or human faculties ('Conscience', 2.191) professional
roles, and the role of winning remains crucial in these visions as it is represented by 'Lady Mede' (or 'reward').[84] Langland is much more anxious
about the role of winning than the author of *Winner and Waster* ('And

modiliche [wrathfully] upon Mede with myght the Kyng loked, / And gan wexe wroth with Lawe, for Mede almoost hadde shent [destroyed] it', 4.173–4), and no appropriate place has been found for Mede in civil society when the first vision breaks off (as the dreamer, Will, awakes) and new subjects are taken up. The estates satire of *Piers Plowman* is insurgent in its own, quieter way, however, as it evokes a social order in which the 'communes' not only provide the king's authority (itself a perfectly standard view) but possess substantive power, in this way taking their place as a class equivalent to 'knighthood' and 'clergy', and even the king himself:[85]

Thanne kam* there a Kyng: Knyghthod hym ladde;*	*came / led*
Might of the communes made hym to regne.*	*reign*
And thanne cam Kynde Wit* and clerkes he made,	*Native Intelligence*
For to counseillen* the Kyng and the Commune	*counsel*
save.*	*protect*
The Kyng and Knyghthod and Clergie bothe	
Casten* that the Commune sholde hem	*arranged*
communes* fynd.	*food*
The Commune contrived of Kynde Wit craftes*	*skills*
And for profit of al the peple plowmen ordeyned	
To tilie* and to travaille* as trewe lif asketh.*	*till / work / demands*
The Kyng and the Commune and Kynde Wit	
the thridde	
Shopen* lawe and leaute* – ech lif to knowe	*created / justice*
his owene.	

(Pro. 112–22)

Such a vision of society bears much more consequential fruit when the personified 'plowman' Piers emerges in the poem's second vision (after a sermon by Reason and a lengthy confession by allegorical representations of the Seven Sins). Not only does this extraordinary figure claim to know the 'Truth' that Holy Church first told Will to seek ('I knowe hym as kyndely as clerc doth hise bokes', 5.538), but he seems capable of organizing the whole of society around himself and his labour, as that society – again, generally represented in estates form – is set to work *plowing* (for Piers must complete this work before he can show others the way to 'Truth'). It was not uncommon to represent peasants as one of the estates, but Langland is unusual in representing this class by means of a plowman, and bold in bestowing such authority on this figure (the ideal plowman in The General Prologue can disguise this innovation but it seems clear that Chaucer's Plowman was meant to honour Langland's invention).[86] In fact, so much authority gathers around Piers in the course of *Piers Plowman* (in the poem's last visions, the Crucifixion is represented as Christ jousting 'in Piers armes' [18.22], and Grace makes Piers his 'procuratour' and 'reve' [19.260]) that 'in contemporary imagination [he] effectively supplanted the author as a putatively actual historical being'.[87] This is nowhere more clear than in the rising of 1381 and the appearance of Piers in the rebel letters as if he were one of their party. I have already quoted one letter in which Piers is so cited, but it is worth quoting the other, for it gives this figure even more political potency by fleshing out his life and his work (he stays home, to plow, while the rebel Jack Carter, his 'brother', 'goes' with the others to 'do' on his behalf):

> Jakke Carter prayes yowe alle that ye make a gode ende of that ye have begunnen, and doth wele ay bettur and bettur, for at the even men heryth the day. For if the ende be wele, then is alle wele. Lat Peres the Plowman my brother duelle at home and dyght us corne, and I wil go with yowe and helpe that y may to dyghte youre mete and youre drynke that ye none fayle. Lokke that Hobbe Robbyoure be wele chastised for lesyng of youre grace, for ye have gret nede to take God with you in alle youre dedes. For nowe is tyme to be war.[88]
>
> [*heryth*: praise   *dyght*: prepare   *lesyng*: losing   *war*: vigilant]

In this way, Langland's extension of estates satire was broadly insurgent as it made that genre available to the rebellion as 'a language and a style'.[89] Not only is 'Hobbe Robbyoure' a kind of estates figure (closely resembling Langland's 'Roberd the robbere' [5.462]), but 'Jakke Carter' is a personification on the exact model of 'Piers the Plowman', an everyman ('Jack') labourer ('carter'). To the extent that this letter envisions the activities of 1381 as doing 'wele' and 'ay bettur and bettur', it also understands the rising as a lived fulfilment of the ethics unfolded at the end of *Piers Plowman*'s second vision, where one must 'do well' in order to be eligible for the pardon sent by Truth to Piers ('Do wel and have wel', 7.112), an activity that is then quickly extended into the comparative and superlative by Thought (as he tells Will, at the beginning of the next vision, 'Dowel . . . and Dobet and Dobest the thridde / Arn thre faire virtues, and ben noght fer to fynde', 8.79–80).

That *Piers Plowman* should have become the watchword for revolutionary sentiments was upsetting to Langland, as some of his revisions in the C-text show,[90] but his latter-day reservations were not enough to stop these sentiments from being absorbed into other works of literature, often in even more strident forms. I have already described the critical realism of one of these poems, *Pierce the Ploughman's Crede*, but it is also worth noting here that, as that poem makes its tour through the four orders of friars, it both conforms to the conventions of estates satire and rends that genre, as it firmly brings together allusions to *Piers Plowman* (Will is 'yrobed in russet' when he sets out to seek 'Dowel' in 8.1), a distinct Lollard vocabulary ('trewe men' was a phrase that Lollards commonly used to identify others of their sect),[91] and something like the urgency of the rebel letters ('loke'), reaching outside of generalities to point to an immediate problem in a localized world:

Thei usen russet* also somme of this freres,	*rough garments*
That bitokneth* travaile and trewthe opon erthe.	*signify*
Bote loke whou* this lorels* labouren the erthe,	*how / scoundrels*
But freten* the frute that the folk full lellich*	*devour / faithfully*
biswynketh.*	*produce*
With travail of trewe men thei tymbren her houses,	
And of the curious* clothe her copes thei biggen*	*fancy / buy*
And als his getynge* is greet he schal	*income*
ben good holden.*	*considered*

(ll. 719–25)

This is not realism but, rather, the subsuming of literary technique to insurgent purpose, and a similar process can be observed, in the same tradition, in *The Plowman's Tale* (*c.*1400). This descendant of *Piers* is mediated through Chaucer's homage to Langland, for its short prologue attaches it to *The Canterbury Tales* as the tale of the Plowman that Chaucer failed to provide, but it is couched as an allegory that this Plowman once heard from a 'prest in pulpit',[92] culminating in a debate between a 'Pelican' who voices almost wholly Lollard views and a 'Griffin' who speaks for the pope. The Griffin is given very little opportunity to speak, and the poem's radical energies push the Pelican's attacks on clerical corruption ever wider until they take in the secular governance that would permit such abuse:

Wonder is, that the Parlyament	
And all the lordes of thys londe	
Here-to taken so lytell entent*	*care*
To helpe the people out of her hond;	
For they ben harder* in theyr bonde,*	*more secure / bonds*
Worse beate, and bytter brende,*	*burnt*
Than to the kyng is understande:*	*known*
God Hym helpe thys to amende!	

(ll. 677–84)

Such satire may not be any more dangerous for the boldness that would finally point a satirical finger at 'alle the lordys of this land', but it is clear that there was sufficient boldness in this period for fearful lords to try to stamp it out.

Ball's brutal death and the rounding up of the leaders of the rising of 1381 turned out, in fact, to be only the beginning of a series of ever more restrictive measures placed on rebels and insurgent expression. The most severe of these was the statute usually called *De haeretico comburendo* ('concerning the burning of heretics'), put on the books in 1401,

> for the eschewing of such Dissensions, Divisions, Hurts, Slanders and Perils in Time to Come, and that this wicked Sect, Preachings, Doctrines and Opinions should from henceforth cease and be utterly destroyed.
>
> [et pro huiusmodi dissencionibus, divisionibus, dampnis, scandalis, et periculis imposterum evitandis, et ut huiusmode nephande secta praedicaciones doctrine et opiniones cessent decetero et penitus destruantur.][93]

This statute is aimed specifically at Lollards ('this wicked Sect') rather than any work or body of literature, but it does proscribe the very sorts of rebel 'opinions' that we have seen making their way into what would also have to be called the English literary tradition; it therefore represents a moment when 'joint ecclesiastical, royal, and parliamentary action' combine to resist what English literature in this period often existed to say.[94] It is a reaction that must be counted as a literary production of sorts (in that negative sense, literature's 'accomplishment'). Censorship of this active kind is a subject I will take up more fully in the next chapter, but it is worth noting here that the satire I have been describing brought about its most dramatic cultural change when it finally foreclosed the possibility of its own writing: estates satire simply disappears as a genre in the fifteenth century.[95]

The rise of English

Although probably written by the clerics who took part in the rising, the rebel letters were insurgent wholly apart from any political claims they made: as texts purportedly written by a class of people who normally did not write – carters, ploughmen and millers – they were 'so many acts of assertive literacy'.[96] As documents that made urgent and political claims in English rather than Latin or French (the customary 'languages of record' in the church, courts and royal administration of medieval England) they were also insurgent for insisting that English had an important share in England's 'intellectual and political life'.[97] Like so many of the views that emerged in and around the rising of 1381, such claims about access to the written word as well as the importance of the vernacular were under-

written by Wycliffite thinking. In fact, among the most important pro-
grammes Wycliffites undertook was a complete translation of the Latin
Bible, since, as a fifteenth-century tract makes clear, such translations were
a natural extension of the view that the 'truth of God' should be available
to the 'common people', and that 'clerks', or the institutional church,
should not have a monopoly on such knowledge:

> Sithen that the trouthe of God stondith not in oo langage more than in
> another, but who so lyveth best and techith best plesith moost God, of
> what langage that evere it be, therefore the lawe of God writen and taught
> in Englisch may edifie the commen pepel, as it doith clerkis in Latyn,
> sithen it is the sustynance to soulis that schulden be saved.[98]

[*sithen*: since   *schulden*: ought to]

Such thinking not only associated the commons with English, but it made
English writing a figure for a certain sort of egalitarianism, as if the sharing
of a language was necessarily an instrument in the sharing out of political
authority.

Once such Wycliffite views were condemned, moreover, simply to
write in English could be regarded as an insurgent activity. In the fifteenth
century 'the primary evidence for Lollardy' often consisted of nothing
more than 'the possession of vernacular books',[99] and even copies of *The
Canterbury Tales* were seen as insurgent in such an environment.[100] So
volatile did matters become in fact that a writer such as the bishop Reginald Pecock (*c*.1392–1459), who condemned Lollard positions, still found
himself accused (and convicted) of heresy partly because he addressed
theological issues in English.[101] The larger, but less visible, consequence
of such volatility, however, was 'self-censorship', and in the fifteenth and
sixteenth centuries this earlier insurgency translated into 'a sharp decline
both in the quantity of large theological works written in English and in
their scope and originality'.[102]

The latter half of the fourteenth century was also a watershed for the use
of English in all quarters, for up until that time any such use was always
overlain with issues of class, less as English might relate to Latin (where
the issue was ecclesiastical authority), but as it related to French, since that
relationship mapped onto social hierarchies put in place by the systematic
dispossession of the English nobility by their Norman conquerors after
1066. Although there were never very many French speakers in England
(probably no more than 5,000 out of a population of 1,500,000 in the years
just after the Conquest, and settlement from Normandy and elsewhere in
France never took the proportion higher than 10 per cent of the popula-

tion), these few speakers held the lion's share of political power.[103] Latin may have remained a crucial 'language of record', particularly in royal administration and the church, but throughout the fourteenth century French remained the language of business or private communication among the aristocracy and upper clergy, the language most often used in baronial administration as well as some royal administration, and the standard language for a large proportion of legal transactions and documents (wills, contracts, deeds).[104] Two hundred and fifty years after the Norman Conquest, Robert of Gloucester was still asserting in his *Chronicle* (*c.*1300) that French was still ('yute') the language of the nobility and English was the only language known by 'low men':

Thus com lo engelond in to normandies hond	
And the normans ne couthe* speke tho* bote her	*could [not] / then*
owe speche	
And speke french as hii* dude atom* and hor*	*they / at home / their*
children dude also teche	
So that heiemen* of this lond that of hor blod come	*highmen*
Holdeth* alle thulke* speche that hii	*employ / this*
of hom nome*	*took*
Vor* bote* a man conne* frenss me	*for / unless / can speak*
telth* of him lute*	*counts / little*
Ac* lowe men holdeth to engliss and	*But*
to hor owe speche yute.**[105]	*yet*

English was, of course, widely – if sometimes fitfully – employed in many quarters throughout this period, but its official use remained an aberration until the early decades of the fifteenth century.[106]

Such restrictions meant that the use of English had insurgent power long before Wycliffite thinking made that use so dramatically controversial. This power is well illustrated by the oldest official document we have in Middle English, a proclamation of 1258 by Henry III, also issued in the other official languages of record, French and Latin. This document is, to be sure, an exception (the next indication we have that official writing occurred in English – though we do not even have that writing – comes from a description in a document from the London Guildhall of 1327 which describes certain provisions having been 'read, published and expounded in English'),[107] and, on the whole, this proclamation responds to, rather than attempts to incite, rebellion. Much in the manner of Magna Carta, it was issued by the king in order to placate a group of strong barons, and it therefore pledges to uphold past 'isetnesses' [agreements], and cedes a great deal of royal prerogative to thirteen of these barons (along with the

Archbishop of Canterbury and the Bishop of Worcester), enrolling them as the king's 'raedesmen' or 'councilors'.[108] But the use of English in this document also (oddly) follows the insurgent logic of the rebel letters, for it widens the remit of Henry's concessions, to the 'unlearned' or 'ileawede' as well as the 'ilarde' [learned]. Henry's strategy for absorbing insurgent energies to his own position was shrewder than it was effective (the Barons' War, which was to cause great bloodshed, soon erupted), but that absorption depended entirely on the potency of the official use of English in this century.[109]

A great deal of English writing in the early fourteenth century claimed to widen its own audience in exactly this way – to write English, as Robert Mannyng also put it in *Handlyng Synne* (c.1303), 'nat to lered onely, but eke to lewed'[110] – but, since the relationship of English and French remained so much an issue of status (and Latin's authority is also a factor here), the use of English in literature remained rebellious, even if not politically charged. Even in the last decades of the fourteenth century, a writer such as Thomas Usk might characterize the English of his *Testament of Love* (1385–6) as both 'rude' and 'boystous', contrasting it to the 'science' of Latin and the 'queynt termes' of French.[111] In such a context, Chaucer's decision to write a lengthy composition in English in 1369, while also borrowing freely (but without comment) from the most sophisticated French poets of the time (Machaut [d. 1377] and Froissart [d. 1410]),[112] and also addressing the most powerful of English magnates (John of Gaunt), was momentous, although he encourages us to mistake the gesture by suggesting that he makes it for no other reason than that he has had some trouble sleeping:

So whan I saw I might not slepe	
Til now late this other night,	
Upon my bed I sat upright	
And bad* oon reche* me a book,	*asked / hand*
A romaunce, and he it me tok*	*gave*
To rede and drive the night away;	
For me thoughte it* better play*	*it seemed to me / activity*
Then playe either at ches* or tables.*	*chess / backgammon*
And in this bok were written fables	
That clerkes had in olde tyme,	
And other poetes, put in rime	
To rede and for to be in minde,	
While men loved the lawe of kinde.*	*nature*
This bok ne spak* but of such thinges,	*spoke [only]*
Of quenes lives, and of kinges,	

And many other thinges smale.
Amonge al this I fond* a tale   *found*
That me thoughte a wonder thing.
(*The Book of the Duchess*, ll. 44–61)

That this simple 'tale' is the story of Ceyx and Alcione from Ovid's *Meta-morphoses* is another way in which this poem quietly enters itself in the company of the most august writing that could, at that moment, be named. *The Book of the Duchess* – an elegy, in the form of a dream vision, which takes up the delicate subject of the death of Gaunt's wife Blanche – seems to have been Chaucer's first independent composition of any length (his first substantial composition was a translation of another poem of high status, the *Roman de la Rose*), and only a decade later such a decision might have seemed almost natural (by 1386 John Gower begins his own ambitious *Confessio Amantis* in English, and it is probably also in this period that the *Gawain* poet's works were produced). But this self-evidence was itself a product of Chaucer's daring.

The more important result of Chaucer's insurgent English, however, was the increasing sense, in the fifteenth century, that English was not 'rude'. As Thomas Hoccleve marked the transformation in his *Regiment of Princes* (1412), Chaucer was the first to make English 'faire' (the 'firste fyndere of our faire langage').[113] And as John Lydgate put the point in his *Life of Our Lady* (1409–11), it was Chaucer who 'fonde the floures . . . our Rude speche . . . to enlumyne';[114] or, as he repeated the point in his *Troy Book* (1412–20): Chaucer 'gan oure tonge firste to magnifie / And adourne it with his elloquence'.[115] While it is all too easy to overemphasize the role of a particular person's creativity in revolutionary change, and the shift to English was general by the fifteenth century, the frequency with which fifteenth-century writers attribute the beauties of their own language to Chaucer suggests that it is hard to overestimate the latter's importance in this cultural change. That change would surely have occurred had Chaucer never written a word, but it took its particular historical form because he wrote precisely as and when he did.

3

Statecraft

Max Weber memorably defined the state as 'that human community which (successfully) lays claim to the monopoly of legitimate physical violence within a certain territory'.[1] This definition may seem both pessimistic and unreservedly modern, but it is not unusual in recognizing force as a key component of political structures, and if stress is laid on the term 'legitimate', then what Weber is describing is not only the importance of violence to the state but the role the state may play in limiting our most destructive tendencies.[2] The term 'statecraft' may describe the procedures of laying such claims and placing such limitations ('the art of conducting state affairs'), but since 'craft' (or 'art') also refers to the broad field in which we might place literary technique, 'statecraft' can also refer to the variety of ways in which literature and its capacities may themselves become state instruments.[3] If violence lies like a steel fist within the velvet glove of these instruments, 'statecraft' can also be the means by which state power distorts, limits, and – where it can instil enough fear – even stops the making of literature.

The various relationships the state may have to art are helpfully explored in the beast fable that concludes the Prologue to *Piers Plowman*. There, a troop of rats and mice who clearly represent the human community (they come together to debate the 'commune profit', Pro. 148) have to decide what to do about a cat who is a figure for lordship (he is 'of a court') as well as the violence that always lies, in potential, at the sharp end of lordship's 'will' (the allegory is governed by the fact that cats naturally eat rats and mice):

For a cat of a court cam when hym liked*	*when he pleased*
And overleep* hem lightliche* and laughte* hem at his wille,	*pounced on / easily / seized*
And pleide* with hem perillousli and possed* hem about.	*played* *pushed*

(Pro. 149–51)

Two responses to the cat's predations are proposed. In the first, his power is to be curbed by art, although not by literary art but, rather, a more ornamental 'crafty work' (Pro. 162), a 'belle of bras or of bright silver' (Pro. 168) that, when placed around the cat's neck, will ensure that the troop of rats and mice can avoid him ('and if hym wratheth [angry], be war and his wey shonye [avoid]', Pro. 174). A second response is proposed when it becomes clear that no rat or mouse dares this belling. A wise mouse ('that much good kouthe [knew]', Pro. 182) urges the troop to let the cat be, on the grounds that this capacity for violence is structural rather than the property of any particular cat ('Though we hadde ykilled the cat, yet sholde ther come another', Pro. 185).[4] Yet a third position emerges as support for this inaction, a quiet but firm advocacy of predatory power as that which rats and mice need to limit their own capacities to do harm:

For may no renk* ther reste have for ratons by nyghte.	*man*
For many mennes malt we mees* wolde destruye,*	*mice / destroy*
And also ye route* of ratons rende* mennes clothes,	*troop / tear*
Nere* the cat of the court that kan	*were it not for*
you overlepe*	*pounce on*
For hadde ye rattes youre will ye kouthe noght*	*could not*
rule yowselve.	

(Pro. 197–201)

In a stunning reinforcement of the second alternative, Langland has Will, the dreamer, insist that he 'dare not' interpret any of this politically charged allegory ('What this metels [dream] bymeneth, ye men that ben murye, / Devyne ye, for I ne dar, by deere God in hevene!', Pro. 209–10).

Langland's caution here is both real and significant, since it is generally thought that, however broadly it diagnoses the various alignments of literature and state power, in its day this beast fable would necessarily have seemed to refer to the volatile political scene of 1376, after the death of the Black Prince, with the heir to the throne, Richard, only nine years old and Edward III in seriously failing health. The cat would then have seemed to represent John of Gaunt, Edward III's eldest surviving son and 'the *de facto* leader of the court', while the rats and mice would have represented the 'Good Parliament' which made serious efforts to curb Gaunt's growing power.[5] Agility was a necessary part of any stance taken even in describing such power, for, as the struggle between Gaunt and parliament unfolded, the site of power moved: by the end of the year Gaunt had strongly reasserted his position, calling a new parliament by his own authority as *regni gubernator et rector* [governor and ruler of the realm], and having those instrumental in the 'Good Parliament' arrested and imprisoned (most notably, that parliament's 'speaker', Peter de la

Mare, the clear basis for that 'ratoun of renoun, moost renable of tonge' [Pro. 158] who first urges the cat's belling).[6]

Langland's real wisdom in this allegory lies not in following the mouse or Will in their political cautiousness, however, but, rather, in telling this story in a way that allows him to occupy, simultaneously, every possible orientation the speaker or poet might take toward state power, the whole thereby offering, as literature's craftiest work, the capacity to seem to kow-tow to authority even while bucking it. As Langland's allegory rings these complex changes on the relationship between art and state power, moreover, it is also wise in showing us that these relationships exist as a ratio rather than as a set of alternatives, constantly sliding along a scale because of the subtlety that literary technique and political manoeuvre share. The discussion that follows will try to follow Langland in illuminating this ratio, by looking, first, as he does, at its extremes: I shall begin with those texts that so forcefully confront state power that they provoke punishment or censure; I shall turn then to those texts in which literature is so aligned with the state that it seems to serve as nothing other than a mouthpiece for its interests. In a concluding section, I will try to analyse a more complicated middle ground in which texts exhibit just the sort of complexity Langland achieves in the passage I have just cited – a complexity often as audacious as it is subtle in the extraordinarily dangerous truths it manages to speak.

There is a historical component to the orientations and movements within these particular categories, and another important task of this chapter is to trace the effects of the historical changes that made *Piers Plowman* so alert to this complex ratio. The teachings of Wyclif and his followers are again important here, but, rather, as points on the continuum rather than as watersheds. Beginning in 1275 there is a strand of legislation which forbids the 'tell[ing] or publish[ing of] any false news or tales whereby discord may grow between the king and his people, or great men of this realm' [ne . . . de dire ne de contier nule fause novele ou controveure dont nul discord ou manere de descord our desclandre puisse sourdre entre le Rey e son pople, ou les hauz houmes de son reaume], legislation that is significantly strengthened in both 1378 and 1388.[7] Legislation against heresy begins in earnest in 1382 (the year after the rising). However, it grows ever more fierce not only in 1401 (with the statute *De haeretico comburendo*), but, also, with that extraordinarily comprehensive set of ecclesiastical provisions usually called the *Constitutions* of Archbishop Arundel (promulgated in 1409), which forbid (among other things) the study of books that have not been examined by a panel of twelve people appointed by the archbishop, the translation of scripture into English, and the proposing of 'any conclusions or propositions in the catholic faith . . . except necessary doctrine'.[8] There is growing evidence that this legislation was not wholly effective – that the Wycliffite Bible remained in widespread production and that a great variety of daring theological writing continued to flourish after the *Constitutions* – but the state's increasing interest in English writing was not confined to matters of religion, and there is no question that this is a period in which statecraft and literature become, both progressively and perniciously, ever more closely entwined.[9]

Censorship

The Middle English period begins with the extensive and determinate physical violence William of Normandy used to legitimate his claim to England's throne (though the Anglo-Saxon nobility emphatically dis-agreed, William claimed this throne as the designated heir of Edward the Confessor).[10] The Norman Conquest targeted the Anglo-Saxon polity rather than its culture, and the effect on writing was, if anything, surpris-ingly slow (I have already described the continuation of the various ver-sions of the *Anglo-Saxon Chronicle* long after the Conquest),[11] but it was really William's determination to take control of the church in England – to appoint Norman bishops to vacated sees, and to fill the monasteries with Norman monks and abbots – that slowly but surely undermined the foundations of Anglo-Saxon literary culture, in part as it was simply replaced by an 'overseas culture', but, largely, as most of the techniques of literary craft in English were forgotten through neglect.[12] The effects are, again, most dramatically illustrated in the surviving versions of the *Anglo-Saxon Chronicle* – not in its prose history, but in the different sorts of poetry that are silted into that prose on either side of its account of the Conquest. In the annals prior to 1066 these poems are either classical in style or they hover somewhere between alliterative metre and rhythmic prose,[13] and, even though some of this rhythmic prose suggests a certain broadening of tradition within Anglo-Saxon culture, on the very eve of the Conquest we still find a wholly 'classical' poem on the subject of Edward the Confessor's death, employing the typical forms of the half-line, the traditional appositional style, and a conservative diction:

> Her Eadward kingc,   Engla hlaford,
> sende sothfæste   sawle to Criste
> on godes wæra   gast haligne.

[Here King Edward, lord of the English, did send his righteous soul to
Christ, and his holy spirit into God's keeping.][14]

By 1067, however, the version of the *Chronicle* kept at Worcester includes
a poem on the virginity of Margaret, sister to Edgar 'the Aethling' (the
descendant of Edward's with the strongest ancestral claims to the English
throne), in which only the vestiges of this technique remain:

And cwæth thet heo hine   ne nanne habban wolde
Gyf hire seo uplice   arfæstnys geunnan wolde
Thet heo on maegth hade   mihtigan drihtne
Mid lichoman heortan   on thisan life sceortan
On clænre forhæfednysse   cweman mihte.

[And she said that she would never have him, nor any husband, if
heavenly mercy should grant it that she might, the mighty lord to
please, keep her heart in her body, in this brief life, and maintain her
chastity.][15]

Alliteration is so light that it is hard to know if it is accidental or vestigial
(a bad implementation of a remembered style, or all that is known of how
alliterative poetry was recently written), and rhyme at the end of some of
the half-lines ('heortan / sceortan') is a sure sign that the classical style is
collapsing. Tracing these consequences further requires that we note just
how very few works of literature there are in the century or so after the
Conquest, a 'hiatus in our literature' that may have satisfied no particular programme of state power (it is nowhere evident that William or his
successors actively suppressed English writing), but which, nevertheless,
means that literature in English was dealt a severe blow by the variety of
cultural changes that the Conquest brought about.[16]

Such absences highlight the paradox of any history of censorship too,
for where it becomes a wholly determinate force there can be no literature
to record its pressures. But writing under conditions of persecution, Leo
Strauss has argued, also 'gives rise to a peculiar technique . . . in which the
truth about all crucial things is presented exclusively between the lines',
so that, rather than hunt for absences and their determinants, what a
history of censorship may also look for are texts that seem divided against
themselves, that seem in some determinate way to be what Paul Strohm
has more recently called 'wounded'.[17] For the paradigmatic employment
of such techniques and such wounds we must jump forward to the end
of the fourteenth century when writing in English is again common, and
in particular to Thomas Usk's *Testament of Love* (1385–6), a text that could
hardly appear more innocuous, but which is everywhere inflected by the
kinds of terror that persecution can produce, not least because Usk was

one of the few Middle English writers put to death by the state (he was drawn, hanged and beheaded in 1388). Usk was not killed for writing the *Testament*, however, although the set of accusations he made against John Northhampton and his associates in the text usually referred to as his 'appeal' severely damaged his position.[18] This legal document was produced after Usk was forced to switch his allegiance from Northhampton, who was mayor of London from 1381 to 1383, to Nicholas Brembre, mayor of London in 1377 and 1383–6, because Brembre had had Usk arrested for treason. The factional politics of London in this period were deeply affected by a bitter conflict between Richard II and his more powerful magnates, and it was really Usk's decision to 'embrac[e] the politics of faction completely' that got him killed: Brembre and his party were closely allied with the king, and the parliament of 1388 was called 'merciless' because it put many people to death for no more than such an association.[19] Usk was deeply involved in these troubles when he produced the *Testament of Love*, and the broadest manifestation of such danger is the text's studied plainness: that it is in prose in this age of verse narrative allows it to avoid almost every common technique for formal complexity. This text also unfolds as the simplest of allegories in which a figure called 'Love' visits a narrator in prison, where he is grieving over the loss of 'a Margarite precious',[20] and, after a wide-ranging but straightforward consideration of misfortune, human free will, and God's omnipotence, it reaches a moving and satisfying apotheosis in which Love is attained ('and with that this lady al at ones sterte in to myn herte', III.vii.910–11). This subject matter owes a great deal to Chaucer's *Boece* (c.1380), a translation of Boethius's *Consolation of Philosophy* (c.524), not least because the *Consolation* is also a work of prison literature, since Boethius too was 'condemned to death' [morti . . . damnamur] for running foul of an equally complex factionalism in the Senate of late antique Rome.[21] Usk also owes a great deal to Chaucer's adaptation of Boethius's philosophy to the subject of 'love' in *Troilus and Criseyde* (1382–5), but the contrast is another way of showing how Usk dramatically simplifies literary possibilities, for his prose is only ever graceful by virtue of its simplicity ('by woodes that large stretes werne in, by smale pathes that swyne and hogges hadden made, as lanes with ladels their maste to seche, I walked thynkynge alone a wonder great whyle', I.iii.268–9).[22]

But the allegory of the *Testament* also creates lines that Usk can then write between, for its simplicity combined with its abstraction amounts to a texture in which controversial things can be said – but hardly understood. Thus, while it would be clear to any reader who knew the position from which Usk wrote that the experiences of the narrator were also Usk's, when Love absolves this narrator of his guilt, it is precisely *unclear* that she is referring to Usk's betrayal of Northhampton:

> Loke nowe what people haste thou served, whiche of hem al in tyme of thyne exile ever thee refresshed by the valewe of the leste coyned plate that walketh in money. Who was sorye or made any rewth for thy disease? If they hadden getten their purpose, of thy misaventure sette they nat an hawe . . . I wene of thy dethe they yeve but lyte. They loked after nothynge but after their owne lustes. And if thou lyste say the sothe, al that meyny that in this brigge thee broughten lokeden rather after thyne helpes than thee to have releved. (I.vii.720–7)

> [*walketh*: circulates   *rewth*: pity   *misaventure*: misfortune   *hawe*: trifle   *wene*: suppose   *sothe*: truth   *meyny*: group   *brigge*: trouble]

In this absolution Love 'is a factionalist herself', as Paul Strohm has put it, but no reader need ever know it, since she is eminently more circumspect than Usk was in life.[23] At the same time, as a benign but ignorant interlocutor, Love not only allows but encourages the narrator (Usk) to complain, drawing further accusations from him with her own questions (and thereby absorbing responsibility for them), repeatedly asking him to clarify an earlier point ('What understondest thou there', quod she, '. . . I not [do not know] what thou therof meanest', I.iv.401–2). Within such complaint, moreover, while the narrator may sketch out situations that could be connected to a contemporaneous English politics, his vocabulary is so anachronistic that such specifics are always projected out of contemporaneous time (Usk complains, for example, not about a London mayor and his allies but about 'myghty senatoures' [I.vi.608]). Usk's technique finally amounts to what has sometimes been called 'functional ambiguity',[24] an obscurity so complete in the end that 'the substance of the *Testament*' and, in particular, the significance of the lost 'Margarite' within it (whether, for example, it represents an object, a concept or a person) has simply 'baffled many readers'.[25]

The threat of the factionalism that so troubled Usk's life as a writer was also both registered and measured by the unlikely places in which fear can be seen to lodge in this period. For example, Chaucer's *Legend of Good Women* (1386–7) takes as its simple premise the proposition that Chaucer's past writing is a 'heresye' in violation of the 'lawe' (F 330), that it has caused such offence to a 'king' that torture and death are trailed as possible punishments ('if that thou lyve, thou shalt repenten this / So cruelly that it shal wel be sene!', F 339–40). To be sure, in the confrontation that takes place in the dream vision that forms the *Prologue* to the *Legend* (the body of the poem seems to be unfinished, but it consists of eight and a half 'lives' of particularly good or scandalously betrayed women all taken from classical myth), the king in question is Cupid, and the law that has been so offensively violated is 'Love'. On the other hand, the texts that have given such offence are texts that Chaucer had actually written:

Thou hast translated the Romaunce of the Rose,	
That is an heresye ayeins* my lawe,	*against*
And makest wise folk fro* me withdrawe;	*from*
And of Creseyde thou hast seyd as the lyste,*	*it pleases you*
That maketh men to wommen lasse* triste.*	*less / trustful*

(F 329–33)

It is also the case that the years in which Chaucer wrote the *Legend* were years in which he emphatically withdrew from London life, resigning his post as Controller of Customs (in 1386) and taking up residence outside the city, in Greenwich (until 1389). Such movements might have had no other goal than to provide him with the time he needed to write a poem as ambitious as the *Legend*, but we need not imagine him in any particular danger to see how this poem 'matches precisely the discursive environment of Richard II's court', how the 'tyrannical and potentially violent environment' in which Chaucer imagines his narrator makes him a figure nearly identical to Usk.[26] It is therefore consequential that the scheme of the *Prologue* also transforms the *Legend of Good Women* into a kind of punishment, a text that the dream-narrator is, in effect, condemned to write:

Now wol I seyn* what penance thou shalt do	*say*
For thy trespas.* Understonde yt here:	*wrong*
Thow shalt, while that thou lyvest, yer by yere,	
The moste partye* of they tyme spende	*part*
In makyng of a glorious legende	
Of goode wymmen, maydenes, and wyves,	
That weren trewe in lovyng al hire* lyves.	*their*

(F 479–85)

Through such a scheme, censorship becomes the very condition of the *Legend*'s making, and a poet presents one of his most ambitious poems as something extracted by violence from his pen. The manoeuvre is both witty and deft, but, given the moment of its production, one must also suspect it of a rather uncharacteristic honesty, the exposure (under the guise not only of wit, but of allegory) of a real and growing cultural danger.

The sense that Chaucer 'really' feared something is further pointed up by The Manciple's Tale, the penultimate narrative in *The Canterbury Tales* (but, in this sense, its last 'tale', since The Parson's Tale is, in form, a treatise on the Seven Deadly Sins rather than a fiction), for it is here, at yet another crucial moment in an important text, that Chaucer again conjures up the nightmare of censorship. The poet is figured doubly in this case, first as the crow who is silenced for telling Phebus Apollo that his wife has cuckolded him ('Ne nevere in al thy lif ne shaltou [you will not] speke', IX.297), and, second, in Phebus himself who, while capable of 'every mynstralcye' (IX.113), gives up all his art in his grief (he 'brak [broke] his mynstralcye', IX.267). The poem concludes with a long series of proverbs on the value of reticence, a large proportion of which are drawn from the common school text the *Distichs of Cato* (as such, they try to fold the tale's nightmarish vision of poetic production back into received wisdom):[27]

My sone, ful ofte for to* muche speche	*too*
Hath many a man been spilt,* as clerkes teche,	*killed*
But for litel speche avisely*	*discreetly*
Is no man shent,* to speke generally.	*harmed*

(IX.325–8)

But the nightmare cannot be put by, since the crow has been punished violently for speaking nothing other than the truth (what he 'sey . . . with his eyen [eyes]', IX.261) – or, rather, for being so 'bolde' (IX.258) as to project a hard truth across the gap between power and subservience.[28] The extraordinary irrationality this gap can breed is clearly demonstrated in Phebus's claim that the crow's 'tale' is either untrue or some sort of betrayal – a *'false tale'* in both senses of the Middle English word (IX.293)[29] – even though Phebus's actions toward his wife (whom he kills for betraying him) and the crow (whom he punishes for informing him of his cuckoldry) prove that he believes the crow and is willing to act on that belief. The self-destructiveness on view in this poem – the extent to which Phebus's censoring actions harm himself as much as anyone else – makes it an equally bold assertion on the part of Chaucer about the nature of power as such, the extent to which the kind of censorship it describes arises less to protect particular interests than to protect a site of power as a means for preventing the less powerful from having *any* say.

Where a writer felt he had such hard truths to utter, however, mere evasiveness became less and less possible in the early decades of the fifteenth century as state and church scrutiny grew ever more restrictive in its attempts to stamp out Lollardy. The text that bears the marks of the resulting pressures most acutely is *The Testimony of William Thorpe* (1407), which purports to be a straightforward transcript of Thorpe's trial for heresy before Archbishop Arundel. The text is organized around five clear 'questiouns' of belief and, rather than allegorize or fictionalize the views that constitute Thorpe's heresy, it simply spells them out:

> And anoon the Archebischop radde this rolle conteynynge this sentence: 'The thridde Sonedai after Ester in the yeer of oure Lord a thousand foure hundrid and sevene, William Thorp cam into the toun of Schrouesbirie, and thorugh leve grauntid to him for to preche, he seide openli in seynt Chaddis chirche in his sermoun that the sacrament of the auter aftir the consecracioun was material breed; and that ymagis schulden in noo wyse be worschippid; and that men schulden not goon in pilgrimage; and that preestis have now no title to tithis; and that it is not leeful to swere in ony maner'. And whanne the Archebischop hadde rad this rolle he rollid it up agen.[30]

> [*radde*: read   *Shrouesbirie*: Shrewsbury   *leve*: leave   *auter*: altar   *ymagis*: images   *wyse*: way   *leeful*: lawful]

Thorpe often evades the archbishop's questions (here, rather than say he does not believe 'these thingis', he says that he never preached them), and a strong sense that this text is more complicated than it is willing to declare emerges as Arundel responds to such evasions with a surprisingly impotent frustration ('And than the Archebischop, smytyng with his fist fersli [fiercely] upon a copbord, spake to me with a grete spirit', ll. 2070–1), even as it is also elsewhere clear that Arundel has the power to torture those who thwart him ('Bi God, I schal sette upon thi schynes [shins] a peire of pillers [manacles] that thou schalt be gladde to chaunge thi vois!', ll. 2191–2), or even to kill them:

> But I seie to thee, lewid losel, eithir now anoon consente to myn ordynaunce and submytte thee to stonde to myn decre, or bi seint Tomas thou schalt be schaven and sue thi felow into Smethefelde! (ll. 406–9)

> [*losel*: wretch, rascal   *ordynaunce*: commandment   *schaven*: shaved   *sue*: follow]

When, at the end of the text, Thorpe refuses to recant, a 'constable' leads him forth into 'prisoun' (ll. 2233–5).

In fact, the *Testimony* hides both its technique and its insurgent agenda in plain sight, for its Arundel is clearly not the historical archbishop but a figure designed to make Thorpe and his arguments more appealing – a near personification of impotent authority, helpless with all its worldly power before the higher truths that Thorpe knows and wields. There is no mention of Thorpe in Arundel's archiepiscopal register, and Thorpe's very existence is difficult to prove.[31] The *Testimony* may therefore be a text that fictionalizes the very act of censorship in order to evade it. Certainly the text manages to invert the procedure by which a fear of retribution might limit the promulgation of heretical belief, for, precisely as it places Thorpe's beliefs under negative scrutiny, it manages to disseminate them in detail and at great length.[32] The same sort of inversion also helps to shape the figure Thorpe cuts within the text, for even as his vulnerability grows in the face of an Arundel who simply exults in his power ('Wel, wel, thou schalt seie othir wise or [before] that I leve thee!', ll. 1053–4), as the trial slopes towards Thorpe's inevitable injury, it is this injury that has already become the warrant of Thorpe's truthfulness: 'in myn herte I thoughte that God dide to me a greet grace if he wolde of his greet mercy brynge me into suche an eende' (ll. 410–11). In this way Thorpe is not so much a man advancing certain beliefs as a martyr prepared to die in their cause, and the *Testimony* is not so much a record as 'a substitute saint's life'.[33]

The techniques of evasion that invert the *Testimony*'s stated purposes may also be said to operate in two poems in the '*Piers Plowman* tradition', *Richard the Redeless* (c.1400) and *Mum and the Sothsegger* (c.1409). *Richard* seems almost foolhardy in the boldness of its political advice, not only pointing out Richard II's many 'myssededis',[34] but also criticizing his tendency to silence or harm those who offer him advice:

And ho-so* pleyned* to the prince that pees shulde kepe	*whoever / appealed*
. . .	
He was lyghtliche* ylaughte*	*easily / seized*
and y-luggyd* of many,	*baited*
And y-mummyd* on the mouthe and	*silenced*
manaced* to the deth.	*menaced*

(III.334, 336–7)

No statement is quite what it appears in this text either, however, and the poem's ostensible boldness is effectively 'y-mummyd' by the important chronological fact it mentions but then utterly ignores: this copious advice is being offered to Richard not only when he could no longer make anyone suffer for it, but when he could no longer really heed it – since it is offered after his deposition ('covetise hath crasid [crashed] youre croune for evere!', I.95), when he was no longer king. The direction of this address might be a strategy for addressing advice, covertly, to the current king, Henry IV, who is also firmly and constantly praised ('Henri . . . / Whom all the londe loved in lengthe and in brede [breadth]', I.11–12), but this could also be a different form in which the poem's fear expresses itself. So extensive did that fear clearly become that it is taken as the central subject of *Mum and the Sothsegger*, where such prudent silence comes to be the norm not only among advisers to kings, but in the universities and among friars, monks, the whole priesthood and every man of the town: in this poem's vision, in fact, 'Mum', the personification of such silence, is 'maister moste uppon erthe'.[35] Like Langland's Will, the narrator of *Mum* discovers this general condition by wandering through a varied landscape peopled with generalizing personifications, but, unlike Will, he does not fall asleep until the middle of the poem, at which point he dreams of a 'gardyner' (l. 976), and the bees that he keeps:

The bomelyng* of the bees, as Bartholomew us telleth,	*bumbling*
Thair noyse and thaire notz at eve* and eeke at morowe,	*evening*
Lyve* hit wel, thair lydene* the leste of thaym hit knoweth.	*believe / language*
The most merciful among thaym and meukest* of his deedes	*meekest*
Ys king of bees comunely,* as clergie us telleth,	*generally*
And sperelees,* and in wil to spare that been hym under,	*without a sting*
Or yf he haue oon, he harmeth ne hurteth noon* in sothe.	*no one*
For venym* doeth not folowe hym but vertue in alle workes,	*venom*
To reule thaym by reason and by right-ful domes,*	*lawful judgements*
Thorough contente* of the cumpaignie that closeth* alle in oone.	*agreement* / *unites*

(ll. 1028–37)

This description concludes with the narrator pretending that he does not know what this vision means ('hit is to mistike for me', l. 1089), thereby absorbing the fear of state power that has been so extensively described even to this revelatory moment, since it seems clear that the beekeeper is the 'sothsegger' [truth-teller] that political England lacks, and this vision not only of a cooperative community (ruled by 'reason') but a *noisy* one – in this sense, wholly free from censorship – is the poem's utopian imagining, although it never actually manages to formulate a political recommendation. When 'conseille' to 'the king' (l. 1343) is finally ventured upon, it is offered not in the narrator's voice, but as the contents of 'many a prive poyse [secret poem]', found, tied up, in a 'bagge' (ll. 1343–4).[36]

The constraining legislation that made the decades around *Mum*'s writing so perilous for the English writer yielded to greater uncertainty in the latter half of the fifteenth century, as England descended into what can only be called civil war, and political life was increasingly characterized by 'a barbarity at once atavistic and new'.[37] Henry VI was deposed (on two separate occasions, in 1461 and 1471), as was Edward IV (when Henry VI briefly supplanted him) and Richard III (in 1485). In between these dramatic changes in kingship, there were also great swings in the power of kings and the magnates who supported and opposed them. The central period of this turmoil (1455–85) is often called the 'Wars of the Roses' after the badges chosen by the two primary sides (the red rose symbolizing the 'Lancastrians' and the white rose symbolizing the 'Yorkists'), but the period was particularly treacherous for any one person to navigate, because factions were so fluid and even the most powerful of magnates repeatedly switched sides: Richard Neville, Earl of Warwick, offers a telling example here, for he not only helped Edward IV depose Henry in 1461, but he also later helped Henry depose Edward, in 1471.[38] The same movements characterized the career of the writer John Fortescue (c.1397–1479): although he was powerful enough in his own right (he was, for a time, Chief Justice of the Court of King's Bench), and was the author of several foundational texts on natural law (*De Natura Legis Naturae*) and the historical basis of the English law (*De Laudibus Legum Anglie* [1468–71]), Fortescue wrote so frequently in support of the Lancastrian right to the throne that, when the Yorkists came to power in 1471, he only survived because he was willing to renounce all his earlier justifications (in a document usually called the 'Declaration').[39] But it was Thomas Malory whose career as a writer was more or less produced by such movements, for he was similarly malleable in his allegiances, and repeatedly found himself in prison as a result (he was jailed for most of the 1450s for opposing the king, as a 'Yorkist', and he was jailed in the period 1468–70 for having supported Henry VI as a 'Lancastrian'), and, as a result, it seems clear, the last of these incarcerations afforded him the opportunity to write most if not all of his *Morte Darthur*.[40] In fact, while prison represents an extreme in the pressures the state can bring to bear on a writer, by an odd paradox, once the state has dealt this particular blow, a writer such as Malory can find himself not only *freed to write* (by the unoccupied time that constituted his punishment), but provided with a subject by the terms of his confinement. Thus, not only does Malory write feelingly about the trials of imprisonment (at one point describing Sir Trystram's 'syknes' as the 'grettist payne a presoner may have' [2: 540]), but his position, somehow both external to as well as deeply ensnared by chivalric ethics and dynastic politics, allowed him to direct a withering scepticism at both.

The best measure of the tumult that beset this period, however, is that 'prison literature' becomes a meaningful category. In addition to the *Morte*, two sequences of delicate and accomplished love lyrics were the fruits of a lengthy imprisonment, in the latter case, of Charles, Duke of Orléans (1394–1465), captured at the battle of Agincourt (1415) and captive in England for the next twenty years (first in the Tower, and then in the guardianship of a series of noblemen); since Charles otherwise wrote in French, his decision to write in English – and probably his ability to do so – was doubtless another unforeseen product of imprisonment.[41] It is also possible to see these circumstances reflected in certain images in these lyrics ('Opressid with thought, langoure, and hevynes, / Forcast in woo and all forwrappid [wrapped up] in payne'), although it is clear that Charles's captivity was not arduous,[42] and, if prison did provide him with a certain vocabulary for pain, such descriptions are also fully licensed by the conventions of the subservient lover in court poetry:

Myn only ioy, my lady and maystres,*	*mistress*
Whiche are the hope of all my worldis wele,*	*well-being*
Withouten whom that plesere nor gladnes	
As may me helpe, god wot,*	*knows*
right nevyr a dele,*	*not at all*
So that* it lust* yow witen of	*provided that / pleases*
myn hele,*	*health*
A noyous* liif y lede in gret turment	*troubled*
And so endewre* it to my caris felle*	*endure / painful*
Only bicause y am from yow absent.	

(ll. 5688–95)

For some prisoners, of course, hardship will not only limit the possibilities for writing, it may so fill a writer's horizon that no amount of convention can control it. George Ashby was such a prisoner (yet another Lancastrian jailed when the Yorkists took power in 1461), and *A Prisoner's Reflections* (1463) is just such a text, for while Ashby tries to present his troubles as an example to others to 'kepe pacience' in the face of any 'gret wrong' or 'iniury',[43] what is wholly 'occupying' him throughout this poem is the difficulty of his wretched 'fate' (l. 339). In fact, what the poem most vividly evokes is the real horror of being placed in 'a sepulture / Of lyvynge men' (ll. 344–5), of having the power to think and speak and write while having nothing for such faculties to act upon but 'strong lokkes' (l. 345) and 'castigacon' (l. 347).

Propaganda

Literature can also align itself so firmly with the state's interests that it
seems to speak with its voice, not only endorsing political orthodoxy, but
becoming, in this process, a craft of state in its own right. In the Middle
Ages, where the vivid rehearsal – and moving reinforcement – of 'a pre-
vailing but adjustable set of commonplaces and beliefs' was often all that
art hoped to be, and where, as we have seen, cultural authority emanated
as much from the church as the king, 'propaganda' was often the norm,
taking in much more than the 'locally political'.[44] Indeed, medieval propaganda may be detected not by a characteristic stridency or persuasive
insistence – as in the modern case – but, rather, by a *generosity* of subject,
an openness to different sorts of concerns through which the 'currents
coming from many wells could flow together', where passions of one sort
could be quietly redirected toward some other end.[45] The literature of
devotion offers the most pervasive example here, since it so often sought to
substitute piety for more earthly goals and ethics, and the poem *The Luve-
Ron* (or 'love song'), copied in about 1270, offers an unusually sustained
example of such redirection. It sings the lengthy praises of a figure who
is, by turns, a 'lefmon' [sweetheart],[46] a 'riche mon' (l. 81), a 'treowe king'
(l. 89), and a 'knyhte' (l. 144) 'ful of fyn amur' [full of courtly love] (l. 182),
but who, nonetheless, is discovered in the poem's last stanza sitting 'heye
in heovene' (l. 208). The identity of this lover is no secret (in its first line
this love song claims to have been written at the behest of a 'mayde Cristes'
[a maid of Christ]), and there is certainly a long tradition of representing
devotion to Christ in the language of romance,[47] but the poem could still
be said to be structurally suspenseful, for it never expressly names Christ
as the desired 'lefmon', and it everywhere insists on evoking this higher
end, even where the contrast is negative, in terms of an amorous and
courtly world:

Hwer* is Paris and Heleyne	*where*
That weren so bryht* and feyre on bleo,*	*bright / face*
Amadas and Ideyne,	
Tristram, Yseude and alle theo?*	*those*

(ll. 65–8)

Luve-Ron has been seen as part of a specific programme, organized by the
friars for 'turning a liking for song into profitable ways of piety', whose
most significant production was the religious 'carol' (a poem in stanzas

with a refrain).[48] Certainly, *Luve-Ron* typifies the defining capacity of propaganda to redirect energies by blurring lines between very different ideas and things: as Kantorowicz put this point, by constantly placing 'interrelated, interdependent arguments . . . on the same general denominator', what propaganda can accomplish – what may define its distinctive capacity as a verbal form – is the 'general equation of anything with everything'.[49]

Such blurring was also possible within the territory of the political, and this is particularly well illustrated by a set of eleven poems written by Laurence Minot to celebrate English victories against the Scots and the French between the battle of Halidon Hill (1333) and the taking of the castle at Guînes (1352). These poems vary in texture (usually narrating key events but sometimes pausing to praise particular acts of bravery), and they employ an extraordinary variety of verse forms (from simple tail-rhyme to much more elaborate alternating and interlocked rhyme schemes) and lines (both long and short, alliterating and not), but their theme is ever one – the bravery and success of the English, and, in particular, the king, Edward III ('oure king and his men held the felde / stalwortly with spere and schelde').[50] It is here, moreover, that we can begin to see propaganda's powers of equation pulling in the opposite direction, as the devotional is annexed to the secular and Edward always succeeds because he is favoured by God:

His redy rout mot* Jhesu spede*	*may / help*
And save tham both by night and day;	
That lord of hevyn mot* Edward lede*	*must / favour*
And maintene him als he wele may	
The Scottes now all wide will sprede,	
For thai have failed of thaire pray*	*their prey*
Now er thai dareand* all for drede	*cowering*
That war before so stout and gay.	
(I.33–40)	

It is not clear whether Minot was commissioned to write these poems, or whether he wrote out of his own patriotic fervour (perhaps for preferment in that case as well), but the governing historical fact is that, while he tends to write from the stance of an eyewitness, these poems were probably written long after the battles they commemorate.[51] They are also propagandistic not simply because politically partisan, but because they mobilize all of literature's resources (rhetoric, narrative, a precision and power of diction) in order to conjure up a political scene in which there is only one side: this involves the claim that these poems contain the only truth ('Lystens now and ye may lere, / als men the suth [truth] may understand', VIII.57–8), the alignment of virtue entirely on one side (so the Scots are 'ful of treson', I.76, the English are 'maintene[d]' by the 'lord of hevyn', I.35–6), and the insistence that there was never any possibility of a bad outcome ('Edward sall have al his will', II.34). Such poems make their case by neither argument nor detailed description but, rather, by the presumption that all the attributes of a positive moral universe (virtue, justice and right) are naturally aligned with Edward's military projects.

It is by creating and then embracing such asymmetries as given facts that propaganda gains its characteristic verbal energy, as can be seen in the unusually exuberant poems of this kind that survive in the early four-teenth-century collection of Middle English in London, British Library, MS Harley 2253. Among the earliest of these must be *A Song of Lewes*, since it celebrates the victory of Simon de Montfort over Richard of Cornwall, Henry III's brother, in 1264, during the 'Barons' Wars':

By god that is aboven ous, he dude muche synne	
That lette passen over see the erl of Warynne;	
He hath robbed engelond, the mores ant the fenne,*	*fens*
The gold ant the selver ant yboren* henne* for love	*brought / hence*
of Wyndesore.	
Richard [thah thou be ever trichard,*	*traitor*
Tricchen* shalt thou nevermore!][52]	*betray*

The projection of 'synne' (rather than merely wrong) onto the other side follows the logic I described above, but this poem is more keen to embrace the various sorts of passion – the self-satisfaction as well as the threats – licensed by the insistence that virtue lies only on one side (a modern edition rightly peppers its strongly declarative lines with exclamation marks). As another poem in the Harley MS, *The Flemish Insurrection*, makes clear, such feeling need not always align itself against an enemy, and could try instead to whip up fellow feeling into hatred for those defined as 'other'. This poem's political point of departure is a general English sympathy for the Flemish weavers, who were in open revolt against an oppressive French rule in 1302 (with a settlement coming only in 1305), but it builds its real passion out of English hostility toward the French and the importance of the Flemish weavers as buyers of English exports of wool.[53] Perhaps because of the complexity of the politics involved, this is a much more narrative poem than any of the other instances of propaganda I have so far mentioned, but it is no different in so far as it uses the inevitability of defeat (and the presumption of French perfidy) as an excuse to gloat:

> Tho* wolde the baylies,* that were come
>> from fraunce,   *then / officers*
> Dryve the flemisshe that made the destaunce;
> Hue* turnden hem ageynes with suerd*   *they / sword*
>> and with launce,
>> Stronge men ant lyht.*   *swift*
> Y telle ou for sothe, for al huere bobaunce,*   *pride*
> Ne for the avowerie* of the kyng of fraunce,   *protection*
> Tuenti score ant fyve haden ther meschaunce,
>> By day ant eke by nyht.[54]

What the Harley MS poems taken together begin to show is that, consequent upon their one-sided equations, is a kind of moral ugliness whereby the most appalling events or difficulties can be celebrated because they befall someone else. *The Execution of Sir Simon Fraser* proves this particularly well, for, in its description of the capture of a number of prominent Scots leaders in the early fourteenth-century campaigns of Edward I (the poem refers to events of 1306), it not only places 'the traytours of scotlond . . . that loveth falsnesse'[55] in direct opposition to 'sire edward oure kyng, that ful ys of piete' (l. 25), but it takes constant pleasure in the description of physical injury – that these 'scottes' are 'nou to-drawe' (l. 9). The poem's story may be said to build to the moment when it describes the gruesome death of Fraser himself:

> Tho he come to galewes,* furst   *gallows*
>> he was an-honge*   *hanged*
> Al quick byheueded, thah* him   *although*
>> thohte* longe.   *it seemed to him*
> Seththe* he was y-opened, is   *afterwards*
>> boweles ybrend;*   *burnt*
> The heved to londone brugge* wes send   *bridge*
>> to shonde.*   *dishonour*
>>   (ll. 185–9)

The spectacle is rendered the more horrifying for the 'gomen' [pleasure] and 'solas' (l. 194) of those who hasten to London Bridge to see Fraser's severed head, and even children are described looking on ('moni wes the wyves chil that ther-on loketh a day', l. 196), as it happens, vindictively (in this poem, they are made to feel sorrow that 'so feir' a man should have ended 'so villiche' [foully], ll. 199–200).[56]

The power of such techniques (one might even call them tactics), both emotional and rhetorical, is also measured by the decision of Pierre Langtoft (d. 1305) to include certain 'soldier's songs' in chronicle descriptions of Edward I's wars on the Scottish border:[57]

The sothe* is to see	*truth*
Without any lesyng,*	*lie*
Alle is thi hething*	*scorn*
Fallen opon the.	
Skaterd be the Scottes,	
Hoderd* in thar hottes,*	*huddled / houses*
Never thay ne the.*	*may thrive*
Ryth if I rede,	
Thai tumbed* in Twede,	*tumbled*
Thet woned* by the se.[58]	*is located*

Langtoft says that these and some other songs are rhymed in English 'in reproval of the Scot' and 'in mockery' ('en reprovaunt le Escot. . . . et par mokerye en Englays rymeyé' [2:234]), and the form of his chronicle seems to authenticate the claim, since it is otherwise in French alexandrines. But the view that these are 'popular' songs, sampled from the very battlefield (or near it), is, Turville-Petre has suggested, only a 'touching theory', and, as Langtoft's editor pointed out, the tail-rhyme form of the verses is itself rather bookish (more suited to writing than singing).[59] Nevertheless, even as no more than a chronicler's confection, such songs bring to historical narrative all of propaganda's capacities to blur the boundaries between victory and moral advantage (so that, when the Scots tumble into the Tweed, it is certainly 'ryth'), all the while hurling abuse ('hething') and taking a pitiless pleasure in the misfortune of others ('hoderd in thar hottes') even as the chronicler takes no responsibility for such views himself. Langtoft could not be more partisan when narrating events in his own voice ('Car de cele part fust unkes une fez, / Denz vile ne dehors, un bon fet esprovez' [For on that side was never once, within town or without, a good deed shown]),[60] but the number of such songs Langtoft added (twelve in all) suggest their rhetorical usefulness, as does Robert Mannyng's decision to retain these songs when he used Langtoft as a source for part of his own *Chronicle* (*c*.1338).[61] Because Mannyng's versions of these songs are sometimes different, it has been suggested that he 'somehow knew fuller versions of the original English'.[62] But what Mannyng clearly knew better were the kinds of emotional weight propaganda could lend a political position, and, sharing Langtoft's politics ('for him the treachery of the Scots was one of the chief lessons of history'), he simply elaborated Langtoft's extraordinarily effective technique.[63]

Poetry aligned with the interests of power need not be vicious, however, and in perfect keeping with its penchant for turning a fact into its opposite, propaganda tends to become positive and celebratory only when power has reached a difficult pass, as, for example, in the set of tricky successions that followed the deposition of Richard II, at which point it became almost obligatory, even for an accomplished poet, to cobble together an obsequy in praise of the current king. Chaucer was in fact the first to get in on this act with a begging poem addressed to the newly crowned Henry IV. The main purpose of this poem, anthologized now as *The Complaint of Chaucer to his Purse*, was to secure the continuation of Chaucer's annuity under the new regime, but it pursued that end in part by setting out Henry's threefold 'right' to a throne that he had, in fact, usurped ('O conquerour of Brutus Albyon / Which that by lyne and free eleccion / Been verray [true] kyng', ll. 22–4). A similarly bold and tendentious argument is made on Henry's behalf by Gower in *In Praise of Peace* ('Thi title is knowe uppon thin ancestrie'),[64] a poem that shows particularly well how a dicey political moment is well served by propaganda's capacity to equate a fact with its opposite: for while the poem argues fervently against warfare of any kind ('if werre may be left, tak pes on honde', l. 83), it understands the war Henry waged in order to claim the crown as that which *produced* peace ('A kyng may make werre uppon his right, / For of bataile the final ende is pees', ll. 65–6). However dubious his father's claim to the throne may have been, the military campaigns of Henry V in France were so successful that celebration had much more to work with, and there are, accordingly, two different poems customarily called the *Battle of Agincourt* (1415), the second of them long enough to be divided into sections named (as in *Piers Plowman*) 'passus'.[65] This success also lets bloodthirstiness back in, and a carol on Agincourt again equates death and slaughter with 'mirth' and 'joy':

> There dukys and erlys, lorde and barone
> Were take* and slayne, and that wel sone,*   taken / very quickly
> And summe were ladde into Lundone,
> With joye and merthe* and grete renone;   mirth
> Deo gracias Anglia
> Redde pro Victoria.*[66]   *England, give thanks to God on account of victory.*

Such poetry also found extraordinarily fertile ground within England after the Wars of the Roses began. In a particularly violent episode, each individual stanza of *The Five Dogs of London* (1456), each speaking in the voice of a 'dog' or 'servant' betrayed by the Duke of York ('Wat planet compellyd me, or what signe, / To serve that man that all men hate?'),[67] was placed in the mouth of a dog's head, and displayed 'upon the Standard in Fletestrete'.[68] By contrast, the Lancastrians become 'dogges' in the *Battle of Northampton* (1460), pursued and defeated by the Yorkist 'bere' (Richard, Earl of Warwick).[69] In such territory the poetry of praise again has a great deal of work to do, although it now unfolds from two directions. There is, for the Lancastrian side, a carol by John Audelay (fl. 1417–26) transforming Henry VI's dangerous youthfulness (he was, at the age of one, putative ruler of the newly forged 'kingdom' of England and France) into a beguiling innocence ('ful yong, tender of age . . . Lovele [lovely] and lofte [noble] of his lenage [lineage], / Both perles prince and kyng veray [true]').[70] There are also John Lydgate's *The Title and Pedigree of Henry VI* (1427) and *Ballade to King Henry VI upon his Coronation* (1429), which forcefully reargue the Lancastrian claim to the throne.[71] On the Yorkist side, however, there was yet another carol annexing divine favour to Edward IV's usurpation ('Sithe God hathe chose the to be his knyt / And posseside the in thi right').[72] And there is also a long poem, *On the Recovery of the Throne by Edward IV* (1471), which attacks those Lancastrians who 'trowbelid the ryalle prynce'[73] with 'myschevus dedes' (277), 'malice' (277) and 'false treson' (278).

Such a war of words also characterizes theological controversies of the period, for Wycliffite views were not only punished by the state, they were emphatically countered by state-sponsored writings that vigorously propounded the orthodoxies challenged by Wyclif and his followers. A great deal of this writing necessarily occurred in Latin, although, as I mentioned in the previous chapter, Reginald Pecock was notable for attempting to reply to the Lollards in the vernacular in a series of tracts (*The Reule of Crysten Religioun, Repressor of Over Much Blaming of the Clergy* and *Donet*).[74] But the most important English text of this kind was the *Mirror of the Blessed Life of Jesus Christ*, a free translation by the Carthusian monk Nicholas Love (d. 1424) of the *Meditationes Vitae Christi* (a Franciscan work of the fourteenth century). Seventeen surviving manuscripts of the work contain a memorandum which insists that the text was submitted to Archbishop Arundel himself for 'inspection and due examination' [ad inspiciendum et debite examinandum] before it was 'published universally for the edification of the faithful and the confutation of heretics or lollards' [puplice communicandum fore decrevit et mandavit ad fidelium edificacionem, et hereticorum sive lollardorum confutacionem].[75] The subject of these meditations is the life of Christ, unfolded in its key episodes, but

Love often expands events in directions that expressly defend those aspects of the institutional church that the Lollards attacked, such as confession before a priest (which is defended in the context of a description of Mary Magdalene's conversion) and the doctrine of transubstantiation (which is worked into a description of the Last Supper):[76]

> And verrey cristies body that suffrede deth upon the crosse is there in that sacrament bodily under the forme and liknes of brede, and his verrey blode undur likenes of wyne substancially and holely, without any feynyng or deceit, and not onely in figure as the fals heritike seith. (151–2)
>
> [*verrey*: true   *substancially*: in substance   *holely*: wholly]

The pressing of orthodoxy could hardly be less pedantic, and yet Love's text acquires all of propaganda's usual urgency in the versions of scripture that frame such disquisitions:

> If thou beholde wele thi lord, thou maiht have here matire ynouh of hye compassion, seynge him so tormentede, that fro the sole of the fote in to the hiest part of the hede, ther was in him none hole place nor membre without passion. (181)
>
> [*maiht*: might   *hiest*: highest]

Polemic and 'the trewe byleve that holi chirche hat tauht us' (152) are in this way made to emerge from the Gospels, and the quiet movement of the text from doctrine to such 'passion' makes propaganda's typically severe equations – in this case between the Gospels' truth and church-authorized sacrament – but with an unusual subtlety.

If Arundel actually persuaded Love to write the *Mirror* (one possible interpretation of such an overt declaration of approval), then this text is also a manifestation of the growing importance of writing produced *by* the state in late medieval England, a blending of political interest and literary ambition that was a direct result of the increasing use of English in official documents. The bureaucratic forum for this blurring was established in the thirteenth and early fourteenth centuries within the 'writing offices' in the central administrative bodies that grew out of the king's household (chancery, the Privy Seal and the Signet). Writing in these offices was mainly in French and Latin, as I suggested in the last chapter, but in the early decades of the fifteenth century English began a slow and steady (and then ever more rapid) encroachment. The result was what Ethan Knapp has called the 'bureaucratic muse', an absorption of the forms, styles and stances of administrative documents to poetry, by a poet such as Thomas Hoccleve, who was also a clerk of the Privy Seal.[77] In fact, Hoccleve creates a kind of

bureaucratic persona for himself in many of his poems, a figure constantly
dogged by the gritty realities of needing to write to earn a living:

> What man that three and twenti yeer and more
> In wrytynge hath continued, as have I,
> I dar wel seyn, it smertith* him ful sore   *hurts*
> In every veyne* and place of his body;   *vein*
> And yen* moost it greeveth, treewely,   *eyes*
> Of any craft that man can ymagyne.[78]

These lines come from a lengthy dialogue between this persona and a
'beggar' in the prologue to the *Regiment of Princes* (the dialogue comprises
2156 of the poem's 5463 lines), and it is also part of Hoccleve's strategy
of self-presentation to emphasize his powerlessness – to stage, quite dramatically at times, the difficulty clerks in his position had in extracting the
payments that had been promised to them:

> His lettre he takith and foorth gooth his way,
> And biddith us to douten* us nothyng;*   *fear / not at all*
> His lord shal thanken us anothir day.
>   . . .
> What shul we do? We dar noon argument
> Make ageyn him, but faire and wel him trete,
> Lest he reporte amis* and make us shent.*   *falsely / ruined*
>   (ll. 1506–8, 1513–15)

The detail itself is beguiling (the portrait feels, for all the world, like autobiography of the most modern kind), although it eventually tails off into
a description of the most general and anodyne difficulties ('The worldly
ryche men, han [have] no knowleche / What that they been of hir condicioun', ll. 1933–4).[79] But it also eventually becomes clear that the abjection
as well as the generality are part of a much larger strategy of positioning
whereby this bureaucratic figure is so enshrined in his 'meekness' that he
may not only address but advise a much more powerful prince (in this
case, Prince Henry, the future Henry V):

> Hy noble and mighty Prince excellent,
> My lord the Prince, o my lord gracious,
> I, humble servant and obedient
> Unto your estat* hy and glorious,   *estate*
> Of which I am ful tendre* and ful gelous,*   *devoted / solicitous*
> Me recommande* unto your worthynesse,   *I recommend myself*
> With herte enteer* and spirit of meeknesse.   *whole*
>   (ll. 2017–23)

Since the bulk of the poem consists of such advice (the mercy or patience proper to a king, the prodigality or avarice he should avoid), it could appropriately be grouped with the poems of 'counsel' I discuss below.[80] It has also been argued that the *Regiment* actually 'constrains the king . . . by its representation of the unruly, potentially unregimented body politic'.[81] But, to my mind, Hoccleve's method of self-fashioning – his thoroughly bureaucratic subservience – tends to annex all of propaganda's characteristic stances and energies to such counsel, most of all as he insists on addressing Henry as a prince whose 'altitude' already exceeds any recommendation his poor 'pamfilet' can make (ll. 2059–62), a king *proved*, rather than made, wise for having sought such advice ('. . . it be no maneere of neede / Yow to consaille what to doon or leeve', ll. 2136–7). In this sense, the *Regiment* is a 'calculated act of self-promotion' – not on the part of Hoccleve, the petitionary poet, but on the part of Prince Henry himself.[82]

So it may come as little surprise that Hoccleve also wrote poems that were more purely propagandistic. In his *Remonstrance to John Oldcastle* (1415), for example, a condemnation of a notorious Lollard and his doctrines, we find the typical bloodthirstiness ('And but yee do god, I byseeche a boone, / That in the fyr yee feele may the sore!'),[83] and these dark wishes also serve as a fulcrum for unfolding an absolute anti-Lollard orthodoxy ('the preest is instrument / Of god thurgh whos wordes trustith this ay, / The preest makith the blessid sacrament', ll. 334–6). Less vicious but equally oriented to the interests of power is a 'balade' praising Henry V for translating Richard II's bones to Westminster in 1413 ('See eek how our Kynges benignitee / And lovyng herte his vertu can bywreye [divulge]', ll. 33–4).[84] The sequence of poems usually called the *Series* begins, in *Thomas Hoccleve's Complaint*, with an extraordinarily vivid self-description, virtually unprecedented in its honest account of mental breakdown,[85] but soon enough, in the next poem, the *Dialogue with a Friend*, such autobiography is again put in the service of praise for a powerful magnate, in this case Henry V's brother, Humphrey, Duke of Gloucester ('Next our lord lige, our kyng victorious, / In al this wyde world lord is ther noon / Un-to me so good ne so gracious').[86]

One of the more extraordinary works of propaganda produced in late medieval England, *The Libelle of English Policy* (1436), also celebrates Humphrey of Gloucester and his success in fighting off Philip, Duke of Burgundy, who had laid siege to the port the English had long held at Calais. The poem is explicitly addressed to 'lordes'[87] of the Privy Council (since it names one of them, 'the wyse lorde baron of Hungeforde' [l. 1151]), and its author was probably a clerk of the Council.[88] Formally, the poem lies in the Chaucerian tradition (it has a prologue and conclusion in rime royal stanzas, and its body is in rhyming couplets), but it is unique in the depth of its engagement with the fine detail of English trading policy and its ramifications. It surveys the various 'commodytes . . . commynge' (51) to England from its most important trading partners (Spain, Flanders, Portugal, Scotland, Venice and Florence), and it also roots current practice in the strong naval policy of a host of English kings (Edgar, Edward III, Henry V), marshalling all of its detail toward the recommendation that all the trade routes around the island of Britain should be seized, and the Channel placed under blockade:

> Kepe than the see abought in speciall,*   *especially*
> Which of England is the rounde wall,
> As thoughe England were lykened to a cite
> And the wall environ* were the see.   *around*
>
> (ll. 1092–5)

As noted in the previous chapter, these recommendations had some literary influence when many of the poem's lines were taken over in the 1460s into the complaints of *A Trade Policy*, but their immediate political effect was negligible.[89] As it calmly but resolutely diverts all poetic resources toward the interests of state power, however, this poem represents something like the triumph of the bureaucratic muse: its most compelling device is neither argument nor overheated passion, but the lists of the commodities which model the richness of things in the profusion of words used to describe them:

> Bene* fygues, raysyns, wyne, bastarde* and dates,   *good / spiced wine*
> And lycorys, Syvyle oyle* and also grayne,   *oil from Seville*
> Whyte Castell sope* and wax is not in vayne,   *soap from Castille*
> Iren, wolle, wadmole,*   *coarse, woollen cloth*
>   goteful,* kydefel* also.   *goat skin / kid skin*
>
> (ll. 53–6)

As it equates 'love of Christ and of his joye' (l. 1064) as well as human 'worshyp' (l. 1070) and 'corage' (l. 1075) with 'profite' (l. 1070), as it insists, in most striking lines, that 'power' necessarily begets 'peace' ('The ende of bataile is pease sikerlye, / And power causeth pease finall verily', ll. 1090–1), this poem not only speaks for the state, it speaks with its bloodless calculation, as if every good will necessarily be served by the aggrandizement of 'kyng, shype and swerde, and pouer [power] of the see' (l. 35).

Counsel

The subtle and complex form in which Middle English literature found itself best able to navigate the demands of state power was the genre sometimes called the 'mirror for princes', or (more traditionally) *Fürstenspiegel*, but perhaps best called – because this is the role it chiefly gives itself – the literature of 'counsel'. Such literature generally took shape as the advice given by a fictive counsellor (or counsellors) to some king, but this advisory stance itself presumed that advising or educating the king would necessarily be of benefit to the state as a whole. At the foundations of this literature, then, is the presumption that the royal will is not only dangerous (that which has to be pandered to or praised) but profoundly effective, that the state is, in essence, the expression of that will, since, as a legal maxim had long had it, 'what is pleasing to the prince has the force of law' [quod principi placet legis habet vigorem].[90] This relationship was often described by a bodily allegory in which the state became a body, the king the governing 'intellect', and counsellors the indispensable appendages who, in mediating the world to the king, also protected him from it:

> When God almyghty made man, and made hym noblest of bestis, He comaunded hym, He for-bade hym, He bihote hym, and He rewarded hym and stablisshed his body as a cité, and his intellect as kyng in it, and sette it in the hyest and noblest place of the man, that is his hede, and made hym counselers to governe hym and to present hym all thyng that is necessarye, helpyng and kepyng hym from all noye . . . Therfor tho 5 counselers forseid ben as 5 wittes that ben these: the eye, the eere, the nose, the tonge and the hande.[91]

> [*bestis*: beasts   *bi-hote*: promised   *noye*: annoyance]

This description is taken from a fifteenth-century translation of the text that was foundational for all medieval literature of counsel, the *Secretum Secretorum* [Secret of Secrets] (its original Arabic title, *Kitāb sirr al-asrār*, translates best as *The Book of the Science of Government, on the Good Ordering of Statecraft*), a text so popular that it survives in its Latin form in 'about five hundred manuscripts dating from the twelfth century onwards'.[92] Such an understanding of the state insisted, with a helpful simultaneity, that the counsellor was as superior to the king in wisdom as he was subservient in power. Such a counsellor – or any poet who could project himself into this role – not only had the right to educate a king, it was his express duty to do so.

Although there is a very long and old tradition of literature emerging from such a stance, its very importance meant that no such literature was written in English until the end of the fourteenth century (when the vernacular was finally making significant inroads in official culture). Although I have already described its important relationship to the literature of confession, John Gower's *Confessio Amantis* (*c*.1390–3) is also the earliest English work of counsel, and it offers an excellent example of the unusual mixture of ambiguity and boldness that generally characterized such writing. Both versions of the poem are dedicated to a 'prince' (the first to Richard II, the second to Henry of Lancaster – later, Henry IV),[93] and even though the poem never couches itself as advice to either of these royal figures, the exemplary narratives the priest Genius uses to instruct Amans in its first six books often concern kingship, and in the last two books they expressly concern 'policie' (7.1710), defined there as the 'lore' a king must have 'to lede / The poeple' (7.1711–14). A good example of how political such teaching becomes can also be found in Genius's account of the debate among three counsellors to Darius, King of Persia, when asked whether 'wyn, the womman or the king' is 'strengest' (7.1812–13). The first of these 'wise men' responds with a bald version of that legal maxim I have already mentioned:

The pouer* of a king stant* so,	*power / stands*
That he the lawes overpasseth;*	*exceeds*
What he wol make lasse, he lasseth,*	*lessens*
What he wol make more, he moreth.*	*increases*
(7.1838–41)	

The second insists that wine is stronger than kings because it 'takth aweie . . . reson' (7.1852–3). The third, however, insists not only that 'trouthe' is the 'strengest . . . of erthli thinges' (7.1953–5), but that it is stronger than any princely will ('trouthe . . . mai for nothing ben overcome', 7.1957–8), and therefore represents a significant limitation upon princely power:

For therupon the ground is leid*	*laid*
Of every kinges regiment,*	*rule*
As thing which most convenient	
Is forto sette a king in evene*	*balance*
Bothe in this world and ek in hevene.	
(7.1980–4)	

The gradual movement from unregulated absolutism to an emphatic regulation of royal power, in which Darius 'can no longer consider himself in isolation' and must 'recognize and allow for the energies and jurisdiction of his subjects',[94] is characteristic of the political thought of the *Confessio Amantis*, but so too is the 'political wariness' inherent in that statement's form – as it is lodged in a narrative, addressed to a 'lover' by the 'priest' to whom he is confessing, in an allegory that does not expressly represent itself as a work of counsel.[95]

This combination of boldness and wariness characterizes almost all works of counsel, and this general fact is well illustrated by the most prolific poet of the genre in Middle English, John Lydgate (d. 1449). His *Fall of Princes* (1431–8), a poem of 36,365 lines, derived from Giovanni Boccaccio's *De casibus illustrium virorum* [Concerning the Falls of Famous Men] via Laurent de Premierfait's French translation, was written 'to yive [give] exaumple how this wold doth varie . . . onto pryncis'.[96] Like Chaucer's Monk's Tale, which may have impelled Lydgate towards this topic (Lydgate was a Benedictine monk),[97] the *Fall* offers both a series of narratives of historical, biblical and literary figures, and their tragic fates, as monitory examples (the story of Samson, for example, who wrongly trusts Delilah with the secret of his strength, 'yeveth in evidence' [1.6490] that 'ye noble Pryncis' [1.6504] know to 'keep your conceitis under coverture [cover]' [1.6508]). In his Prologue Lydgate presents the *Fall* as another commission by Humphrey of Gloucester, the younger brother of Henry V and Protector of England during Henry VI's minority (1422–37), and a certain boldness is evident in the long 'envoy', which does not hesitate to remind Humphrey of his own dangers:

Though your estat lyk Phebus wer shynyng,	
Yit,* for al that, ye have no sewerte,*	*yet / surety*
How longe tyme is here your abydyng;*	*living*
Age, with hire cosyn callyd Infirmyte,	
Wyl cleyme hire ryght of verry* dewete;*	*true / necessity*
Deth takith no mede;* afform* he wyl not sende.	*reward / in advance*
Provide your-sylff whyl ye have liberte,	
Dayly in vertu tencresyn* and ascende.	*to increase*

(9.3565–72)

There is some wariness in the way the main issue is made to be 'vertu' rather than the proper use of power, and the dangers Humphrey is meant to fear are the inevitable predations of age and infirmity rather than the more political sorts of destruction that can befall a hapless prince in the *Fall*'s narratives (Cyrus, lord of all Asia, for example, is taken by death 'thoruh perced with many mortal woundis, / On pecis rent, as beris been with houndis', 2.3875–6). But the most common form of wariness Lydgate exhibits in the *Fall* is 'a humility topic of an intensely specific kind',[98] a protestation of inability that could be understood as radical qualification of his own capacity to offer meaningful advice:

Thouh* that I have lak*off eloquence,   *although / lack*
I shal procede in this translacioun,
Fro me avoidyng al presumpcioun,
Lowli submyttyng everi hour and space
Mi reud* language to my lordis grace.   *rude*

(1.437–41)

Where Lydgate later roots such a 'lack' in his own age, he describes himself
as 'fordullid [completely dulled] with rudnesse' (8.190), and it is 'dullness'
more generally that not only characterizes Lydgate's stance in the *Fall*,
but, since that stance so generally epitomizes the political circumspection
necessary to write at all in this period, it has been argued that it was 'the
mark of a fifteenth-century poet'.[99]

To be sure, Lydgate has also been felt by many commentators to be
truly dull, diffuse in his language ('no poet . . . can so readily make
twenty words do the work of one'), overblown in his rhetorical style
('which can easily make a stanza out of a line' in his source), and
everywhere hampered by the 'unselectivity' and 'essentially uncurious
nature of [his] mind'.[100] But the generality of Lydgate's touch – the capacity for such a diffuse style and attention to take anything and everything
in – also allows him scope to venture onto difficult territory, while only
seeming to have blundered there. The best example here is the *Siege of
Thebes* (1420–2), perhaps significantly, one of the only major works Lydgate
wrote without patronage (his exact source is unknown too), framed not
with a dedication to a powerful prince, but as a supplement to *The Canterbury Tales*: in the frame narrative that begins it Lydgate places himself
on the fictional pilgrimage to Canterbury, where he is persuaded by the
Host to tell the first tale on the return journey ('"Come forth, daun
John be your Cristene name, / And lat us make some manere myrth or
play!"').[101] This poem is not a mirror for princes, but its central incident
is the quarrel between the brothers Eteocles and Polynices, over who
'oght of resoun . . . to be crowned kyng' of Thebes (ll. 1086–7), and its
conclusion describes a fall like no other (the utter destruction of Thebes
after interminable civil war). In the midst of the cyclical violence that
follows from this quarrel, a priest, Amphiorax, tries unsuccessfully to persuade Adrastus, King of Argos, not to help Polynices in his attack on
Thebes (2800–988), and Jocasta, the mother of Eteocles and Polynices,
also fails to persuade either of her sons to settle their differences peacefully
(ll. 3648–708). Such failures of counsel within the narrative also allow
Lydgate to move, quietly, into the position of counsellor, from where he
roundly condemns warfare as such:

For in the werre is non excepcioun
Of hegh estat nor low condicioun,
But as fortune and fate both yffere,*   *together*
List* to dispose with her* double   *are happy / their*
   chere,*   *countenance*
And Bellona the goddes in hir char*   *chariot*
Aforn* provydeth; wherfor ech man be war   *first*
Unavysed* a werre to bygynne.   *rashly*
(ll. 4645–51)

This counsel also slowly but surely connects itself to current English politics as it turns from the problems of war to the benefits of what it calls 'pees and quyet, concord and unyte' (l. 4703), a phrase that strongly echoes the phrase 'concordia, pax, et Tranquillitas' in the Treaty of Troyes (1420), the settlement negotiated by Henry V in order to conclude his lengthy and costly war with France.[102] To condemn a war at the moment of that war's conclusion is of course the height of political wariness, but to observe, at this particular juncture, that it is 'unavysed' to 'bygynne' a war is bold in ways that might shock (were we more prepared to find Lydgate shocking). Moreover, with every passing moment after the Treaty of Troyes was agreed, the peace Henry achieved seemed more costly, and Lydgate's counsel would have acquired increasing bite: the central proposition of the treaty made Henry V's heir king of both England and France, but, after Henry's untimely death in 1422, this left the one-year-old Henry VI as ruler of an extraordinarily divided kingdom, 'a constitutional and conceptual monstrosity' that led, almost immediately – as Lydgate may well have known when he was finishing this poem – to renewed warfare.[103]

One might still suspect such boldness of being the kind of political risk only a dullard would take, but the extent to which Lydgate concerned himself with the errors of the powerful suggest, instead, that he reserved his sternest thoughts for texts whose form (or subject) tended to pull away from any obvious application in fifteenth-century statecraft. This is particularly well demonstrated by *Reson and Sensuallyte*, usually ascribed to Lydgate, a courtly love allegory with almost no overt political concerns, but which James Simpson has shown 'explores the propensity of aristocratic love to revisit and repeat the catastrophes of history'.[104] The poem is a partial translation of the French poem *Les Echecs amoureux*, and, like the *Siege of Thebes*, it is not immediately addressed to any patron. Its dreamer-narrator not only needs counsel, he demonstrates its value by being unable to accept the sound advice he continually receives. Urged by Nature to avoid the road of sensuality 'ful of plesaunce and fals delyte'[105] in favour of the road of reason, the advice is instantly 'clene out' of his 'remembraunce' (l. 971), and he sets off down the road of earthly delights. Urged by Diana to avoid the dangerous pleasures of Venus (as detailed in many examples of lovers who came to a bad end) and to dwell, instead, with her in 'ryghtwissnesse [righteousness], hoonour and trouthe' (l. 3108), the dreamer hastens into Venus's 'lusty herber [pleasure garden] delytable' (l. 4797). If the poem is not overtly political, as C. S. Lewis observed, its 'psychology is excellent', and it therefore tends to suggest that the real battle for princes lies on no battlefield, but in their 'ful gret stryf / with reson' (ll. 768–9).[106]

Since the poetry of counsel must always look for some middle way between pandering to power and falling foul of princely displeasure, it is hardly surprising that it should grow increasingly timorous in the tumultuous decades of the Wars of the Roses. Fortescue is again an important example, for in *The Governance of England* (1471), a text addressed to the recently restored Edward IV, he seems incapable of offering any substantive advice. In fact, while he usually speaks *as if* with the voice of a counsellor, he always argues from the king's position: he offers him that commonplace licensing princely absolutism ('quod principi placuit, legis habet vigorem') as the universal law that 'first began in Realmes',[107] and he focuses, in particular, on the necessity of a king's financial 'indowment' ('but sithyn . . . the kyng hath not at this day sufficiant therto, it is most convenient that we nowe serche, how is hyghnes mey have sufficiant' [134]). Even when he seems to be cautioning against impoverishing the commons his arguments tend to favour even heavier taxation ('But owre commons be riche, and therefore thai give to thair kynge' [139]). Fortescue's most prudent gesture, however, is slyly structural, for near the end of the *Governance* he does offer some advice on how a king's counsellors 'may be chosen' (145); however, this very gesture makes 'counsel' a possible consequence of this treatise rather than what it actually is ('yff the kyng have such a Consell . . . his lande shall not only be ryche and welthy . . . but also is hyghnes shalbe myghty', 149–50).

Another example of such cowed advice comes, unsurprisingly, from George Ashby, for even though his *Active Policy of a Prince* (1463) rather boldly addresses itself to the heir to the throne (Edward IV's son Edward, Prince of Wales), it was, like his *Prisoner's Reflections*, written in prison, and so it does nothing so well as tell the prince what he would most wish to hear, urging him in the direction of the kind of ruthlessness towards perceived enemies that had been so harmful to Ashby ('Ye must subdewe with al suppressing / Every persoune withoute submission / Pretendyng right to your coronacion'),[108] insisting that he act more generally with reference only to himself and his power ('Put no ful truste in the Comonalte, / Thai be ever wavering in variance', ll. 870–1). The *Policy* also takes no chances with the kind of narratives that lent Lydgate's political thinking its depth and complexity, and so, even though its Latin prologue promises an account of policy in the past, present and future ('preterito, presenti & futuro'),[109] the only past kings mentioned are Edward's 'noble progenitours' (l. 148), some of whom just happen to have been 'seintes' (l. 141). Ashby also describes the importance of listening well to counsel, but he projects all the qualities of the best counsellor onto the prince:

Heere every man is* counseil and advise	*his*
Paciently and chese therof the best,	
And than I wold youre highnesse advertise	
That ye sholde kepe youre entent in your brest	
As ye wolde your owne tresoure in youre chest.	
And so shall ye youre estate magnifie,*	*increase*
And youre grete wisdam daily multiplie	

(ll. 359–65)

The emergence of a princely figure whose 'estate' is guaranteed only by his powers of dissimulation – his capacity to 'kepe' his 'entent' in his 'brest' – is hardly surprising at a moment when the role of the prince was as fraught as the role of his counsellor (where not only were counsellors imprisoned, but the former king, Henry VI, was on the run from the current king – and would, by 1465, find himself in prison as well), but the conceptual evolution is as dramatic as it is (typically, for this genre) quiet. For what Ashby also marks, as he insists that a prince must be 'circumspect in his actes' and of 'discrecions ful sure' (ll. 207–8), is not only the way that the characteristics of counsel are being absorbed *into* the prince but that, in this dividedness, in his 'ability to effect a divorce . . . between the tongue and the heart', the prince has begun to engage in those sorts of 'role-playing' and 'improvisation' that have been seen as fundamental to the fashioning of the 'self'.[110]

The best exemplification in our period of such a self in princely form – the real culmination of the tendencies Ashby begins to document – is to be found not in the literature of counsel then, but in dramatic performance, not in a poem addressed to a prince, but in a play that describes him, John Skelton's *Magnyfycence* (1519).[111] The play is allegorical, so the 'noble prynce of myght' *is* Magnyfycence,[112] and the central concern of its action is the importance of generosity or 'Lyberty', that 'presydent of prynces' (l. 2082). It is an exuberant literary performance, by turns

elaborately rhetorical ('O feble fortune, O doulfull destyny!', l. 2048), dog-
gerel ('Spare for no coste; / And yet in dede / It is coste loste / Moche
more than need / For to exceed / In suche aray. / Howe be it, I say', ll.
891–7), vulgar ('Torde! . . . She is made for the malarde fat', ll. 925–7),
and high-flown ('Alexander, of Macedony kynge, / That all the oryent
had in subjeccyon', ll. 1466–7). It is also a play that often seems to praise
as princely virtue exactly what it would suit a prince to hear: 'measure'
is repeatedly an important component of liberality ('I warne you beware
of to moche lyberte, / For *totum in toto* [all in all] is not worth an hawe
[hawthorn berry]', ll. 2088–9). But Magnyfycence is also assailed, not only
by a host of dissimulating counsellors ('Flattery', 'Crafty Conveyaunce'
and 'Clokyd Colusyon'), but – precisely because he can trust no one – by
'Dyspare'. So it is small wonder that Magnyfycence is only led to success
and contentment by the figure called 'Sad Cyrcumspeccyon', like Ashby's
prince, a figure whose wisdom consists in his capacity for self-protection.
Magnyfycence finally comes to seem less like the centre of state power
than its victim, for all the world a figure very much like the censored or
conscripted or punished writer ('Goddes grace hath vexed you sharply /
And payned you with a purgacyon of odyous poverte, / Myxed with bytter
alowes [aloes] of herde adversitye', ll. 2352–4). Such a prince is probably
no easier for the less powerful to deal with, but he certainly represents a
fitting culmination to the relationship between statecraft and literature that
I have been tracing, a site of power almost wholly defined by the capacity
for subtlety and dissimulation that literature in this period had had to refine
in direct response to the dangers such power posed.

4

Place

Middle English varied greatly in morphology (the grammatical shape of words), phonology (the pronunciation of words) and lexis (the words themselves), and this variation, although often uneven in its distribution, tended to map very firmly onto place. As Ranulph Higden (d. 1364) described the resulting situation in his *Polychronicon*, England was a territory divided into three large linguistic regions that corresponded neatly to the physical divisions of the kingdom (the translation and elaboration I quote is John of Trevisa's, from 1385):

> Englisch men, they hadde from the begynnynge thre manere speche, northerne, sowtherne, and middel speche in the myddel of the lond, as they come of thre manere peple of Germania, notheles, by commyxtioun and mellynge firste with Danes and afterward with Normans, in meny the contray longage is apayred, and som useth straunge wlafferynge, chyterynge, harrynge and garrynge, grisbayting.
>
> [*mellynge*: mixing *apayred*: damaged *wlafferynge*: stammering *chyterynge*: jargon *harrynge*: snarling *garrynge*: clicking or chattering *grisbayting*: grinding of teeth]
>
> [Angli . . . quamquam ab initio tripartitam sortirentur linguam, austrinam scilicet, mediterraneam, et borealem, veluti ex tribus Germaniae populis procedentes, ex commixtione tamen primo cum Danis, deinde cum Normannis, corrupta in multis patria lingua peregrinos iam captant boatus et garritus.][1]

Higden's history is accurate as far as it goes, although in modern accounts it is now customary to subdivide Middle English into five dialectal areas ('Kentish' or 'Southeastern', 'Southwestern', 'East Midland', 'West Midland' and 'Northern').[2] Since variation in forms, vocabulary and pronunciation is the norm in any language without some strong standardizing force, it is also significant that Higden should find language difference in his day not only worthy of comment but so distasteful.[3] Dialectical variety in Middle English was often so great, however, that, despite an underlying unity of grammatical structure and a largely common vocabulary, there were indeed problems of mutual intelligibility between speakers from different regions. In 1490, Caxton is still complaining that English is 'ever waver-ynge', and in the prologue to his *Eneydos* (a translation of a French version of Virgil's *Aeneid*) he offers an amusing illustration of the kinds of trouble this could cause:

> Certayn marchaunts were in a shippe in tamyse for to have sayled over the see into zelande, and for lacke of wynde thei taryed atte forlond and wente to lande for to refreshe them. And one of theym named sheffelde a mercer cam in to an hows and axed for mete, and specyally he axyd after eggys. And the good wyf answerde that she coulde speke no frenshe. And the marchaunt was angry for he also coude speke no frenshe, but wold have hadde egges, and she understode hym not. And thenne at laste a nother sayd that he wolde have eyren, then the good wyf sayd that she understod him wel.[4]

[*tamyse*: Thames   *zelande*: Zealand   *forlond*: a promontory   *mete*: food *frenshe*: French]

Eggys was the form for modern 'eggs' derived from Old Norse, which had taken hold in the North of England (where there had been extensive Viking settlements), while *eyren* was the Southern form (singular *ei*), derived from Old English. That this confrontation of forms could occur at all is evidence that dialect was not wholly wedded to place, but that the resulting mis-understanding could only be resolved by an act of translation shows how tenacious variation could be, even when forms were so frequently mixed in particular populations (the teeming crowds of the Thames estuary) and by certain activities (trade).

Place is therefore often an important shaping fact in the production of every Middle English text, and this makes it possible to construct a liter-ary map of England to some extent.[5] *The Ayenbite of Inwit* is our firmest landmark here, since it survives only in a copy (London, British Library, MS Arundel 57) in the 'englis' of its author's 'oghne hand', and this copy locates its wholly Southeastern forms in Kent (at the 'boc-house of saynt Austines of Canterberi').[6] Laurence Minot's political poems (1333–52) are similarly easy to locate, for they survive in only a single manuscript (London, British Library, MS Cotton Galba E.ix) which matches their wholly Northern subjects with wholly Northern dialect forms.[7] The sole copy of the York mystery plays (British Library, Additional MS 35290) was clearly written in the city of York.[8] Robert Mannyng associates himself with Bourne in Lincolnshire, and one of the earliest manuscripts of his *Chronicle* (London, Inner Temple Library, MS Petyt 511) was evidently produced in this area.[9] A number of manuscripts of the writings of Richard Rolle

(Cambridge, University Library, MS Dd.5.64; Oxford, University College, MS 64; Oxford, Bodleian Library, MS Hatton 12) were definitely copied in Yorkshire, near Hampole, where Rolle sometimes locates himself.[10] We do not know who wrote *Ancrene Wisse* (1215–24) or the clutch of saints' lives (*St Katherine, St Iuliene, St Margaret*) and related texts (*Hali Meidhad*, a treatise on virginity, and *Sawles Warde*, an allegory on the 'custody of the soul') usually called the *Katherine*-group (1190–1220), but we can be sure these texts were produced in the 'same cultural centre' because Cambridge, Corpus Christi College, MS 402 (an early manuscript of *Ancrene Wisse*) and Oxford, Bodleian Library, MS 34 (an early manuscript of the *Katherine*-group) not only employ the same West Midland dialect but share a regularized spelling of Western forms:[11] 'AB language', as this dialect was termed (after the symbols conventionally used to represent the two similar manuscripts), could only have arisen as the result of circumstances that not only sponsored devotional writing in English (when almost all such writing in this period occurred in Anglo-Norman and Latin) but also directed its production (in this particular location and time, there clearly was a standardizing force).[12]

The placing of most Middle English texts is much more complicated than this, however, since any given speaker's dialect might become mixed through travel. Both authors and scribes moved about, and even texts were mobile, sometimes traversing great distances before they were recopied: thus, any given copy of any given text might have several dialects superimposed over its original forms, and those original forms might themselves be mixed. Where such movements can be clearly traced for an author, we have something like *St Erkenwald*, a poem very much 'of' London – not only set there, but very concerned with its affairs – but in what is doubtless the original dialect of its poet, that of the West Midlands (perhaps, more precisely, of Cheshire).[13] Where it is the dialect of scribes that predominates, we have something like the two manuscripts of *The Owl and the Nightingale* (London, British Library, MS Cotton Caligula A.ix, and Oxford, Jesus College, MS 29), both of which are reasonably consistent in their West Midlands forms, but where the occasional slip or rhyme make clear that *The Owl and the Nightingale* was originally written in Kent.[14] So important was such movement, in fact, that it is finally absorbed to the allegory of *Piers Plowman*, which begins 'on a May morwenynge on Malverne Hilles' (Pro. 5), in the heart of the West Midlands, but moves, within a few hundred lines, to an 'assemblee' of merchants gathered in London (Pro. 218–30), a geographical movement that is only the first and most graphic instance of the kind of wandering and exploration that characterizes this allegory as a whole. And small wonder, for various versions of this poem 'were subject to so many different forms of copying in different dialects' that there is simply 'no surviving manuscript . . . [which] can be proved to be in [Langland's] language'.[15]

Paradoxically, then, the deep importance of place to each and every Middle English text, at every stage of its production and dissemination, tends also to diminish the importance of any *one* place for any particular text. In fact, insisting that 'place' is equivalent to geography, as I have so far been doing, can result in a kind of facile metonymy whereby the text becomes a product of a region (so *The Owl and the Nightingale* becomes a 'Southern' text), with the result that the complex mixtures inherent in Middle English dialect are stripped away and geography comes to substitute itself for all the other places that have a direct and shaping effect, on a text's words, literary form and style. As I shall try to show in this chapter, moreover, the places that exerted a much more extensive shaping force on texts were the institutions and communities, the organized practices and social structures, what might more generally be described as the *cultural* places, in which they were produced. The five places I have chosen to focus on here – the schoolroom, religious communities, the household chamber, the city and (what I will call) the way or the street – are not exhaustive. But, individually, they were sufficiently important to such a substantial body of Middle English writing that, taken together, they may be said to 'place' that writing much more precisely than aspects of dialect or region ever could.

The schoolroom

Although only a small proportion of people learned to read and write in the Middle Ages, wherever that learning was at all formalized (where it consisted of more than a tutor and the children of a particular nobleman) it occurred in a place described as a 'school' [scola].[16] Such schools emerged first within monasteries and cathedrals,[17] but public and independent fee-paying schools, which any boy with the necessary means could attend, became 'the major schools of medieval England . . . from the twelfth century onwards'.[18] Early in this period, many of these schools were referred to as 'song schools' and tended to teach basic reading and plainsong to boys destined for a clerical life.[19] Later, schools teaching 'business skills' (letter writing, the drafting of deeds and charters, the proper method for keeping accounts) became increasingly common.[20] But the most common sorts of schools throughout the medieval period were the grammar schools where Latin was taught through the rigorous memorization of both long grammatical texts (the

Ars Minor of Donatus [fourth century] was the most important of these, supplemented by Priscian [sixth century])[21] and a set of exercises in imitation that quickly merged the study of language with training in the structuring of ideas (dialectic) and verbal patterning (rhetoric), as students learned to write their own texts by means of exercises that at once helped them analyse and reconstruct what they were reading.[22] The curriculum of authors read was remarkably consistent across the whole medieval West, comprising many classic Roman writers (Cicero, Ovid, Horace, Virgil),[23] as well as a core of six texts that are now much less read: the *Distichs of Cato* (a collection of simple instructions for good behaviour of a proverbial sort), the *Eclogue of Theodulus* (a debate poem which pairs pagan and Christian myths), the *Fables* of Avianus (proverbial wisdom in story form), the *Elegies* of Maximian (an old man's account of his past sexual conquests), Claudian's *On the Rape of Proserpina* (a brief, because unfinished, but dramatically gripping epic) and the *Achilleis* of Statius (a brief, but typical, classical epic).[24] It is worth naming such texts not only because they provided such a distinctive (and, to modern sensibilities, different) literary foundation for medieval writers, but because they were so intensively studied, at such a basic level, that they became part of every medieval writer's 'mental furniture'.[25] Langland acknowledges this early on in *Piers Plowman* when 'Reason', summoned to counsel the king, and preparing to ride off, calls 'Caton his knave' (4.17) to assist him, and the *Distichs* acquire particular authority at important moments throughout *Piers Plowman* (e.g. 7.71–73a).[26] But it is Chaucer who shows just how closely held this early learning remained, for, despite the wide range of his own learning, *The Canterbury Tales* in particular are simply 'saturated' with references to the core school texts.[27]

It is therefore not surprising that Middle English writers should have translated the *Distichs of Cato*, the most basic of these school texts, but it is a different sort of illustration of the cultural importance of this learning that such a translation was made on at least seven different occasions in the fourteenth and fifteenth centuries alone.[28] The earliest of these texts (from *c*.1390) assimilates the most basic schoolroom practices to literary form, unfolding, distich by distich, as if it were itself a translation exercise. So, each distich is printed first as the original Latin couplet:

> Contra verbosos noli contendere verbis:
> Sermo datur multis, animi sapiencia paucis.

Then, as if it is the crib the student is turning to for assistance (that is, to a translation in a language whose syntax is closer to the syntax of English), the distich is given in Anglo-Norman:

En-countre ianglour,
Ke ne eyez deshonour,
Ne voyelles estriuer:
Kar meynt homme ad iangle
En vertu de sa lange,
Est poy de sauer.

Finally – as if it is the English version the student has finally banged out – the distich is given in an English quatrain that renders the Latin, but generally, with the form and syntax of the crib:

Ageynes* men ful of wordes	*against*
Stryue thow riht nouht:*	*not*
Wordes is given to alle men,	
And wisdam selden* brouht.[29]	*seldom*

The sensibility that might have found any sort of pleasure in *reading* such an enactment of schoolroom practice is not easy for modern readers to recapture, but its key term is that other aspect of the schoolroom that this version of the *Distichs* absorbs, the teacher, and, with him, the pedagogic experience – the sense that these 'wordes' are not simply pithy maxims, but that they carry within them a 'wisdam' proved as such because, on its way in and out of books, it has passed through lived experience. The figure of the teacher enters the *Distichs* in a distinctly paternal form ('now I will teach you, dearest son, how to fashion a system for your mind' [nunc te, fili karissime, docebo quo pacto morem animi tui componas]),[30] while the attribution of such wisdom to a particular Roman statesman (probably Cato the Censor [234–159 BC]), however apocryphal (the text seems to have originated in the third century AD), seems to place such wisdom somewhere out of the classroom.[31] But the false attribution to *some* person – the need for schoolroom teachings to come *as if* dispensed by some person – is simply another way in which the schoolroom scene is absorbed to the schoolroom text, as if the teacher had been absorbed to the text he taught.

The fundamental importance of the *Distichs* to schoolroom training explains the deep investment Middle English writers made in this basic text, but it also has a great deal to do with the widespread importance of the proverb in general. *The Owl and the Nightingale* (c.1216) illustrates both of these tendencies particularly well, for not only is it a debate poem whose form and content owe a great deal to schoolroom training in dialectic,[32] but the two birds (the debaters in this case) continually appeal to proverbs for their authority, and many of those proverbs are drawn from the *Distichs* (the nightingale, for example, cites a version of the distich I quoted above:

'Loke that thu ne bo thare, / Thar chavling both and cheste yare / Lat sottes chide and vorth thu go!' [Watch that you aren't around where there is babbling and brawling at hand; Let fools bicker and you walk away]).[33] None of these proverbs is attributed to 'Cato', but on thirteen occasions they are said to be the 'words' of 'King Alfred', the Anglo-Saxon king famous for his learning, and, more particularly, remembered for copying wise sayings out of books.[34] Since there is no traceable link between the proverbs the owl and the nightingale cite and anything Alfred wrote, the importance of the attribution seems to be, again, to attach wisdom to a person, to insist that the proverb come complete with the pedagogic scene. This simple gesture governs the whole of the form of *The Proverbs of Alfred* (c.1150), a text with no demonstrable historical connection to anything King Alfred wrote[35] but which insists, nevertheless, that Alfred was responsible for its every line (each of its stanzas begins with the phrase 'Thus queth Alvred' [Thus said Alfred]). The poem also begins with a stanza that presents Alfred as a good and brave king, but, above all things, as a teacher:

> At Sevorde
> Sete theynes monye,
> Fele Biscopes,
> And feole bok-ilered.
> Eorles prute,
> Knyhtes egleche,
> Thar was the eorl Alvrich.
> Of thare lawe swithe wis
> And ek Ealvred
> Englene hurde,
> Englene durlyng.
> On englene londe
> He wes kyng.
> Heom he bi-gon lere,
> So ye mawe i-hure.
> Hw hi heore lif
> Lede scholden.[36]

> [At Seaford many thanes gathered together, many bishops, and many book-learned men; proud earls, valiant knights. The earl Ælfric was there who was very wise about the law. And also Alfred, guardian of the English, darling of the English. He was king in the land of the English. He began to teach them, as you may hear, how they should lead their lives.]

The scene is often understood as a political gathering, since Alfred's audience consists of bishops, earls and knights, but what gives the game away – what makes clear that this is yet another pedagogic scene – is that Alfred's teaching guides none of the political roles in which we might expect to see bishops, earls and knights instructed (making war or giving counsel, devising laws or handing them down); it is, rather, teaching of the most basic sort, guidance in how to 'lead . . . lives'. This poem is also often described as transitional, since it retains certain elements of the alliterative style of Old English poetry (just as the citation of 'Alfred's' words seems an attempt to retain at least the image of Anglo-Saxon learning), but it also looks forward to newer forms, as rhyme also encroaches on its long lines ('He wes the wysuste mon / That wes englelonde on', ll. 23–4), breaking them in half.[37] The more significant cultural transition executed here, however, is the tricking out of the most basic schoolroom learning as the stuff of poetry, for while presuming to speak in the voice of a king and to dispense truths important enough for 'book-learned men' (bok-ilered), this nostalgic text offers nothing other than the learning of the schoolroom, often the proverbs of the *Distichs of Cato*, including a version of that distich which I have now quoted several times on the importance of guarding one's tongue:

> Thus queth Alvred:
> Ne gabbe thu ne schotte,
> Ne chid thu wyth none sotte,
> Ne myd manyes cunnes tales,
> Ne chid thu with nenne dwales.

> [Thus said Alfred: Do not mock or bluster, nor quarrel with a fool, nor with too much talk quarrel with any fools.]
> (ll. 449–53)

Some measure of the importance of *The Proverbs of Alfred* is provided by the four different manuscript versions in which it survives: this is a relatively high number for such an early Middle English text, and these versions are so different from one another (it is clear that none of these manuscripts is a copy of any of the others) that we can be sure there were many more.[38] The popularity of *The Proverbs of Alfred* may also have helped to inspire the poem called *The Proverbs of Hendyng* (c.1275), where every stanza's proverbial teachings are also represented in a refrain ('quoth Hendyng') as the direct speech of some authoritative figure ('Hendyng' seems to be a personification generated from the word *hende* ['skilled, clever'], and seems to mean something like 'the clever one').[39] The structural similarities are more probably evidence of the hold schoolroom practices and sensibilities had over writers, the nearly reflexive connection between wisdom and an instructing person, and the embrace of repetition, almost primal in its need, which means that we can again find in *The Proverbs of Hendyng* yet another version of the distich on the importance of reticence:

Wis mon halt* is wordes ynne;*	*holds / within*
For he nul* no gle* bygynne,	*will not / song*
Er* he have tempred* is pype.	*before / tuned*
Sot* is sot, and that is sene;*	*fool / evident*
For he wol speke wordes grene,	
Er then hue* buen rype.	*they*
'Sottes bolt is sone shote';*	*shot*
Quoth* Hendyng.⁴⁰	*says*

The verse forms of this text are not in any way transitional – aside from their refrain, these stanzas are more or less those of the tail-rhyme romances commonly written in this period. However, to precisely the extent that this poem is stylistically up to date, its contents show just how conservative was the schoolroom's influence, and how broadly the traditionalism of both its activities and its curriculum were capable of defining knowledge itself as that which did not change.

The durability of this old knowledge as well as the heavy hand the schoolroom laid on the most ambitious of literary and intellectual endeavours is best exemplified in Middle English by Chaucer's Tale of Melibee, although this text is almost never associated with the schoolroom and is most usually assimilated to the 'mirror for princes' tradition.⁴¹ The range of authorities cited in the text does extend far beyond the *Distichs* and its sphere (Seneca, Cicero and Petrus Alfonsi are often mentioned), but 'Cato' is also frequently cited, and a surprising number of the most learned references simply conceal (or quietly elevate) a schoolroom text that is its real source ('Senek', for example, often means another common school text, *Publilius Syrus* [e.g. VII.1185, 1488, 1866]).⁴² The Melibee is, on the whole, a close translation of Renaud de Louens's *Livre de Melibée et de Dame Prudence* (1336), itself a close translation of a Latin text by the jurist Albertano of Brescia, and its central issues are not a schoolboy's: after Melibee's 'olde foos' invade his house and beat his wife, 'Prudence', and injure his daughter 'with five mortal woundes in five sondry places' (VII.970–1), Melibee must decide whether to 'biginne werre' (VII.1020), as a group of 'hise neighebores' (VII.1018) urge him to, or to yield to Prudence's advice and sue for peace. Chaucer particularly insists on the schoolroom origins of the wisdom that is then trotted out in support of these two positions when he introduces the text by saying that he has added 'somwhat moore / Of proverbes than ye han herd before / Comprehended in this litel tretis' (VII.955–7), and it also matters that Chaucer's is the only version of this text that names Melibee's daughter 'Sophie' (VII.967), or 'wisdom'[43] – and therefore that the task of Chaucer's text becomes, centrally, the discovery of how an injured wisdom may be repaired. With the tradition on which The Melibee's sources extensively draw in clear view, it is easy to see that to whatever extent Melibee resembles a 'king requesting advice from men chosen as counsellors' he is an allegorical figure; and the material of that allegory is, again, the schoolroom, with Prudence yet another version of the teacher, instructing a wayward but familiar pupil.[44] In the lengthy interaction between Melibee's formidable resistance (he may be stubborn, but he already knows a lot) and Prudence's powerful insistence, The Melibee also becomes an uncommonly powerful illustration not only of the educative force of proverbs, but of the drama of pedagogy. In fact, the real pleasure of this text must be that of any teacher, watching 'techinges' acquire sufficient power to change both views and a life, as Melibee is brought round 180 degrees from his original position and yields, finally and completely, to Prudence's wisdom ('Whanne Melibe hadde herde the grete skiles and resons of dame Prudence, and hire wise informaciouns and techinges, his herte gan encline to the wil of his wif', VII.1870–1). Although the subject of this text and its manner is extremely serious, it is also clear that Chaucer wanted it to be understood in terms of pleasure (he insists, before beginning the tale, that it will be, above all things, 'mirye', VII.964). If we are sometimes inclined to insist on our own distance from such merriment – to say that it was only 'in the Middle Ages when readers did not entirely distinguish between pleasure in literature and pleasure in being edified'[45] – it is also because we lack the kind of literature that celebrates the process of edification with anything like the passion and painstaking detail that the *Melibee* provides.

Such celebrations survived into the fifteenth century, and a good way to continue to trace their importance is through the English translations made of the *Liber philosophorum moralium antiquorum* [The Book of the Ancient Moral Philosophers], a thirteenth-century Latin text that was (via a Spanish intermediary) a translation of an eleventh-century Arabic collection of wisdom, the *Mokhtar el-Hikam*.[46] That such a work could still be eagerly absorbed into the English poetic tradition by George Ashby (1390–1475) testifies to the conservatism of the schoolroom, its defining capacity to sustain the oldest forms of learning in the repetitions that constituted its activities. And nothing is ever lost, for while the embrace of wisdom becomes truly stately in the rime royal stanzas of this text ('Of al the yeftes [gifts] that ever god made / Wisedam is the most excellent by name, / By whiche vertue wol encrece [increase] and not fade'),[47] that embrace remains fully rooted in schoolroom practices, and this poem also unfolds as if it were a translation exercise, with English verses continually alternating with the original Latin of the *Liber philosophorum*. Ashby's translation survives in only one manuscript,[48] but we must add to it the thirteen manuscripts, and the one printing (by Caxton, as one of his first English books), of the four *different* prose translations made between 1450 and 1473 of the same text (sometimes via a fourteenth-century French translation called *Dits moraulx*) under the name *Dicts and Sayings of the Philosophers*.[49] Although these texts often include a short potted biography of the authoritative figures they cite (e.g. 'Socrates', 'Pythagoras', 'Hermogenes'), they resemble The Melibee with all allegory and narrative stripped out: a similar flood of the kind of proverbs that Melibee and Prudence address to one another, but innocent of anything like the arguments in which those figures embedded them. The purity of such contents as well as the continued popularity of this wisdom in such a stripped-down form testify to the paramount importance of this particular brand of wisdom. These contents also further demonstrate the conservativism that defined such learning, for even this number of centuries after the *Distichs of Cato* the *Dicts* is still insisting on the importance of guarding one's speech (e.g. 'Beware that thi tunge speke no vilons [villainous] thinge and also here theime [them] not').[50]

Alongside the broad movements I have been tracing, there is also a general narrowing of schoolroom traditions in a genre of texts that equate the proverbial with the practical, which always tends to rob such teachings of their weight, transforming them from a substantive and world-changing knowledge into a kind of veneer, what is then understood as guidance in 'manners' or 'courtesy'.[51] The *Distichs* certainly concern themselves with mundane matters ('Mundus esto' [Be tidy], I.8; 'Vino tempera' [Be moderate with wine], I.22), but what we see in a poem such as *How the Good Wife Taught her Daughter* (mid-fourteenth century) is a new focus on the most minor matters of self-presentation:

Whanne thou gest* in the gate, ne go thou noght to faste	*go*
Braundiy* noght thin heved, thine schuldres	*toss*
thou ne caste*	*shrug*
Be noght of mani wordes, ne swer thou noght to grete;*	*greatly*
Alle swiche maneres, douter,* thou most lete.*	*daughter / leave*
Evil lat,* evil name,	*manners*
Mi leve* child.[52]	*dear*

This text consists of twenty-eight stanzas in exactly this domestic vein ('Housewifliche schal thou gon on the werkedai', l. 95) and, since the schools 'catered chiefly for boys', whereas most girls were taught, informally, by their mothers at home, it could also be said to open out schoolroom traditions by acknowledging, and thereby absorbing, not only the household's role in pedagogy, but a whole new class of educated people.[53] Equally narrowing in such cases are the trivializing views of women drawn in as part and parcel of this domesticity, so that, in this version of 'wisdom', even the most casual social interaction becomes fraught with the possibilities for sin ('Aquinte noght with ilka [that] man thou metest in the street . . . That he thorugh no vilenie thin herte nothing chonge', ll. 65–8). But it is really the narrowness of its vision that distinguishes the courtesy book from wisdom literature in the main, as is particularly well proved by a fifteenth-century translation of a Latin poem attributed to Robert Grosseteste (*c*.1170–1253) usually called *Stans Puer ad Mensam* [A Boy Standing at Table]. Here, the standard recommendations on governing one's tongue are brought down to the mechanics of eating:

Lett not your mowth of metis* ben full replete.	*food*
Defoyle not yoursylfe with bestiall	
rebomynacyon,*	*abomination*
In eythere syde of your mowth ete not your mete.	
Nother with a fulle mouth have no cowmunycacion,	
Ne laught not lest it twrne to abomynacyon,	
Or hurt yoursylfe by soden aventure*	*accident*
Whych is ayen all connyng* and norture.*[54]	*refinement / breeding*

The triviality of such literature was also clearly the grounds of its appeal, as is proved by the number of such texts that survive from the fifteenth century (e.g. *An ABC Morality, How the Wise Man Taught his Son, Myne Awen Dere Sone*),[55] but the point is made most dramatically by the behaviour the fifteenth-century *The Book of Curtesye* is willing to commit to its elegant rime royal ('Purge youre nase [nose], lete hit not combred be / Wyth foule matiers ayenst all oneste [honesty], / But wyth your bare hande no matier from it fecche / For that is a foule and an uncurtays teche [characteristic]'), and, also, by the size of the audience expected for such advice, since the *Book* was printed by Caxton in 1477.[56]

Religious communities

Religious communities were central to literate life in England because clerics were so generally literate and wrote so much and, at the time of the Conquest and for some time after, monasteries were the most important of these communities. Monastic life was often described as 'regular' because it was lived according to a 'rule' [regula], but in the case of the Benedictines, for six centuries the dominant monastic order, literacy stood at the very centre of that regularity, since life was built round a single text, the *Regula Monachorum* (*c*.530–40) by Benedict of Nursia (d. 547), which I mentioned in chapter 1. This text ruled every aspect of Benedictine life, not least by insisting on complete adherence to its every provision ('in all things, therefore, let all follow the Rule as master' [in omnibus igitur omnes magistram sequantur regulam]).[57] All monastic communities sought to purify devotion by isolating their members from worldly distractions in part by becoming largely self-sustaining (the Benedictine monastery was to contain 'all necessary things . . . so that monks may not be compelled to wander outside it, for that is not at all expedient for their souls' [omnia necessaria . . . ut non sit necessitas monachis vagandi foris, quia omnino non expedit animabus eorum] [152–3]). In this environment, whatever time the Benedictine monk did not spend providing sustenance for himself he was meant to spend in devotion, often in the *lectio divina* or 'sacred reading' ('the brethren . . . must be occupied at stated hours . . . in sacred reading' [et certis temporibus occupari debent fraters . . . in lectione divina] [110–11]). The Benedictine Rule never mandates writing as part of this regular activity, but, as I have said, the literacy necessary to follow the Benedictine Rule ensured that these communities were rich sites of textual production. This is well proved at the beginning of our period by the *Anglo-Saxon Chronicle*, always a project of the Benedictine monasteries and, as I have mentioned, the most important bridge between Old English and Middle English writing, since institutional continuities allowed its composition to continue in a number of places right across the Conquest.[58] Much Benedictine writing was in Latin, but both the generality and the durability of the Benedictine commitment to letters is later proved by the rich fruit it bore in the fifteenth century in the roughly 145,000 lines of English verse penned by John Lydgate, a monk of the Benedictine house at Bury St Edmunds.[59]

The Benedictine idea of the regular life was the oldest in England, but from the twelfth century onward such life, the communities it founded, and the kind of writings it fostered varied greatly as a result of the waves of reform that swept into England from the Continent. The Cluniac, Cistercian and Carthusian movements were probably the most important of these new monastic orders to English letters,[60] but to these should be added the Augustinian canons, who were also expanding enormously in this same period. Although the Augustinians were not 'monks' but, rather, the priests who worked in the service of a single bishop, a 'rule' for their conduct slowly emerged, and they came to live in well-defined communities, less cloistered than those of monks, but still 'regularized' by their common devotional practices.[61] Since these communities were at once so self-contained but so different in their needs, the various orders can often be mapped across Britain, with some more dominant in certain areas (the Cistercians, for example, were so concerned to isolate themselves that their monasteries were founded in the sparsely populated North, or the far west of Cornwall and Wales), and others favouring particular sorts of places (the centrality of the Benedictines ensured that either they located themselves in or near large towns and cities, or those towns and cities formed around them).[62] The effects of such varied regularity on Middle English must be as complex and various as it was pervasive,[63] but it can also be traced with some concision by looking at both the diffusion of, and the variation in, the *idea* of regulation as it passed from these orders into the surprising variety of rules, or guides, or instructions for a religious life (in addition to those translations of the Benedictine Rule itself) that proliferated in Middle English from the thirteenth century onward.

Ancrene Wisse (1216–20) is the earliest and most important of these, and, although I have already mentioned it for its important discussion of confession, it also offers a particularly clear illustration of the strong connection such texts make between devotion and regulation ('Theo beoth rihte the livieth efter riwle' [They are right who live according to a rule]).[64] Anchorites lived in an 'anlich stude' [solitary place] (60/75). However, they particularly required the help of such a rule, for, unlike hermits, they did not live alone in a remote area, but, rather, in an enclosure (an 'anchorhold') in the centre of some community, often attached to a church, and it was never easy to navigate the complications of remaining separate from the social world around them.[65] Although it is not itself affiliated with any monastic movement, *Ancrene Wisse* draws heavily on the *De Institutione Inclusarum* [On the Conduct of Enclosed Women], a rule written by a Cistercian monk, Aelred of Rievaulx (1110–67), for his sister.[66] In addition to a common emphasis on the body, *Ancrene Wisse* draws deeply on the connections between solitude and introspection in Cistercian spirituality, and on the way its modes of devotion isolated the individual so as 'to lay bare the recesses of the soul'.[67] In *Ancrene Wisse*, entering the anchorhold provides 'sikernesse' [safety] (63/80), but most of all it takes the anchorite away from the material trappings of the world, so that she may cultivate spiritual or *im*material parts of herself:

> Ha deth hire in [to ancre-hus] to huden hire from hise kene clokes; ha hud hire in hire hole ba from worltliche men ant worltliche sunnen, ant for-thi ha is gasteliche Davith, thet is strong toyein the feond ant hire leor lufsum to ure Laverdes ehnen . . . Treowe ancres beoth briddes icleopede for ha leaveth the eorthe, thet is, the luve of alle worltliche thinges, ant thurh yirnunge of heorte to heovenliche thinges fleoth uppart toward heovene. (52/65)

> [She goes in [to the anchor-house] to hide herself from [the fiend's] sharp claws; she hides herself in her hole both from worldly men and worldly sins, and therefore she is spiritually David, who is strong against the devil, and her face is lovely in Our Lord's eyes . . . True anchor[ites] are called birds, for they leave the earth – that is, love of all worldly things – and through yearning in heart for heavenly things fly upwards towards heaven.]

Regulation of this kind tends to create the interior space it presumes to govern simply by imagining it, but, by insisting on the importance of thought to devotional practice, it also tries to reach inside minds and, as a way of fashioning a deeper and more consequential relationship with God, it also regulates *thought*:

> Thench ofte with sar of thine sunnen,
> Thench of helle wa, of heoveriches wunnen,
> Thench of thin ahne death, of Godes death o rode,
> The grimme dom of Domesdai mune ofte i mode,
> Thench hu fals is the worlt, hwucche beoth hire meden,
> Thench hwet tu ahest Godd for his goddeden. (91/113)

> [Think of your sins with sorrow often,
> Think of hell's misery, of joys in heaven,
> Think of your death, of God's death on the cross,
> Call to mind the fierce judgement of Judgement Day oft,
> Think how false is the world, what is its meed,
> Think what you owe God for his good deeds.]

The English of *Ancrene Wisse* served not only to draw such ideas out of a purely monastic world, but also in some measure to popularize them: *Ancrene Wisse* was revised by its original author for a larger audience,[68] and there was also 'an extraordinarily early multiplication of copies', very soon after the text was first written, as if it was very much in demand.[69] It was clearly very well regarded too, since it was one of the few English texts in this period to have been translated 'up' the linguistic hierarchy, into Latin as well as (on two different occasions) French.[70]

As this equation of devotion and thoughtfulness moves further from the monastery it becomes less a matter of demanding certain sorts of thinking and more a matter of cultivating a certain emotional stance, less a question of probing ever deeper into mental states the better to shape them than of finding a set of strategies for inspiration and persuasion. In this vein, such thinking is sometimes called 'mysticism' because of its intense focus on the immaterial, although 'vernacular theology' is a term that better credits its rigour as a body of thought, and Richard Rolle (d. 1349) is usually taken to be this theology's founding figure.[71] Rolle was a hermit, withdrawn from the world, and he too wrote a rule for the 'solitary lyf', called *The Form of Living*.[72] But the real energies of this rule and Rolle's theology generally lie not in any specific strictures for conduct, but in describing the state from which an interiorized spirituality could emerge, as if spontaneously (as 'God enspires' believers 'to forsake this worlde' and 'ledes tham by thar ane, and spekes til [th]ar hert' [118]). Most characteristic of Rolle's method, then, is not the imperative ('Think often . . .'), but the literary techniques that will lead to a particularly emotional response. In *The Form of Living* and *Ego Dormio* this often takes the form of inset lyrics in which contemplation is equated with the longings of a more earthly love:[73]

For lufe my thoght has fest,* and I am fayne*	*laid hold of / eager*
to fare.*	*to go*
I stand in still mowrnyng.* Of all lufelyst of lare*	*mourning / lore*
Es lufe langyng, it drawes me til* my day,	*to*
The band of swete byrnyng,* for it haldes me ay*	*burning / always*
Fra* place and fra plaiyng til that I get may	*from*
The syght of my swetyng,* that wendes*	*sweetheart / goes*
never away.	

(107)

Also characteristic of Rolle is the extravagant metaphor that draws together the most mundane objects with the most sacred imagery, using the shocking mixture of levels to insist upon their proximity, on the immanence of the deepest spirituality in the everyday and, in that sense, its attainability:

Efte, swete Jhesu thi body is like to a dufhouse. For a dufhouse is ful of holys, so is thy body ful of woundes. And as a dove pursued of an hauk, yf she mow cache an hool of hir hous she is siker ynowe, so swete Jhesu, in temptacion thy woundes ben best refuyt to us. Now, swet Jhesu, I beseche the, in euche temptacion graunt me grace of some hoole of thy woundes, and lykynge to abide in mynd of thy passioun.[74]

[*dufhouse*: dovehouse *holys*: holes *mow*: might *siker*: safe *refuyt*: refuge *euche*: every *lykynge*: pleasure]

This image comes mid-way in a series of similes in the *Meditations on the Passion*, which also compare the wounded body of Jesus to a 'nette', a 'honeycombe' and a 'boke written al with rede ynke', and which culminate in an image that converts all of these wounds into the 'swet savorynge' of the grace it represents, 'lyk to a medow ful of swete flours and holsome herbes' (35–6).

The monastic roots of such practices are well illustrated by another writer and text usually categorized as 'mystic', Julian of Norwich and her *Revelation of Love*, for this set of meditations on visions Julian had in 1373 begins with a demand for regulation:

> The secunde [revelation], come to my mind with contrition, frely without any seking: a wilful desire to have of God's gifte a bodily sicknes. I would that that sicknes were so hard as to deth that I might, in that sicknes undertake all my rightes of holy church, myselfe wening that I should die, and that all creatures might suppose the same that saw me. For I would have no maner of comforte of fleshly ne erthely life.[75]

[*sicknes*: sickness *undertake*: receive *wening*: believing]

Monastic life was often very easy, particularly in the large abbeys of the larger orders where there was wealth aplenty,[76] but the connection Julian makes between bodily hardship and spiritual improvement – the extent to which she equates the strictness of regulation with devotional rigour – can be understood as a passionate embrace of the restrictive logic at the heart of any *ruled* life. And though her wish for a 'more true mind in the passion of Christ' (127) is separate from her wish for sickness, she realizes, in her sickness, that it is the state of the body that prepares her mind for such visions, for her own pain not only connects her to Christ's 'blessed passion' ('his paines were my paines, with compassion', 133), but she is also like Jesus ('that for love would become a deadly man', 133) in having chosen to suffer. These preparations are described in two chapters, and this is followed by sixteen 'shewings' or visions which share with Rolle both an extravagance of imagery and an extraordinary capacity to extend into metaphor the defining amalgam of the material and the immaterial, the body and the mind:

> In this same time that I saw this sight of the head bleeding our good lord shewed a ghostly sight of his homely loving. I saw that he is to us all thing

that is good and comfortable to our helpe. He is our clothing, that for love
wrappeth us and windeth us, halseth us and all becloseth us, hangeth about
us for tender love, that he may never leeve us. And so in this sight I saw
that he is all thing that is good, as to my understanding. Also in this, he
shewed a little thing, the quantity of an haselnot, lying in the palme of my
hand as me semide, and it was as round as any balle. I loked theran with
the eye of my understanding, and thought: 'What may this be?' And it was
answered generally thus: 'It is all that is made'. I marvayled how it might
laste, for methought it might sodenly have fallen to nought for littlenes.
And I was answered in my understanding: 'It lasteth and ever shall, for God
loveth it. And so hath all thing being by the love of God. (139)

[*halseth*: embraces   *becloseth*: encloses   *haselnot*: hazelnut]

Julian chose a regular life at some point (when Margery Kempe visits her,
about 1413, Julian is as an 'ankres' [anchoress] in Norwich),[77] but the most
monastic quality of her *Revelation* is the extent to which spiritual improvement is made a function of intelligence and study, no matter how 'homely'
the imagery or 'little' the subject, a progress always rooted in 'understanding'. In this same way, while Julian insists upon her own meekness as a
person (she calls herself a 'simple creature' [125]) and she always represents
herself as a passive recipient of these 'shewings' ('And then our good lord
opened my gostely [spiritual] eye and shewde me my soule in the middes
of my harte', 335), the whole of her theology is extraordinarily penetrating,
a series of bold and original acts of mind.

The mind remains the fundamental territory for the other fourteenth-
century writers usually regarded as 'mystics', but the theology they develop
is decidedly less intellectual than Julian's. In the *Scale of Perfection*, by Walter
Hilton (d. 1396), for example, while the monastic life still continues to
provide a basic formal principle – the work is a kind of 'rule' for meditation
addressed to a 'goostli suster in Jhesu Christ'[78] – and spirituality is still defined
against the body, an extraordinary premium is placed on *not* knowing:

Alle men and women that speken of the fier of love knowe not wel what it
is, for what it is I can not telle thee, save this may I telle thee, it is neither
bodili ne it is bodili feelid. A soule mai fele it in praiere or in devocioun,
whiche soule is in the bodi, but he felith it not bi no bodili witt. For though
it be so, that yif it wirke in a soule the bodi mai turne into an heete as it
were chafid for likynge travaile of the spirit, neverthelees the fier of love
is not bodili, for it is oonly in the goostli desire of the soule. (59)

[*fier*: fire   *witt*: sense   *yif*: if   *chafid*: warmed   *likynge*: pleasant]

The anonymous, late fourteenth-century *Cloud of Unknowing* takes this idea
of devotion one step further and, by means of what is usually called an

apophatic or negative theology in which any attempt to specify God or the spiritual is seen to err precisely in the act of specification, true 'understanding' is, again, the opposite of 'subtle thought':

> And for this skile it is that I bid thee put doun soche a scharp sotil thought, and kever him with a thicke cloude of forgetyng, be he never so holy, ne hote he thee never so weel for to help thee in thi purpos. For whi love may reche to God in this liif, bot not knowing. And al the whiles that the soule wonith in this deedly body, evermore is the scharpnes of our understonding in beholding of alle goostly thinges, bot most specialy of God, medelid with sum maner of fantesie; for the whiche oure werk schuld be unclene, and bot if more wonder were, it schuld lede us into moche error.[79]

> [*skile*: reason   *sotil*: clever   *hote*: promise   *for whi*: because   *wonith*: dwells   *deedly*: mortal   *medelid*: mixed   *bot if*: unless]

This text's extraordinary image for this spiritual state of ignorance, the 'cloud of unknowing', just like Hilton's 'ghostly desire', does not, however, wholly deny the role of the mind, for it emphasizes a person's cognitive and perceptual capacities in order to cultivate a certain feeling: it is no accident that the common term in the passages from Hilton, the *Cloud* and Julian that I have quoted is 'love'.

The appetite for guidance in lay devotion ensured that not only the Benedictine Rule but monastic rules of all sorts were translated throughout the Middle English period. Five different English translations were made of the *Rule of Saint Benedict* between the thirteenth and fifteenth centuries.[80] Aelred's *De Institutione Inclusarum* was translated into English twice, once in the fourteenth century and once in the fifteenth.[81] The rule organizing the Bridgittine order of nuns, the *Rule of Saint Saviour*, was translated in the fifteenth century.[82] The vernacular interest in the ruled routines of religious communities is perhaps best captured by the lengthy prose description of every word and movement of the Bridgittine Latin service, called the *Mirror of Our Lady*, which was prepared in the fifteenth century and finally printed in 1530.[83] But it is, again, in mysticism that the rigour that defines monastic life found not only its most passionate and thoughtful expression but also its greatest popularity. There are forty-two surviving manuscripts containing one or both of the books of the *Scale*[84] and nineteen surviving manuscripts of the *Cloud of Unknowing*.[85]

The household

Beyond monastic walls and anchoritic enclosures the fundamental unit of social life was the 'household', which divided up the whole English community into a 'symmetrical array' of units, each very different in size and complexity, but all fully commensurable in terms of structure and function.[86] Because our own society is similarly divided up, we tend to think of the household as a given, both fundamental and irreducible, the common component of *any* social existence, the formative influence on every person's basic beliefs ('family values' is the modern phrase that insists upon this connection by presuming it). But the household as we know it did not yet exist in imperial Rome and the Christian empire that succeeded it, largely because Roman and later law allowed slavery, polygamy and concubinage: these societies 'lacked a clear sense of the primary descent group as a distinct moral unit, and lacked too a concept of family or house-hold that could be applied across all social levels'.[87] A structure resembling the modern household only began to take shape in European society from the ninth century onward, as a result of an increasing insistence on monogamy as well as changes in the land law favouring 'dynastic lineage', which ensured that land was not parcelled up among a group of descen-dants but, rather, moved, en bloc, from father to a sole male heir.[88] Feudal-ism complicated the commensurability of these units, since it allowed the most wealthy households to annex other households as dependent units, partially absorbing members of such subsidiary households by extracting their labour (for the performance of a variety of services) in exchange for land rights or money. It was on this scale, often described as a 'court', that the household became an important site of literary production, for it not only gathered together sufficient numbers of people to create a significant audience, it also had the resources to pay for entertainment at meals, for minstrels and tale-tellers who might sing or recite 'verse intended primarily to amuse and divert'.[89] In the twelfth century and afterwards, romances became an important source of such diversion, not least because these texts so generally represented the very household practices in which they played such a significant part. This is particularly clear in those Middle English romances, such as *Havelok the Dane* (c.1280), which begin with the kind of attention-grabbing shout designed to cut through the postprandial noise of a dining hall:[90]

> Herkneth* to me, gode men,   *listen*
> Wives, maidnes, and alle men,
> Of a tale that ich you wile telle,
> Who-so it wile here and there-to dwelle.*[91]   *wait*

The broadly chivalric concerns of romance focused most precisely on household concerns as its gaze withdrew from the large hall and more public matters, looking ever inward toward the household 'chamber', that 'household within the household' which developed in the largest aristocratic dwellings (and particularly the household of the king) in the later Middle Ages.[92] This withdrawal left the minstrel outside in the hall where his function became almost exclusively musical,[93] while a new sort of household writer arose, a more aristocratic figure, sometimes called a 'court poet' (where his political function is emphasized), a figure whose writings were increasingly compounded of strategies for articulating and valuing the heterosexual bond around which even the largest medieval household was organized, a relationship that might or might not be amorous but which was fully ideological (in fact, and in this poetry) in its insistence that such a bond was defined by 'love'.

The necessary transformation in household structures can be located with some precision, in England, in the latter half of the fourteenth century, for it is then that Langland not only describes but laments the recent movement of 'lord' and 'lady' into a 'pryvee parlour' (10.99), since this also separates the servants and lesser members of the house from easy opportunities for casual largesse from the high table in their own 'wretched' hall ('elenge is the halle', 10.96). This withdrawal is also carefully described in Chaucer's *Troilus and Criseyde* (c.1381–6), when Pandarus comes to look for Criseyde in her 'palays' [palace], and finds her 'within' her parlour, listening (not surprisingly) to a 'romaunce' (2.100):

When he was come unto his neces place,	
'Wher is my lady?' to hire folk quod he;	
And they hym tolde, and he forth in gan pace,*	*proceed*
And fond two othere ladys sete* and she,	*seated*
Withinne a paved parlour, and they thre	
Herden a mayden* reden hem the geste*	*girl / story*
Of the siege of Thebes, while hem leste.*	*they pleased*

(2.78–84)

Despite its ostensibly ancient setting, the households in *Troilus and Criseyde* are very precisely modelled on those in medieval England (the romance read out here is doubtless meant to be the *Roman de Thèbes* [1150–5], a retelling of the events of Statius' *Thebaid*), and this poem is also very much set in parlours and bedchambers, concerned above all with tracing the evolving relationship of Troilus and Criseyde (it is no accident that this poem's spatial centre – in the middle of the third of its five books – is a bed in a bedroom, in which Troilus and Criseyde lie, wound in each other's arms 'as aboute a tree, with many a twiste, / Bytrent [encircles] and writh [twines around] the swote wodebynde [honeysuckle]', 3.1231–2).[94]

The English poem that partakes most dramatically of the contrast between hall and chamber, however, is *Sir Gawain and the Green Knight*, where an extended sequence at the court of Bertilak entwines a public agreement in which Gawain promises to 'swap'[95] his daily winnings with his host, and Gawain's lengthy temptation by Bertilak's wife, who invites him to intimacies in his bedroom that he can neither accept nor too brusquely refuse:

'Ma fay',* quoth the meré* wyf, 'ye may not be werned;*	*my faith / gay, fair* *denied*
Ye ar stif* innoghe to constrayne wyth strenkthe yif yow lykes,	*strong*
Yif any were so vilanous that yow devaye* wolde.'	*refuse*
'Ye, be God', quoth Gawayn, 'good is your speche,	
Bot threte* is unthryvande* in thede* ther I lende,*	*force / ignoble / country* *live*
I am at your comaundment, to kysse quen* yow lykes;*	*when / it pleases*
Ye may lach* quen yow lyst,* and leve* quen yow thynkkes,*	*take / like / abstain* *like*
in space'.*	*in due course*

(ll. 1495–1503)

In its attention to what it calls 'luf-talkyng' (l. 927) of the kind Gawain engages in here, that delicate conversational dance through which Gawain's tact and goodness are tested by what he manages *not* to say, the poem also shows some of the ways in which intimacy was formalized in the large household as a quasi-public game, elaborated not so much as a set of rules but as a *display* of social skill which could be enjoyed (apart from the ethics that constrained it, and the feelings that it described) as an art form in its own right. It is not only in these bedroom scenes, moreover, that *Sir Gawain and the Green Knight* insists that the most intimate gestures and experiences bear consequentially on public performances – that a household ethics worthy of the name takes in both hall and chamber.

Such a 'game of love' was a late medieval phenomenon, but its source was the kind of lyric that had long been recited or sung by the minstrel in hall, and it depended upon the rhetorical techniques such lyrics had developed for describing intimate thoughts and acts in a crowd.[96] The earliest of these lyrics were written by the 'troubadors', in Occitania (or, roughly, the south of France) in the eleventh century,[97] but the furthest back we may reach in Middle English for such poetry is the set of lyrics that survive in London, British Library, MS Harley 2253. In such poetry the game often consists in the displacement of a powerful affection on to a virtuosity of style, as in the poem usually called *Annot and Johon*, where lines that both alliterate and rhyme (on a single syllable for a whole stanza) spin out a long series of comparisons between Annot and the most desirable things:

Ichot* a burde* in a bour* ase beryl* so	*I know / a girl / bower/ beryl*
bryht,*	*bright*
Ase saphyr in selver semly* on syht,	*fair*
Ase jaspe* the gentil* that lemeth* with lyht,	*jasper / genteel / gleams*
Ase gernet* in golde and ruby wel ryht,*	*garnet / true*
Ase onycle* he* ys on yholden* on hyht,*	*onyx / she / held / high*
Ase diamaund the dere* in day when	*costly*
he* is dyht,*	*she / set*
He is coral ycud* with cayser* ant knyht,	*known / emperor*
Ase emeraude amorewen* this may*	*in the morning / girl*
haveth myht.	
The myht of the margarite* haveth this	*pearl*
mai mere;*	*noble*
For charbocle* ich hire ches* bi chyn and	*carbuncle / recognized*
by chere.*⁹⁸	*expression*

In another Harley MS lyric, usually called *Alysoun*, the game resides not only in formal intricacy but in the displacement of a described passion into the rhythmic intensity of the words describing it (a rhythm which either reflects accompanying music we have lost, or models it):

An hendy* hap* ichabbe*	*excellent / fortune / I have*
yhent,*	*received*
Ichot* from hevene it is me sent –	*I know*
From alle wymmen mi love is lent,*	*removed*
And lyht* on Alysoun.⁹⁹	*alights*

Such lyrics often set themselves outside, in gardens, but this pose does not so much take them away from the chamber as project the ethical freedom that was the fundamental condition of such intimate playfulness into a setting. That setting was also, often, a legacy of the other crucial foundation for this sort of household poetry, in this case as much a particular poem as the genre that it founded, the allegorical dream vision the *Roman de la rose*, begun by Guillaume de Lorris (*c.*1230) and completed by Jean de Meun (*c.*1275). This poem begins in the chamber of the dreamer who narrates it ('Couichez estoie / Une nuit, si cum je souloie / Et me dormoie mout forment' [I lay down one night, as usual, and slept very soundly]),[100] but the chamber's amorous games are unfolded into an allegory set in 'a large and roomy garden' [un vergier grant et lé] (130/32), where the uneven and amorphous attributes and movements of love are disaggregated into a set of fixed stages, each represented by a personification ('Idleness', 'Mirth', 'Courtesy', 'Fair Welcoming', 'Disdain', 'Jealousy'), and the desired person is hypostatized, as a target, 'the Rose' itself. This allegory also provides a kind of sportive script for the figures who read it (or had it read to them) in some chamber, a social and emotional choreography which not only reflected, but which could in turn be drawn upon for enacting, this household 'game':

Upon the karoll wonder faste*	*intently*
I gan biholde, til atte laste	
A lady gan me for to espie,*	*spy*
And she was cleped* Curtesie,	*called*
The worshipfull,* the debonaire –	*honourable*
I pray to God ever falle hir faire!*	*it goes well for her*
Ful curteisly she called me:	
'What do ye there, beau ser?'* quod she,	*good sir*
'Come and, if it lyke* you	*pleases*
To dauncen, dauncith with us now'.	
And I, withoute tariyng,*	*delay*
Wente into the karolyng.	

(ll. 793–804)

The English translation I quote from here is Chaucer's, and its very existence is testimony to the importance of this poem and its vision of love in fourteenth-century England (this is probably the first extended piece of writing Chaucer attempted in English).[101] In his early poems, many of which were also allegorical dream visions, Chaucer relied heavily not only on the *Rose*, but also on the other French love allegories very largely modelled on it, which provided further techniques for such intimate revelry (in particular, *Le Jugement dou Roy de Behaingne* and *Le Dit de la fonteinne amoureuse* by Guillaume de Machaut [*c.*1300–77] and *Le Paradys d'amours* by Jean Froissart [*c.*1337–1404]).[102]

In the middle of the last century criticism was particularly alarmed by the indulgence of appetite that lies at the heart of this household ethic (or of 'courtly love', as this ethic was usually described in such criticism), and it was C. S. Lewis who most influentially registered this alarm when, in an uncharacteristic lapse of judgement, he erroneously insisted that 'adultery' was a key element of such behaviour (the others he adduced were 'humil-

ity', 'courtesy' and the sense that love was itself a 'religion').[103] In an allegory as schematic as the *Roman de la rose*, marriage is an irrelevance, while,
in some of the most important games of love, marriage – and marriage
choice in particular – is very much at issue. Chaucer's *Parliament of Fowles*
(*c*.1380) offers a sustained affront to any view that courtly love was 'anti-
matrimonial in principle' (as Lewis also put it), for the chief question before
its playful assembly, convened under the watchful eye of Nature herself, is
which of three male (or 'tercel') eagles is worthy of the hand of the female
(or 'formel') eagle.[104] The game in this case is particularly madcap, as the
ensuing debate maps marriage choice onto bird sexuality and imagines the
difference between bird species as a difference in class (' "Lo, here a parfit
resoun of a goos!" / Quod the sperhauk', ll. 568–9), but the poem also
traces the lines of a more realistic social game as the formel eagle defers her
decision for a teasing year. Since the formel eagle's decision frees the lesser
birds of the poem to choose a mate, the *Parliament* is also free to end with a
rhapsodic description of the bliss of the resulting couplings:

And whan this werk al brought was to an ende,	
To every foul Nature yaf* his make	*gave*
By evene acord,* and on here way they wende.	*mutual agreement*
And, Lord, the blisse and joye that they make!	
For ech of hem gan other in wynges take,	
And with here nekkes ech gan other wynde,*	*entwine*
Thankynge alwey the noble goddesse of kynde.*	*nature*
(ll. 666–72)	

As this stanza shows, Middle English poetry could be very frank about
sexuality, and one can see how a more modern puritanism might recoil
before a poem such as Lydgate's *The Complaint of the Black Knight*, which
remains schematically allegorical in describing the dance of Love ('So
that Dispite now haldeth forth her reyn, / Thro hasty beleve of tales that
men feyn'),[105] but is also frank about the sex that underlies even a love so
stylized:

For I loved oon ful* longe sythe* agoon	*very / time*
With al my herte, body and fulle myght.	
(ll. 316–17)	

Even in these playful contexts, moreover, medieval thought about both
marriage and adultery could be surprisingly sophisticated and complex.
In Lydgate's *Temple of Glass*, for example, marriage is a problem, but only
because it is so loveless that the lady is therefore led to love another
knight:

Devoide of joie, of wo I have plente:*	*plenty*
What I desire, that mai I not possede:*	*possess*
For that I nold* is redi aye* to me,	*do not want / always*
And that I love, forto swe* I drede:*	*follow / am afraid*
To my desire contrarie is my mede.*	*reward*
And thus I stond, departid* even on tweyn,	*divided*
Of wille and dede ilaced* in a chaine.[106]	*laced*

Where the marriage bond is precisely what prevents the satisfaction of adulterous 'desire' ('For I am bounde to thing that I nold', l. 335), literature can hardly be said to celebrate extramarital affection, and, indeed, Lydgate's description is sufficiently vague about the particularities of the relationship (sex is never in prospect) that it seems clear that adultery was something he actually found it hard to think about.

Even when it elaborates such games, the literature of the household becomes increasingly conservative, as we might in fact expect, since it was devoted not to critique or analysis but to a kind of glorious reflection whereby the household was given an image of itself, both outsized and decorated, but, above all, as a stable and stabilizing structure. This proves to be especially true of the most important exemplifications of the game of love in the last decades of the fifteenth century, *The Floure and the Leafe* and *The Assembly of Ladies*. The former unfolds as the allegorical vision of a female narrator who falls asleep, finds herself in a 'herber' [arbour] shaped like a 'prety parlour',[107] and watches as two companies of ladies and knights pass before her – the first, which is devoted to the leaf, 'kepte alway her maidenhede' (l. 478) and was 'aye stedfast' (l. 487), while the second, devotees of the flower, 'loved idelnes' (l. 536) and frivolous pleasures ('for to hunt and hauke, and pley in medes', l. 538). The poem's predictable conclusion reveals the narrator's allegiance 'unto the Leafe' (l. 576). In *The Assembly of Ladies*, another dream vision, Lady Loyalty hears bills of complaint by a sequence of ladies who have been wronged in love, and then, in a dramatic act of retributive justice, orders all of these wrongs put right:

And in al this wherein ye fynde yow greved*	*aggrieved*
There shal ye fynde an open remedy,	
In suche wise* as ye shul be releved	*manner*
Of al that ye reherce heere triewly.	
As of the date ye shal knowe verily,*	*truly*
Than ye may have a space in your comyng,	
For Diligence shall bryng it yow bi writyng.[108]	

This wish-fulfilment upends the normal stasis of the love complaint (where the complainant is more usually, like the lady in Lydgate's *Temple of Glass*, irremediably caught between contraries), and it also amounts to a quiet advocacy for the resolving powers of the loving woman. The self-possession of the voice that insists upon this change seems to reflect a very real knowledge of women's lives, as indeed does the dutiful stance adopted by the narrator of *The Floure and the Leafe*, and such realism may be the direct consequence of female authorship (since both poems are unusual in their use of a female narrator, it has long been assumed that they were written by women).[109] Certainly, in a book that we know to have been produced within the household, the 'Findern Manuscript' (Cambridge, University Library, MS Ff.i.6), we find love lyrics by women that also pull away from the conventions of the thwarted complainant, returning matters of love to a satisfied and stable daily life,[110] taking their language, on one occasion, straight from the standard marriage service ('To hym I woll be trywe and playn, / And evyr his owne in serteyn, / Tyll deth departe us to').[111] These lyrics also tend to embrace marriage as a fundamental fact and virtue:

> Where Y have chosyn, stedefast woll Y be
> Nevyre* to repente in wyll, thowth,* ne dede,   *never / thought*
> Yow to sarve* watt ye commaund me,   *serve*
> Never hyt withdrawe for no maner drede.
> Thus am Y bownd by yowre godelyhede,*   *goodness*
> Wych hathe me causyd and that in every wyse*   *way*
> Wyle Y in lyfe endure to do yow my servyse.[112]

When we are in a position to see the kind of writing actually produced in a particular household it is also very much in this vein, as, for example, the letter that Margery Brewes wrote to John Paston, her 'ryght wele beloved Voluntyne', in February of 1477 (that is, probably on Valentine's Day). Here, in order to stress her devotion and loyalty, Margery draws on the stance of the servant-lover and the game of love's allegory (as she briefly envisions her heart speaking to her body) and her prose shifts into a stuttering rhyme:

> And yf ye command me to kepe me true where-ever I go,
> I-wyse* I will do all my myght you to love and never no mo, *truly*
> And yf my freendys say that I do amys, thei schal not me
> let* so for to do,   *stop*
> Myn herte me byddys ever more to love yowe,
> Truly over all earthly thing.
> And yf thei be never so wroth,* I tryst it schall be bettur *angry*
> in tyme commyng.[113]

Such poetry does not so much restore the elaborate artificialities of 'luf-talkyng' to real household practices as show how a language committed to dramatizing intimacy – to parading its stages and aspects on both a large and a wholly artificial scale – could be both useful and effective in bringing real intimacy about. In fact, by the end of 1477 Margery and John Paston were married.[114]

Cities and towns

Throughout the Middle Ages, England remained a largely agrarian society with as much as 90 per cent of the population living in very small gatherings of households about the size of a village.[115] Medieval England also shared in a general process of urbanization that affected all of Europe, and from the twelfth century onward there was a proliferation of market towns, a growing density of population in such places and, finally, in certain areas (particularly in London) a sufficient collection of people to warrant the name 'city'. The causes of this growth are usually said to be the re-establishment of active trade routes to the East (largely in abeyance since antiquity), a steeply rising population[116] and, connecting these (as landlords increasingly required cash payment in the form of rents and taxes rather than services in exchange for tenancy), a steady emergence of an economy based on money rather than feudal service.[117] Market towns provided tenant farmers with a way of converting an increasing surplus in agricultural production into such money, and these markets also actively promoted a cash economy since they were structurally inclined to growth (providing a host of opportunities for the money they disbursed to be spent by farmers, and then spent again – and again and again – by the merchants who grew up to tend to the needs of those who had come to trade).[118] Too much has sometimes been made of the resulting difference between the lives lived in these market towns and the lives of those who farmed, since, despite a basic difference in their daily labour, the household remained both a common social structure and the fundamental unit of production (even urban craftsmen worked largely out of their homes).[119] The growth of urban populations was also a relative phenomenon, and 'urbanization' in the Middle Ages bore no relation to the kind of exponential growth we mean by that term today: calculations from poll tax returns for 1377 (that is, roughly the middle of our period) suggest that approximately half of the urban population of England lived in 500 different market towns with a population of no more than 500 people apiece (at this point London itself had a population of only 50,000 people).[120] The growth of towns and cities was not steady either, and after a severe famine in 1315–18, which killed nearly 15 per cent of the English population, and an outbreak of bubonic plague (or the 'Black Death') in 1348–9, which killed about half of the entire population, many towns went into a steep decline, and some never recovered.[121]

In earlier Middle English writings towns and cities are usually incidental, entering texts as little more than locatives, mentioned only because they help to anchor a new text to a familiar topographical point. *The Peterborough Chronicle* (completed 1154) gains its name, and reveals its local perspective, by its unemphatic but frequent references to Medehamstede (Peterborough's Old English name). The 'roberd' who names himself in the text now usually known as Robert of Gloucester's *Chronicle* (c.1300) slightly thickens his hazy identity by orienting events in the latter portion of this text in relation to 'gloucestre'.[122] The 'Roberd' who wrote *Handlyng Synne* (c.1303) expands such a locative into a short autobiography: he not only says that he is 'of Brunne' (or 'Bourn', a market town in Lincolnshire), but he gives very specific geographical references ('syxe myle be syde sympryngham evene / I duelled yn the pryorye / Fyftene yer yn companye / Yn the tyme of gode dan Jone').[123] The very casualness of such gestures – their relative unimportance to the meaning of a given text – becomes fodder for a joke in *The Owl and the Nightingale* (c.1216), where the association of the 'tune' [town] of 'Portesham . . . ine Dorsete' with 'Maister Nichole of Guldeforde' gives it all the trappings of an autobiographical locative which is then simultaneously undermined (for Nicholas is actually presented as the poem's ideal audience, rather than its author).[124]

It is in saint's life that cities and towns first gain thematic importance in English literature, for it is in such texts that a knowable place lends both weight and substance to the actuality of the saint – otherwise so unreal in his or her capacity to suffer and survive – as well as the miracles associated with him or her. Bury St Edmunds is an English town in Suffolk that even now bears the traces of such processes in its name, and the account of St Edmund in the large collection of saints' lives usually called the *South English Legendary* (c.1300) is a paradigmatic example of how these associations were produced in literature. This life begins in 869 with the gruesome dismemberment of Edmund, King of East Anglia, by a host of invading Danes, and it then describes the miraculous reassembly of his body as the very foundations of the town:

Hi ladde him to seint Edmundesbury as me* clepeth* thane toun	*men / call*
This holi man al isound* and leide him theradoun	*sound*
In noble schryne hi him broughte as right was to do	

Ther he lyth al hol and sound as hi seoth that cometh him to
For his bodi that was so todrawe* bicom al hol anon   *dismembered*
As the while he was alyue bothe in flesch and bon
His heved* as faste to the bodi as hit was euer er*   *head / before*
In al his bodi ther nas wem* as meni man isey* ther.[125]   *blemish /saw*

The *South English Legendary*'s life of St Kenelm (by legend, a child-king of the Mercian kingdom in the ninth century) provides a similar foundation myth for Winchcombe, in part by substantially aggrandizing the place (this small Cotswold village becomes a 'gret cite'), in part by allowing Kenelm's saintliness to emerge directly from that place: after Kenelm is killed at the behest of his treacherous sister, the location of his body is revealed only by the miracles it produces in that very spot (a cow, who spends all day sitting in the valley where the 'holy bodi' lies, eats nothing, but comes home 'fat and rond . . . and so fol of milk also').[126] Such miracles substantiate the holiness of the body with the solidity of the very earth, but such sanctity is made a permanent presence because it is connected to – made a manifestation of – a real and permanent place:

This holy bodi was forth ibore* with great honur   *borne*
   atte fine*   *the end*
To the abbeie as he lith yute* and ido* in noble ssrine.   *yet / put*
(ll. 361–2)

'Yet' is the key word in this and all such localizing legends.

These substantiating techniques reach their apotheosis in the late fourteenth-century alliterative poem *Saint Erkenwald*, where they are employed not only in relation to the most prominent of places, London, or, as the poem describes it, 'the metropol and the mayster-toun',[127] but in order to underpin the poem's broader theological concerns. The point of departure for this underpinning is the discovery of a body, richly attired, 'unchaungit' (l. 95) and 'unwemmyd' (l. 96), in the foundations of St Paul's Cathedral, when the cathedral was being rebuilt ('beten doun and buggyd efte new', l. 37) in the seventh century. The discovery of this holy body in the foundations of a particular church suggests that its meaning bears on the foundations of the church as such, and that meaning is explored in a conversation between this miraculous body and Erkenwald (Bishop of London from 675 to 693). The bishop learns that this pagan's body has survived intact because he was so uncorrupted in life, administering 'paynymes laghe' [pagans' law] (l. 203) but with an intuitive compassion ('I remewit [departed] never fro the right by reson myn awen [own]', l. 235), although his soul languishes 'in sorow and sike ful colde' (l. 305) because he lived too early for the sacrament of baptism to redeem him ('fulloght [baptism] in fonte wyt faitheful belive', l. 299). The sacrament is then administered by the tears Erkenwald sheds in his own compassion for the suffering of this good soul ('The bysshop balefully [with grief] bere doun his eghen / That hade no space to speke so spakly [soon] he yosked [sobbed]', ll. 311–12), and, as the pagan's soul is redeemed ('was sesyd [seized] in blisse', l. 345), his body turns to dust. At that point, however, the poem insists on a recip-rocal movement, whereby the discovery of such spiritual goodness within the 'mayster-toun' assures that this goodness accrues to the whole of the city. One of the poem's most powerful images is, then, its most urban, for, as those present in St Paul's move out into the city, celebrating the pagan's redemption while also mourning his loss ('Meche mournynge and myrthe was mellyd to-geder / Thai passyd forthe in processioun and alle the pepulle folowid', ll. 350–1), the whole of the city seems to join in, as 'alle the belles in the burghe [town] beryd [resounded] at ones' (l. 352).

Sitting just behind such sacralizing locatives is an ideal wherein the city, as both the newest and the most complex form of human habitation, becomes as much an idea about people as a kind of place, an instrument for envisioning a better social order as if that order were necessarily the same thing as the city's elaborate and built structure.[128] The place most often freighted with such idealism was what the Parson, at the end of Chaucer's *Canterbury Tales*, calls 'Jerusalem celestial' (X.51), a city that emerges as the aspirational opposite of the kinds of human imperfection associated with London in many of the *Tales*, and which, accordingly, even begins to replace Canterbury as the pilgrims' more appropriate spiritual goal (in what was clearly meant to be the last of the *Tales* the Parson promises to 'shewe' the pilgrims the 'wey' in their 'viage' to this city [X.49]). But the most important description of this city in Middle English in this idealized form comes in the last movements of *Pearl* (c.1380), that rich vision by the *Gawain*-poet in which a dreamer, locked in melancholia because of the death of his young daughter, is offered a series of visions of the afterlife, the last of which allows Jerusalem, in its elaborate structure, to embody the bliss in which his daughter now resides:

As John the apostel hit syy* with syght,	*saw it*
I syye that cyty of gret renoun,	
Jerusalem so nwe* and ryally dyght,*	*new / adorned*
As hit was lyght fro the heven adoun.*	*descended*
The borgh* was al of brende* golde bryght,	*city / glittering*
As glemande* glas burnist* broun,	*gleaming / burnished*
Wyth gentyl* gemmes anunder* pyght;*	*noble / adorned / below*

With banteles* twelve on basyng* boun* –	*tiers / base / built*
The foundementes* twelve of riche tenoun* –	*foundations / joinery*
Uch* tabelment* was a serlypes* ston;	*each / tier / separate*
As derely* devyses* this ilk toun	*splendidly / describes*
In Apocalyppex* the apostel John.[129]	*the Apocalypse*

This description may have also evoked some of the elaborate pageants staged in London both to flatter Richard II and to celebrate the city's wealth, but, as in those pageants, many of the details in this description are drawn from the Book of Revelation, and the richness of ornament and the complexity of numerical design that characterize that city are not only intrinsic to its beauty, but manifestations of an underlying spiritual perfection.[130] And that perfection also extends to the social organization this elaborately built environment contains: so, after this description of the city's glass and stone, the dreamer is shown a 'prosessyoun' (l. 1096) in which hundreds and thousands come together happily ('wyth gret delyt thay glod [glided] in fere [together]', l. 1105), and make their way through the city, despite their numbers, with 'no pres in plyt' ['with no crowding in their order', l. 1114]. As an earlier passage in the poem has already made clear, such harmony is made possible by a social ordering whose governing principle (paradoxically, but importantly) annuls all the problems of hierarchy that trouble social ordering in the temporal world:

The court of the kyndom of God alyve*	*living*
Has a property in hytself beyng:	
Alle that may therinne aryve	
Of alle the reme* is quen other kyng	*realm*
And never other* yet schal depryve.	*[one] another*
(ll. 445–9)	

Such ideas make the description of the heavenly Jerusalem an exercise in imagining a better world, but a certain realism is annexed to this idealism when it becomes clear, as part and parcel of this vision, that such perfection is unattainable: when the dreamer actually tries to have some share in this heavenly scene by trying to cross the 'strem' [stream] (l. 1159) between him and the 'mirthe' (l. 1149) of the 'meyny' [company] (l. 1145) he sees, he is jolted right out of his dream and back into his mournful sorrow.

This jolt has much larger meanings in the complex vision that comprises *Pearl*, but it is equally relevant to the ideas collected around the heavenly Jerusalem as well as the English cities and towns mentioned in Middle English literature, for they also often appeared there, not simply in a darker light, but in precise *contrast* to the aspirations of the idea of the city – places of profound disappointment, defined by all the promises they were unable to keep. This is doubtless one of the reasons that London forms a crucial backdrop to *The Canterbury Tales* (the pilgrims begin their journey just outside it, in Southwark) even as it is also 'absent', particularly as the one tale that seems most likely to describe the city's most negative aspects, The Cook's Tale, breaks off at just the moment it seems about to detail them (the Cook has just introduced prostitution as a normal form of London work: or a 'wif that held for contenaunce / A shoppe, and swived [had sex] for hir sustenaunce', I.4421–2).[131] The kind of disappointment from which Chaucer and his Cook recoil is met head on, however, in the late fifteenth-century ballade usually called *London Lickpenny*, which offers up the city as a supreme instance of social *disorder*, where, as Marx would later observe of the capitalism already making huge inroads in London life, all relations between people are converted into relations between 'products'.[132] The fundamental fact of the poem is that its speaker cannot enter London society because he has nothing to trade (as the poem's refrain goes, 'For lacke of money, I may not spede [succeed]').[133] In his attempt to break in he moves, first, from law court to law court, where he is unable to obtain a hearing because all the procedures of justice seem to require substantial palm-greasing (the refrain is here modified so that a judge may insist: 'Ley downe sylvar [silver], or here thow may not spede', l. 48). The poem then moves out into the various sites of trading in the city (Cheapside, Candlewick Street, Cornhill), where it offers a moving picture of just how isolating urban life can be when one is part of an enormous crowd whose interests and energies one also fails to share:

> Then went I forth by London Stone
> Thrwgh-out all Canywike* strete.   *Candlewick*
> Drapers* to me they called anon;   *clothiers*
> Grete chepe* of clothe, they gan me hete;*   *bargains / offer*
> Then come there one and cried, 'Hot shepes fete!'*   *sheeps' feet*
> 'Risshes* faire and grene', an othar* began to grete;   *rushes / another*
> Both melwell* and makarell I gan mete,   *cod*
> But for lacke of money I myght not spede.

> (ll. 81–8)

The poem is, above all, a general critique of corruption, and it understands the market as an instrument for larger ethical failures, but that these failures are uniquely connected to urban life is made clear when the poem concludes with a prayer for London itself ('Jhesus save London, that in Bethelem was bore', l. 125) and represents the country as the only place the speaker *can* function ('By-caus no man to me would take entent, / I dight me [set myself] to the plowe, even as I ded before', ll. 123–4).

The distance between the aspirations that cities held out and the more bitter realities with which their inhabitants had to cope was also modelled in both literature and life by the one form of human community generated *by* the market, those guilds or 'crafts' (as they were then known) which segmented urban populations according to common forms of work. Like cities, guilds were aspirational structures, 'seed-bed[s] of fraternity' which medieval political thinkers often hoped could extend their community-forming powers to the city as a whole.[134] But guilds also tended to segment the city (since people engaged in the same line of work tended to live near each other, most craft guilds originated as 'parish fraternities'),[135] and, by definition, they territorialized labour, ensuring that competition over resources, or space, or rights of various sorts, led to bitter and extended rivalries.[136] In the latter decades of the fourteenth century, as craft associations gained control over elections to London's Common Council (from 1376), such rivalries played themselves out not so much in but very much *as* London's politics.[137] It is in this negative sense that Chaucer may seem to depict 'craft' in The Canon's Yeoman's Tale, where alchemy is presented – not incidentally 'in London' (VIII.1012) – as an entirely empty enterprise ('This cursed craft whoso wol exercise / He shal no good han [have] that hym may suffise', VIII.830–1), wholly defined by secretiveness and deceit, an 'elvisshe craft' that makes its practitioners seem 'wonder wise' (VIII.750–1). In yielding to the Host's invitation to 'telle a myrie tale or tweye' to 'glade' the Canterbury company (VIII.597–8), the Canon's Yeoman's decision to share the secrets of his craft severs his connection to that craft:

> And whan this Chanoun saw it wolde nat bee,
> But his Yeman wolde telle his privetee,*   secrets
> He fledde awey, for verray* sorwe and shame.   real
>   (VIII.700–2)

In fact, many of the rivalries between pilgrims are cast as 'craft' differences (for example, 'Osewald' the Reeve is offended by the Miller's tale of a cuckolded carpenter 'bicause he was of carpenteres craft' [I.3861]), even if they are not in fact truly urban rivalries (as in this case, where the Reeve and the Miller are simply two different sorts of manorial servant). In this broader version of professional conflict such rivalries frequently provide the occasion for the telling of a tale throughout the Canterbury pilgrimage (so, for example, the Reeve tells a tale to 'quite' [I.3864] or 'pay back' the Miller for the perceived affront).

Because crafts and craft members often managed to work together despite their rivalries, craft structures proffered a surprisingly realistic theory for urban life, a different sort of vision of community wherein social bonds could be forged simply by acknowledging and accepting substantial difference. This is, finally, the key insight of The Canon's Yeoman's Prologue and Tale, for the Yeoman's movement out of one (extremely jealous) craft community is simultaneously his mode of entry into another, the community of pilgrims eager to hear his revelations. Such an overt and searching discussion of craft at what seems to be the end of the pilgrims' journey (the Canon and his Yeoman happen on the Canterbury company 'at Boghtoun under Blee' [VIII.556], which is about 5 miles from Canterbury) also acts as a pointed gloss on the importance of craft to the conception of the *Tales* as a whole, as well as to each pilgrim. Only five of the original 'nine and twenty' in the 'compaignye' (I.24) are proper guildsmen ('An Haberdasshere and a Carpenter, / A Webbe, a Dyere and a Tapicer', I.361–2), and they are clearly late additions to The General Prologue, since they are never described in any detail and none is ever assigned a tale. On the other hand, every one of the pilgrims is defined by his or her work – they are *named*, in almost every case, by means of that work – as if every form of daily activity (even, say, the acts in the life of any 'wife') constituted a commensurable and professionalized 'craft'.[138] In this larger sense, then, even if no part of the pilgrimage is set in any city, *The Canterbury Tales* are fundamentally urban, and they therefore also provide a vision of urban life, based on 'craft' – the pilgrims are often identified as a 'compaignie' (I.24, 331, 717, 764; III.189, 1278; VII.2789; IX.27; X.14), a common term for craft groupings[139] – but a 'craft' very much held together by the accommodations and adjustments that follow from the articulation and recognition of defining and intractable difference (as 'diverse folk diversely they seide' [I.3857], as Chaucer puts it in The Reeve's Prologue).

The Canterbury Tales is the most elaborate literary version of this ideology, but a further testimony to its general importance is the prominent part it plays in the Prologue to *Piers Plowman*, where Langland also portrays London, not as a set of buildings or (as he will in passus 2–4) an allegorized set of administrative structures, but as a crowd whose members are both identified and differentiated from one another by their professions, even as they are all joined together in a single 'assembly':

I seigh* in this assemblee, as ye shul here after;	*saw*
Baksteres* and brewesteres* and	*bakers / brewers*
bochiers* manye,	*butchers*
Wollen webbesters* and weveres of	*wool-weavers*
lynnen,*	*linen*

Taillours* and tynkers and tollers*   *tailors / toll-collectors*
    in markettes,
Masons and mynours* and many othere craftes.   *miners*
                    (Pro. 218–22)

This urban world returns in the assembly of drapers, weavers, spinners and brewers who define the social world of 'Coveteise' in his confession (5.196–227), and 'Gloton' also moves through a world peopled by such crafts – a 'Souteresse' [shoe-maker], 'Warner' [warren-keeper], 'Tynkere', 'Hackneyman' [horse-hirer], 'Ribibour' [fiddler], 'Ratoner' [rat-catcher], 'Rakiere' [scavenger], 'Ropere' [rope maker or seller], 'Dysshere' [dish-seller] and 'Cobelere' (5.307–57). But Langland is closest to Chaucer in passus 6, where the dreamer finds Piers Plowman assembling a community of 'alle kynne crafty men' (6.68) for the purpose of going on a pilgrimage ('And I shal apparaille me . . . in pilgrymes wise [garments] / And wende [go] with yow I wile til we fynde Truthe', 6.57–8), but it turns out that 'craft' differences are complementary rather than competing. For Piers says that he will offer his guidance in the pilgrimage to Truth only after he has 'eryed' [ploughed] his 'half acre and sowen [planted] it after' (6.5), and this task is only accomplished by dint of cooperative labour:

Now is Perkyn and thise pilgrimes to the plow faren.*   *gone*
To erie* this half-acre holpen* hym manye;   *plough / helped*
Dikeres* and delveres* digged up the   *ditchers / cultivators*
    balkes*;   *unploughed land*
Therwith was Perkyn apayed* and preised hem faste.*   *pleased / highly*
Othere werkmen ther were that wroghten ful yerne:*   *eagerly*
Ech man in his manere made hymself to doone,
And somme to plese Perkyn piked* up the wedes.   *hoed*
                    (6.105–11)

The displacement from city to country here may seem a utopian move, but it is clear that the vision is deeply thoughtful about urban problems, particularly when many of these workmen lose interest in their common task ('Thanne seten [sat] somme and songen atte nale [ale], / And holpen ere [plough] his half acre with "How trolly lolly!"' [6.115–16]), and Piers takes the severe decision to unleash 'Hunger' on the reprobates (6.172). In fact, the plowing of the half-acre also provides a surprisingly practical image for, and illustration of, all the ways that difference may be *required* for cooperative activity, where a complicated task can only be accomplished by means of those varied skills and gifts that distinguish members of any community (as Langland so perfectly puts it, as 'each man in his manere' does his work).[140]

English literature played an active role in uniting the complicated populations of cities, as it might provide the occasion for bringing large numbers of people together for ceremonial and dramatic occasions. Lydgate describes such pageants in the poem called *Henry VI's Triumphal Entry into London*, detailing the 'noble devyses' and 'dyvers ordenaunces'[141] employed in the allegorical pageant that staged the young king's progress into the city in 1432 ('so as the Kyng gan ryde, / Midde off the Brigge ther was a tour on loffte . . . And at his komyng . . . Ther yssed [came] oute emperesses three', ll. 99–108). Lydgate also wrote seven such pageants or 'mummings' of his own, most of them at the behest of a particular craft (the mercers and goldsmiths), or city or town (Hertford and London), each providing both script and commentary for an unfolding allegorical scene (e.g. 'Loo here this lady that yee may see, / Lady of mutabilytee, / Which that called is Fortune . . .').[142] The most effective urban poetry of this kind, however, were dramas known collectively as the 'mystery' plays, those enactments of episodes from the Old and New Testaments customarily staged in many major towns and cities on the Feast of Corpus Christi (that is, somewhere between 21 May and 24 June) by a particular craft ('mystery' in such usage is yet another medieval term for craft).[143] This drama was 'cyclical', as it moved through biblical history progressively throughout a given day, but also as the individual plays enacting each biblical episode were staged, repeatedly, throughout a town or city, as pageant wagons moved from station to station in a kind of circuit that transformed the whole of the city into a revolving stage.[144] We have only fifteenth- and sixteenth-century manuscripts of the two cycles from York and Chester, although we have, in addition, two very similar cycle-like compilations, the 'Towneley' plays (probably connected with Wakefield) and the 'N-town' plays (from an unknown location in East Anglia).[145] It is clear, however, that plays of this kind were performed in many places in Britain, as well as Ireland, from the late fourteenth century onward. Such drama was written in a grand style, generally favouring lengthy speeches over action, but this grandness also accommodated urban reality as plays were assigned – and then written to bring out – the connections between a given craft and the events portrayed in a play, in this way collapsing the distinction between, say, the builders of Noah's Ark and the 'shipwrites' of York who performed it:[146]

Take high trees and hewe thame cleyne,*	*neatly*
All be sware* and noght of skwyn,*	*squarely / on a slant*
Make of thame burdes* and	*planks*
wandes* betwene,	*battens [strips of timber]*
Thus thrivandly,* and noght over-thyn.*[147]	*skilfully / too thin*

There is obviously a wit to such self-consciousness, but it also made a doctrinal point, underscoring the 'universal' or 'figural' nature of biblical action (its implication in every subsequent event in human history),[148] even as it connected the here and now of any Christian present to the larger pattern of a redemptive history.[149] At its most pointed, this wit could even carry the play's drama, bringing momentous events back to the flesh and blood of lived lives. This is most simply true in so far as the York play on the death of Christ was assigned to the 'Bocheres' (butchers), but the association of the 'Pinners' – makers of wooden and metal pegs – with the York play of the crucifixion made the process of fixing Christ to the cross, the play's main action, truly harrowing. Although this 'work' (as the play often calls it) is only visible once the cross is finally set up on stage, the suffering of Christ is rendered the more gruesome as it is objectified in the details and the difficulties of 'pinning' limbs to wood, as Christ's flesh is treated like so much lumber:

[First soldier:] Strike on than harde, for hym	
the boght.*	*suffered for*
[Second soldier:] Yis, here is a stubbe* will	*short thick nail*
stiffely stande,	
Thurgh bones and senous it schall be soght* –	*applied*
This werke is well, I will warande.*	*affirm*
[First soldier:] Saie, sir howe do we thore?*	*there*
This bargayne* may not blynne.*	*undertaking / end*
[Third soldier:] It failis* a foote and more,	*falls short*
The senous are so gone ynne.*[150]	*shrunken*

The actions of the plays so fully connected themselves to urban life, it has been suggested, that a successful performance of the cycle was a way of realizing certain urban ideals ritualistically, resolving intractable problems, at least for the duration of the feast day, by bringing the whole social body together for a shared and cooperative activity.[151] For the same reason, the very process of mounting the plays also brought out certain tensions, and crafts often argued intensely about who should bear the costs of various aspects of the pageant,[152] just as individual citizens often argued over (or attempted to pay for) the right to have particular stations established in front of their houses.[153]

The way or the street

The growth of English cities and towns in medieval England was largely a function of migration. Urban environments offered more social mobility than the countryside as a direct result of the economic opportunities that defined them, and this was particularly true in the thirteenth century, when a general rise in population led to a glut of labour in the countryside.[154] On the other hand, there was as much movement from the city back to the countryside in the fourteenth and fifteenth centuries as population density in cities made problems of poverty worse rather than better, and as a rural cloth industry drew workers back to the villages.[155] Also, as wage labour increasingly replaced feudal service, and famine and plague caused massive depopulation in the first half of the fourteenth century, there was simply more movement through every part of England, as workers of all kinds gained and exercised the freedom to seek out the best wages.[156] Such freedom produced much of the mixing and overlapping of dialect that I noted at the beginning of this chapter, but it left its strongest mark on English literature as it carried poets who learned their craft in the West and Northwest – who therefore wrote in the alliterative style that was clearly important in these regions in the latter half of the fourteenth century – into Southern cities.[157] I have also already mentioned the ways in which *Piers Plowman* builds these movements into its allegory, but the lived complexity of such movements is best captured by another alliterative poem in a dialect of the Northwest that seems to have London concerns, *Winner and Waster*, whose first lines include the poignant image of a parent watching his child immigrate 'southward', knowing that he will never see him again:

> Dare never no westren wy   while this werlde lasteth
> Send his sone southeward   to see ne to here
> That he ne schall holden byhynde   when he hore eldes.

> [While this world endures, no western man may venture to send his son southward, neither to see nor to hear, without having to stay behind while he grows old and grey.][158]

Such movements were sufficiently troublesome to employers as to be extensively restricted in the Statute of Labourers of 1388 (an updating of the similar, but less restrictive provision of 1349), which insisted that any 'servant or labourer', male or female, who wished to depart from the jurisdiction where he or she lived and worked, was required to carry a passport ('lettre patente'), under seal of the king, explaining the reason for his or her movements and the date of his or her return; should such a 'servant or labourer' [servant ou laborer] be found in 'a city or borough' [citee ou burgh] or some other place where they were not entitled to be according to such a letter, the statute also gave 'mayors, baillifs, seneschals and constables' [meirs, bailiffs, seneschalx, ou conestables] the power to seize such workers until they could produce 'surety' [seuretee] of their return.[159] It is no wonder then that *The Canterbury Tales*, the text that most fully absorbs these movements to its own structure, begins by collapsing the whole set of economic motives that might bring such a large number of people together into a single movement, which was, in turn, represented as natural as the coming of spring:[160]

Whan that Aprill with his shoures* soote*	*showers / sweet*
The droghte* of March hath perced to the roote,	*drought*
And bathed every veine* in swich licour	*sap-vessel*
Of which vertue* engendred is the flour . . .	*power*
. . .	
Than longen folk to goon* on pilgrimages.	*go*

(I.1–4; 12)

The 1388 Statute of Labourers insisted that pilgrims have passports too,[161] and, because they were adamantly opposed to the veneration of images and relics (which they regarded as idolatrous), Lollard writers in particular inveighed against pilgrimage from the end of the fourteenth century onward.[162] Some of this discomfort makes its way into *Piers Plowman*, where another representative assembly of workers vows 'to go to Truthe' (5.512) but seem robbed of sense by this decision ('there was wight noon [no person] so wys . . . but blustreden [strayed] forth as beestes over baches [valleys] and hilles', 5.513–14). But as is usually the case in *Piers Plowman*, the problem is less with the traditional mode of observance than with its corruption, as is clear when these pilgrims eagerly seek knowledge of the way to Truth from a man 'apparailled . . . in pilgrymes wise' (5.516), fresh from the widest of travels ('in Bethlem and in Babiloyne, I have ben in bothe, / In Armonye, in Alisaundre, in manye othere places', 5.527–8), but clearly none the wiser for them, since he has no idea where 'Truth' can be found (5.534–6). Langland is following the restrictive logic of the 1388 statute when he displaces pilgrimage of this ineffective sort into cooperative agricultural labour (as I discussed above), but he also captures the conditions to which the statute responded when that ploughing is in turn abandoned in favour of the dreamer's extensive wanderings ('Thus yrobed in russet [coarse woollen cloth] I romed about / Al a somer seson for to seke Dowel', 8.1–2).[163]

The idea of travelling to a sacred place as a mode of devotion was underwritten in Christianity by the tendency to venerate not only people but their bodies ('And the Word was made flesh, and dwelt among us'; John 1: 14), and therefore to venerate the physical remains of particularly holy people wherever such relics were kept.[164] In saint's life, veneration of the body often becomes grounds to travel *to* the body, as, for example, in the legend of St Edmund, which I discussed above:

Wele whiche fair pelrynage* is thider forto fare	*pilgrimage*
To honury* that holi bodi that hath ibeo* ther	*honour / been*
so yare.*[165]	*long a time*

Pilgrimage was not exclusive to Christianity: travel to Mecca (the *hajj*) was obligatory for all medieval Muslims who could make the journey,[166] and where the journey was too hazardous or expensive Muslims were still expected to travel to the shrines of important 'imams' or teachers.[167] But Christianity was unusual among medieval world religions, not only for having so many sites of pilgrimage, but in its appetite for multiplying such places, as the life and martyrdom of ever newer saints sacralized more and more ground.[168] The expansionist warfare of the medieval West also multiplied such destinations after the first 'crusade' recaptured Jerusalem (in 1099), and this holiest of cities was again within reach of the Western traveller.[169]

Pilgrimage was therefore both common and important enough to spawn its own genre of medieval literature, and the kind of journey Chaucer fictionalized was also documented in travelogues which combined practical attention to the details and difficulties of such journeys – in this way providing guidance to future pilgrims – while in addition celebrating the spiritual rewards of enduring such difficulty. *The Stacions of Rome*, for example, a very popular text probably written at the end of the thirteenth century (but frequently copied in subsequent centuries), offers a detailed itinerary to the important holy sites of Rome and, like a modern tour guide, recounts the history that makes those sites important. It also offers, in the very same register of helpful fact and beneficial detail, a precise enumeration of the spiritual benefits that will accrue to any visitor to these sites:

Therfore passe we forth an othur way	
To seynt powle, as y wene,*	*believe*
Fowr myle ys holden* be-twene;	*thought to be*
In that place ys grette pardon,	
And of many synnis remyssyoun;	
Sawle was his nome* by-fore,	*name*
Syth* the tyme that he was bore;	*since*

> Hethen he was, and cristened noghth,*   *not*
> Tyll criste hit putte yn his thowghth
> And that holy mon Ananyas
> Crystened hym thorow goddis grace,
> And called hym paule, petur* brodur,   *Peter's*
> That eche of hem shuld comforte othur;
> And yn the worshyp* of that convercyoun   *value*
> Ys graunted a Mlle* yere of pardon,   *thousand*
> And at the feste* of his day   *feast*
> Two Mlle yere have thou may.[170]

Although most of them remain unedited or difficult to obtain, texts of this kind grew in number in the fifteenth century:[171] some of them are even more purely practical than the *Stacions*, focusing on the do's and don'ts of foreign travel as such (*Advice for Eastbound Travellers*, *Information for Pilgrims Unto the Holy Land*);[172] others offer narrative maps that guide the reader over a complex route, with directions to and between intermediate towns and cities (*The Way unto Rome and So to Venice and Jerusalem*, *The Way to Italy*);[173] a third sort of travelogue combines these more practical functions with a first-person narrative, unfolding both advice and useful information as a function of personal experience (*Guide to the Holy Land* and John Capgrave's *The Solace of Pilgrims*).[174] All of these generic tendencies were stretched out into the most extraordinary of travel narratives, usually described as *Mandeville's Travels*. Nothing is known of the 'John Maundevylle, knyght' who signs this text and says that he began the journey it describes in 1322 and that he wrote this account in 1356,[175] but textual evidence suggests that it was first written in French about 1357 (although versions of the text exist in all the main European languages), and that it was translated into English for the first time in 1375.[176] The work begins as if it is no more than an itinerary for a journey to the Holy Land, showing the prospective pilgrim 'the weye out of Englond to Constantynoble' (4), drawing attention to spectacular sights along the way ('At Constantynoble is the palays of the Emperour right fair and wel dyght [ornamented]', 12), picking out important shrines ('In Cipre . . . in the castell of Amours lyth the body of seynt Hyllarie, and men kepen it right worschipfully [reverently]', 20), while offering a helpfully specific route for such travel ('From Cypre men gon to the lond of Jersualem be the see. And in a day and in a nyght he that hath gode wynd may come to the havene of Thire [Tyre], that now is clept [called] Surrye', 20). There is, throughout, an interest in sensational facts, particularly about the natural environment ('whan it reyneth [rains] ones in the somer in the lond of Egipt, thanne is all the contree full of grete myzs [mice]', 34–5), but, given its general interest in projecting Christian interests out into the non-Christian world, the text's most extraordinary quality is its sustained and careful interest in cultural difference. The most remarkable expression of that interest comes in an account of 'the customes of Sarasines and of hire [their] lawe', for, despite a certain patronizing praise for the Islamic acceptance of key elements of Christian doctrine ('Also thei beleeven and speken gladly of the virgine Marie and of the Incarnacioun', 96), there is a surprisingly clear-eyed and dispassionate account of Islam's critique of Christianity:

> Thei seyn that the Cristene men erren . . . and that thei beleeven folyly and falsly that Ihesu crist was crucyfyed. And thei seyn yit that, and He had ben crucyfyed, that God had don ayen His rightwisness for to suffre Ihesu Crist that was innocent to ben put upon the cros withouten gylt. And in this article thei seyn that wee faylen and that the gret rightwisness of God ne myghte not suffre so gret a wrong. (98)

[*erren*: are wrong   *folyly*: foolishly   *don ayen*: gone against   *rightwisness*: justice   *suffre*: allow]

Such views are also firmly rejected ('and in this fayleth here fyeth [their faith]', 98), but the capacity of this author to inhabit beliefs he does not endorse is perhaps no less remarkable than the popularity of this text, given these capacities.[177] Curiosity about the whole of the world and its varied forms is the impulse that most fully underlies this book, and it is in this sense that its second part bursts the seams of pilgrimage and moves on from an account of the Holy Land to the furthest realms that could be reached or heard of (India, China, Turkestan, Russia).[178]

Although it would be wrong to categorize *The Book of Margery Kempe* (1433–8) as such an itinerary, it does describe an extraordinary number of pilgrimages (to Jerusalem, Rome, Compostela, Wilsnak and Aachen, and many sites in England), and it is probably right to conclude a section on the space between places with the narrative of a woman who was so frequently on the move and who, often as a direct result of those movements, remains so difficult to assimilate to traditional categories.[179] Kempe's *Book* is itself hard to classify: it is sufficiently concerned with Kempe's inner states to have the feel of an autobiography (it is 'a booke of hyr felyngys [her feelings] and hir revelacyons'),[180] but Kempe is always referred to in the third person (often, also, as 'this creature'), since the *Book* was actually dictated to scribes rather than written down by Kempe herself (see 47–50). It is also an extraordinarily detailed account of one person's journey through the world and her own idiosyncratic spirituality, but it was written, by its own account, 'for the examplyl and instruccyon' of other Christians

(41). And, while Kempe is at pains to stress the sincerity of her piety and to root her behaviour in scripture or right belief, the form her piety takes often sits athwart more typical forms of Christian observance, not least in its extraordinary intensity. In the following passage, for example, Kempe describes the genesis of her passionate and uncontrollable weeping, or 'cryings', during her visit to Mount Calvary:

> And sche had so gret compassyon and so gret peyn to se owyr Lordys peyn that sche myt not kepe hirself fro krying and roryng, thow sche schulde a be ded therfor . . . And this maner of crying enduryd many yerys aftyr this tyme, for owt that any man myt do, and therfor sufferyd sche mych despyte and meche reprefe. The cryeng was so lowde and so wondyrful that it made the pepyl astonynd, les than thei had herd it beforn and er ellys that thei knew the cawse of the crying. And sche had hem so oftyntymes that thei madyn hir ryth weyke in hir bodyly myghtys, and namely yf sche herd of owyr Lordys Passyon. (163–4)

> [*peyn*: pain   *a be*: have been   *owt*: anything   *reprefe*: reproof   *les than*: unless   *beforn*: before   *er ellys*: or else   *hem*: them [these cryings] *weyke*: weak   *bodyly myghtys*: physical strength]

Kempe clearly made her own social situation the more straitened by such behaviour, for she was, in fact, born into the easiest of circumstances (the daughter of an alderman and, later, the wife of a merchant), and she spent a great deal of her life in the Norfolk port city of King's Lynn (then called Bishop's Lynn), living in much more conventional ways (she mentions, off-hand, that she gave birth to fourteen children). But her *Book* also offers many vivid evocations of the anxious sort of travel pilgrimage could be, so very unlike the sportive tale-telling along the way that Chaucer envisions, of necessity ensuring that the pilgrim was removed from her community, placing her on what was not only unfamiliar, but deeply unsafe ground:

> And on nyghtys had sche most dreed oftyntymys, and peraventur it was of hir gostly enmy, for sche was evyr aferd to a be ravischyd er defilyd. Sche durst trustyn on no man; whedir sche had cawse er non, sche was evyr aferd. Sche durst ful evyl slepyn any nyth, for sche wend men wolde a defylyd hir. Therfor sche went to bedde gladlich no nyth, les than sche had a woman er tweyn wyth hir . . . Sche was so wery and so ovyrcomyn wyth labowr to-Caleysward that hir thowt hir spiryt schulde a departyd fro hir body as sche went in the wey. Thus wyth gret labowrys sche cam to Caleys, and the good frer wyth hir, the which ful goodly and honestly had ben govérnyd to-hir-ward the tyme that thei went togedyr. And therfor sche yaf hym reward as sche myth ateyn, so that he was wel plesyd and content and departyd asundyr. (412)

[*dreed*: fear *peraventur*: perchance *to a be*: to have been *durst*: dared *durst ful evyl*: hardly dared *wend*: thought *les than*: unless *wery*: weary *to-Caleysward*: towards Calais *hir thowt*: it seemed to her *frer*: friar *to-hir-ward*: towards her *yaf*: gave *departyd*: parted]

The arc from despair to the comfort traced here is, however, also typical, for what Margery's *Book* everywhere insists upon is the extent to which hardship suffered as an act of Christian devotion necessarily *produces* solace:

> Than owyr blysful Lord Crist Jhesu answeryd to hir sowle and seyd:
> 'My derworthy dowtyr, I swer be myn hy mageste that I schal nevyr forsakyn the. And dowtyr, the more schame, despite, and reprefe that thu sufferyst for my lofe, the bettyr I lofe the, for I far liche a man that lovyth wel hys wyfe: the more envye that men han to hir, the bettyr he wyl arayn hir in despite of hir enmys. (184)

[*owyr*: our *lofe*: love *far*: act, proceed *arayn*: dress, adorn]

At such moments what Kempe shows best of all is what every medieval pilgrim hoped to discover through the strength of her belief and the extremity of her actions: that no matter how far from her own community she travelled, or how meagre her material resources, she was never alone.

5

Jurisdiction

The word 'literature' first appears in English with something like its modern meaning right at the end of the Middle English period, in Henry Bradshaw's *Life of St Werburge* (*c*.1513):

> What were* mankynde without lytterature?   *would be*
> Full* lyttell worthy blynded by ignoraunce.   *very*
> The way to heven it declareth ryght sure*   *very clearly*
> Thrugh perfyte* lyvynge and good   *perfect*
>   perseveraunce;*   *persistence*
> By it we may be taught for to do penaunce
> Whan we transgresse our lordes
>   commaundyment;
> It is a swete cordyall* for mannes entent.*[1]   cordial / purposes, wishes

Bradshaw was a Benedictine monk, and this monumental poem (it is over 5500 lines long, in elaborate rime royal stanzas) describes the miraculous life of the patroness of his abbey, while also tracing, in chronicle form, her illustrious forebears and the history of the city of Chester. In the lines that introduce the poem's second part, however, Bradshaw steps back and tries to describe, in what was then still an unusual manner, the properties of the *kind* of writing he is trying to produce. Those properties appear as familiar to us as the name that Bradshaw gives them, but the Middle English word *litterature* was as rare in Bradshaw's day as the idea it is here meant to convey.[2] In the few fourteenth-century uses of *litterature* that precede Bradshaw's the word simply means 'books' or 'learning' – that which is made of letters [*litterae*] – the words on the page themselves.[3] Bradshaw gives the word a new importance by insisting on it (he uses it in each of the first three stanzas of this book), and the stanzas surrounding these uses also stretch the word toward its modern sense. The first attribute of this new meaning is ethical, for, in the stanzas preceding the one I quote *litterature* is said to produce 'good maners' (2.7) and 'morall vertues' (2.13), while in the stanza I quote *litterature* declares the way to 'perfyte lyvynge' (giving it, in all these ways, the sense this word now has when we say that literature is 'improving' or 'educational'). The second attribute of this modern sense is affect: *litterature* is a 'great conforte' and 'endeles pleasure' (2.11), a 'swete cordial', distinctive in its capacities to produce an emotional response (this is what we mean when we say that literature 'moves' us). The most important new sense that Bradshaw gives to *litterature*, however, is that of supreme *value*, a way of describing writing as so uniquely 'good' that it is something 'mankynde' cannot do 'without'.

Bradshaw's language represents the culmination of a gradual change in practices and attitudes, and the category of 'literature' that is clearly assembling itself under this new term also remains imprecise. As Raymond Williams observed, 'literature' is 'a difficult word', not least 'because its conventional . . . meaning appears, at first sight, so simple' while, at the same time, concealing a host of 'confused distinctions' about what legitimately counts *as* 'literature'.[4] On the other hand, to watch Bradshaw define *litterature* so extensively and with such care is also to witness both a clarification and a significant emergence, not least because 'literature' is a category that is *still* defined by a certain vagueness, an uneven overlapping of two equally broad and vague categories (where what is improving meets what is pleasurable), and an abstraction of the practical products of physical and intellectual labour into qualities and values that could never be specified (the 'swete', the 'good', the 'perfite').[5] Bradshaw includes any 'wrytyng' (2.34) made valuable by the 'lernynge' (2.25) it has 'preserved' (2.34) in the new category he is assembling, but as he begins to specify the various genres in which this preservation has occurred ('auncient histories and cronycles olde . . .', 2.28), and as he slowly bends this list toward his chosen genre ('the lyves of saintes many a noble storie', 2.35) and then toward his own work ('Of whiche histories we purpose speciall / To speke of saint Werburge under your protection', 2.36–7), his justifications become not just a new definition of an English word but a whole new way of looking at – accounting for, and also valuing – English writing. This is hardly the 'birth' of English literature, not least because Bradshaw's confidence is a fairly strong indication that this birth has long ago occurred. But it is the emergence of a new self-consciousness, a new clarity about the nature and function of English writing *in* that writing, an *awareness* that is itself a significant cultural change.

Bradshaw could also be said to mark a slow and fitful but, now, fully accomplished shift in 'jurisdiction', a change in status that amounted to a change in implicit authority, a new sense of the areas English writing might legitimately inhabit. 'Jurisdiction' is a word that normally describes matters of law (its roots are the Latin *ius*, 'the law', and *dicere*, 'to say'), and so it is most usually used to refer to state power of some kind.[6] But the term has been profitably used of late to describe the variety of manners and concerns that counted as legitimate to Middle English writers and readers and to call our attention to the 'jurisdictional heterogeneity' that characterized Middle English as well as the drastic narrowing of this range in the period of literature normally called the 'early modern'.[7] In this sense, the cultural change that Bradshaw marks is the addition of yet another area to those that Middle English writing had long claimed. But it is also an issue of authority, because, in the new area that Bradshaw describes, English writing is defined by its independence from other cultural functions, by its capacity to exist on its own or *as such*. English literature with the supreme value that Bradshaw attributes to it is, we might say, a law unto itself.

It is significant too that such strong claims for literature's autonomy should have emerged first in English in a saint's life, since the subject that English writers first claimed for themselves was doctrine and the sacred, insisting that the vernacular was a crucial mode of access to religious truth for those who did not know Latin. In fact, although the story is never told in this way, it is simply the case that English literature first gathered momentum in both ambition and popularity in texts and then collections of texts where all those qualities and capacities that we might call 'literary' were absorbed to larger doctrinal ends – to writing that was first, and above all, 'religious'. The first section of this chapter will tell this story. Orthodox religious subjects retained their importance well beyond the Middle Ages, of course, but in the second section of this chapter I will describe one of the more important and pervasive techniques used to challenge the church's jurisdictional authority from within – the humour or laughter that remains a still valuable solvent for all forms of textual authority. Such challenges were more constant than new – as ever, Middle English writers drew on Latin and French traditions for their material – but humour is particularly important to the third area of literary jurisdiction I want to explore in this chapter, 'pleasure', and the concomitant sense that enjoyment is *all* that literature need provide. This more challenging sort of independence, more implicit than claimed, was, of course, the key element to the understanding of *litterature* that Bradshaw recognized, named and, in that naming, claimed. A rich set of classical traditions was important to this emergence as well, but the change also involved both a general moment and a number of significant acts of real 'creativity' which I will associate with the work of Geoffrey Chaucer, not so much because he was extraordinarily innovative (although he was), but because the new forms, practices and ideas he introduced into English poetry were hugely significant as they became 'in their turn models'.[8] Although it is a little surprising to end a history of 'culture' with the view that a particular writer made a crucial difference, it is clear that Chaucer made that difference, not least because so many of the Middle English writers who followed him insisted that he had – and, in that sense too, *made* his influence paramount.[9]

The church

The first evidence of anything like a concentrated concern with the production of Middle English writing occurs in that clutch of thirteenth-century religious texts that I described at the beginning of the last chapter as evidence of a certain common culture: in two of their earliest manuscripts, *Ancrene Wisse* and the *Katherine*-group share a regularized dialect, and a number of other closely related manuscripts add to this grouping a further set of texts on common themes, the meditations and prayers usually called the *Wohunge*-group (*The Wohunge of ure Laured, On Lofsong of ure Lourede, On Ureisun of ure Lauerde, On Lofsong of ure Lefdi, On Ureisun of ure Lefdi*).[10] Since priority in time is less relevant to the importance of this category of writing than quantity and proliferation in sites of production, however, it is really in the last decades of the thirteenth century and the beginning of the fourteenth century that we see a true eruption in such writing, as well as the emphatic jurisdictional claims that justify it. A prologue affixed to an 'expanded version' of the *Northern Passion* (originally *c.*1300, expanded *c.*1350), a vernacular account of the betrayal and crucifixion of Christ, states the new position clearly, grounding its authority in 'populism', which it defines as the growing sense that Christian truths ought to be communicated to all rather than just to those few who know French or Latin:

And for the passioun of	
ihesu crist	
Es medeful* forto be	*spiritually beneficial*
puplist,*	*commonly known*
And nedful* to all cristen men	*necessary*
Clerely forto kun* and ken*	*understand / know*
Tharfore thus es it ordand* here,	*ordained*
In iglische land men forto lere.*	*teach*
Als* haly* writ witnes and sais.*[11]	*as / holy / says*

The octosyllabic couplets of this text as well as its language are sometimes reminiscent of the Middle English romances which were beginning to be written in quantity in this period ('A non they gafe [gave] dyntys [blows] sore / And bounde hys hondys more and more'),[12] and, like these romances, this text also has a French source.[13] The poem also makes good on its populist claims through its broad reach, for it not only circulated in a large number of manuscripts, in both original and expanded versions, but it was soon absorbed by the massive *Northern Homily Cycle* (*c.*1375), a collection of (roughly) 117 verse sermons, covering the *temporale* (the movable feasts, centred on the life of Christ) and a few other relevant saints' days, stretching to 20,000 lines in all (there are sixteen surviving manuscripts of an early version of this text, and then two each of two successive expanded versions).[14] In the last version of this text (the only one that has been edited) homily has begun to overwhelm the Gospel narrative, or *narratio*, that lies at the heart of every sermon, but the popularizing impulse is still very clear in the simple clarity of these narratives:

When oure Lord Jesu so fre*	*noble*
Was born in Bedleem* of Jude	*Bethlehem*
In Herodes daies to understand	
That lord was than of al that land	
Over Bedlem stode a stern* ful bright,	*star*
Over ilka* land lasted the light.[15]	*every*

The *expositio* or interpretation that follows each of these stories extends that populism into an allegorical interpretation which tries, above all, to transform Gospel events into injunctions guiding individual belief:

So suld* we folow the kinges three,	*should*
Ilkone* unto oure awin* cuntre,	*each one / own*
That es, to the kingdome of hevyn	
Whare more mirth es than men may nevyn.*	*speak of*

(ll. 4265–8)

The *Northern Passion* is only one of the free-standing narratives that this cycle absorbs, but other accretions also tend to insist on this text's jurisdictional reach, gathering stories both lurid ('the devil in church', ll. 11,785–820) and local ('a clerk that Tiophill hight [is called]', ll. 18,057–854) not only the better to pique the interest of a wide audience, but so as to transform this cycle of sermons into a rich conspectus of religious material – to give 'all cristen men' a rich fund of narrative and explanation on which to found their beliefs and practices.

All of the techniques that abet the populism of the *Northern Homily Cycle* can be described as literary in so far as they shape these texts with a view toward certain effects, and this is also true – but even less apparent – in those texts of religious instruction where those techniques consist largely of a *practical* imagining, a programme of explanation that does not so much simplify doctrine as try to head off the believer's confusions by anticipating them. In the *Lay Folks Mass Book* (c.1300), for example, an account of the standard church service that unfolds in 600 lines of rhyming couplets, there are translations of basic texts (such as the Lord's Prayer) as well as specific guidance for the believer who does not understand what the priest is either doing or saying:

For he wil saie with hegh steven*	*voice*
Pater-noster* to god of heven;	*Our Father*
Herken* him with gode wille,	*listen*
And whils he saies, hold the stille,	
Bot* answere at *temptacionem*	*only*
Set libera nos a malo, amen.	*['But free us from evil']*
Hit were no nede* the to this to ken,*	*necessary / understand*
For who con not* this are lewed* men	*do not know / unlearned*
When this is done, saye prively*	*privately*
Other prayer none ther-by.	
Pater-noster first in Laten,	
And sithen* in englishe als here is wryten.[16]	*afterwards*

This text survives in nine manuscripts, and the considerable variation in their dialects also shows that it was disseminated widely throughout England.[17] Although the connection in their titles is only modern (the creations of editors, not medieval authors), the impulse and techniques of the *Lay Folks Mass Book* are extended to clergy in the *Lay Folks Catechism* (1357), a translation by John Gaytryge of the set of instructions on the most important articles of doctrine (the Pater Noster, the Apostles' Creed, the Ten Commandments, the Seven Sacraments, etc.) issued to priests by John Thoresby (d. 1373), Archbishop of York. The very existence of such a text shows that even the learned might need help with the Latin of the liturgy (and the popularity of this text is indicated by its twenty-two surviving manuscripts),[18] although it is also artful, employing light but constant alliteration throughout ('We schull be-leve that this pater noster, that Crist hym self techis to alle cristyn men, passys other prayers in these thre thynges').[19] Such an ornament made the *Catechism* suitable for oral delivery, and it is clear from its introduction that it was directed at the 'commune profet' (46), in this way not only useful to priest but preached 'openly on Inglis opon sononndaies' (49).

Religious instruction of this popularizing kind continues to grow in importance and quantity well into the fifteenth century,[20] and the whole of that growth can be summed up in the work of John Mirk (fl. 1382–*c*.1414). His *Instructions for Parish Priests*, written in the last decades of the fourteenth century, uses octosyllabic rhyming couplets to make a particularly urgent link between spiritual purpose and the use of English ('Yef [if] thou plese thy savyoure / Yef thow be not great clerk / Loke thow moste [must] on thys werk'),[21] while also presuming that English has a central role in the liturgy ('Englissch or latyn, whether me [men] seyth / Hyt suffyseth to the feyth / So that [as long as] the wordes be seyde on rowe', ll. 131–3); the poem is, accordingly, filled with English translations of basic Latin prayers. The *Instructions* survive complete in seven manuscripts,[22] all of them dating from the fifteenth century, but it is in Mirk's *Festial* (*c*.1382–90), a cycle of sixty-eight sermons covering all the feasts in the church year, that the real massiveness of this instructional project can be readily observed. Like the *Northern Homily Cycle* these sermons wear their popularizing purpose in the simplicity of their language as well as a mode of address that is as ingratiating in its homeliness as it is helpful in assuming nothing:

> *Hortamur vos, ne in vacuum graciam Dei recipiatis. Corintheos [Sex]to.* Good men and woymen, thes wordes that I have sayde yn Lateyn, byn thus to say yn Englysch: 'We amonechen you, that ye take not the grace of God yn vayn'. Thes ben the wordes of Seynt Paule, Cristys holy apostull that ben red yn the pystyll of thys day.[23]
>
> [*amonechen*: admonish   *pystyll*: epistle]

The *Festial* is also full of localized stories with an immediate, homely appeal ('I rede [relate that] ther wer two chapmen dwellyng bysyde the cyte of Norwych . . .', 91). The text survives in twenty-three manuscripts, and there are a further nineteen manuscripts containing extracts (some of them stretching into the sixteenth century), but the real testimony to the success of such populism is Caxton's edition of the *Festial* in 1483 (itself reprinted several times).[24]

The importance and centrality of such instruction in English literature of this period is also proved in the way that poets so deeply comfortable in the variety of literary kinds available by the end of the fourteenth century also placed such weight on instruction of this kind. Chaucer makes the more emphatic gesture when he gives the Parson a treatise on the Seven Deadly Sins to conclude *The Canterbury Tales*, a surprisingly didactic turn in the context of the general narrative vivacity of the tale-telling contest, but, even more importantly, one that all of the pilgrims agree is 'fitting' ('Upon this word we han assented soone; / For, as us semed [it seemed to us], it was for to doone / To enden in som vertuous sentence [content]',

X.61–3). The *Gawain*-poet makes the more significant commitment to such instruction, however, for two of the four poems we have in his hand, *Patience* and *Cleanness*, retell significant biblical episodes (the former, the story of Jonah, the latter, in linked succession, the stories of the fall of Lucifer, the fall of Adam, the flood, the sins and destruction of Sodom, and Belshazzar's feast) in forms that can loosely be described as 'homily' or 'sermon'. These poems are not only too rich but too experimental to be reduced to doctrine. Among the surprises of *Patience*, for example, is the narrative scope given, first, to God's frustration in persuading Jonah to go to Nineveh ('Nylt [will not] thou never to Nunive bi no kynnes wayes [by no route]?'),[25] second, to Jonah's exasperation when things go just as badly as he predicted ('I biseche the, Syre, now thou self jugge / Was not this ilk my [my very] worde that worthen is nouthe [has now happened], / That I kest [said] in my cuntré', ll. 413–15) and, finally, to Jonah's rage when God destroys the woodbine that has been sheltering him and then has the nerve (as Jonah sees it) to describe the loss as 'little' ('Hit is not lyttel', Jonah replies, 'bot lykker to ryght' [rather a matter of justice], l. 493). Similarly, in *Cleanness* the poem's central teaching, that 'the hathel [man] clene of his hert hapenes ful fayre [gains good fortune]',[26] is everywhere complicated – and, in this sense, everywhere interrogated – by the degree to which it must be illustrated in the negative, as the horror of *un*cleanness of 'filth' ('And thenne founden thay fylthein fleschlych [fleshly] dedes, / And controeved [contrived] aayn kynde [against nature] contraré werkes', ll. 265–7). In the main *exempla* that expand on this theme, moreover, this sense of conceptual exploration is displaced on to a God who appears less than all-knowing, who seems, in fact, to have some difficulties discovering just what is happening in the world he created:

The grete soun* of Sodamas synkkes* in myn eres,	*clamour / reaches*
And the gult* of Gomorre gares* me to wrath;	*guilt / makes*
I schal lyght* into that led* and loke myselven	*go down / people*
If thay haf don as the dyne* dryves* on lofte.*	*noise / reaches / high*
(ll. 689–92)	

But all of these radical versions and interrogations of biblical narrative and example give it additional weight, not only by teasing out its complexities, but by engaging so deeply with its meanings in such a richly wrought vernacular: although neither of these poems could ever be reduced to the doctrinal principles around which they are built, they are, fundamentally, vernacular instruction in that doctrine, popularizing to precisely the extent that they everywhere enrich what they so carefully dispose.

As I began this section by saying, however, religious subjects dominated English writing in this period partly through weight of numbers, and the genre of text most fully dominant in this way was saint's life. This is clear enough in the way the *Katherine*-group of lives bulks so large in the earliest Middle English religious writing, or the way saints' lives are themselves absorbed to the *Northern Homily Cycle*, as illustrative narratives,[27] but the monument that most fully testifies to and ensures this centrality is what we now call the *South English Legendary* (so called because the dialect of its earliest survivals was emphatically Southern), a collection of lives for the whole of the *temporale* as well as the fixed saints' days of the *sanctorale*, mounting to over 20,000 long lines (if the verse is set out in septenary couplets). The *Legendary* grew by accretion, probably from the last decades of the thirteenth century, since its contents and order change from manuscript to manuscript, but the earliest manuscript survival (Oxford, Bodleian Library, MS Laud Misc 108) already contains a collection that is more or less complete,[28] and shortly thereafter (in London, British Library, MS Harley 2277) the collection has acquired a prologue, absorbed an elaborate and skilful account of the Gospels from Palm Sunday onward, usually called the *Southern Passion*, and has achieved something of its standard order.[29] In this early form, moreover, the text is already making jurisdictional claims by presenting its central subject in the language of romance. That Christ 'gaf is lyf'[30] in sacrifice is also understood as a 'bataille . . . to holde up Cristendom' (ll. 21–2), and that the saints followed afterwards and 'hare [their] lyf gaf' (l. 18) makes them into an 'ost' [host] eager 'to fight' (l. 24). In the collection's prologue the availability of this language to saint's life becomes proof that these narratives have a similar interest, but in an infinitely superior form, since saints' lives are true:

Men wilneth* muche to hure* telle	of bataille	*want / hear*
of kynge		
And of knightes that hardy were	that muchedel*	*for the most part*
is lesynge*		*lying*
Wo so* wilneth muche to hure*	tales of suche	*whoever / hear*
thinge		
Hardi batailles he may hure	here that nis*	*is not*
no lesinge		
Of apostles and martirs	that hardy knightes were	
That studevast* were in bataille	and ne fleide*	*steadfast / fled*
noght for fere		
That soffrede that luther* men	al quik* hare	*wicked / alive*
lymes totere*		*tore apart*

Telle ichelle* bi reuwe* of ham	as hare dai	*I shall / the order*
valth* in the yere		*falls*
Verst* bygynneth at Yeres day	for that is the	*first*
verste feste		
And fram on to other so areng	the wile*	*as long as*
the yer wol leste.		

(ll. 59–68)

Readers may not have assented so readily to a comparison made in these terms, not least because the flatness inherent to saint's life as a form is increased by their proximity to each other in such a massive collection (where martyrdom is the inevitable trajectory of every story, narrative is robbed of almost every technique for generating drama). But the most ambitious of the *Legendary*'s narratives certainly make good on the prologue's promise to portray martyrdom as warfare. In the long legend of St Thomas Becket, for example, the moment in which a 'clerk' throws himself in the way of the knights attacking Becket on the altar of Canterbury Cathedral unfolds as combat:

Sire Reynaud le Fiz Ours	mest* sorwe of echon	*greatest*
Forto smite this holyman	is* swerd he	*his*
drou anon		
Ac Edward Gri that was is clerk	of Grantebrugge	
ibore*		*born*
To help is lourd yif he mighte	pulte* is arm	*thrust in*
byvore		
He wonded is arm swuthe sore*	that blod	*very badly*
orn* adoun		*ran*
Mid thulke dunt* also he smot	sein Thomas	*blow*
ope* the croun		*upon*
That the blod orn bi is face adoun	in the	
right half of the wonde		
Loude gradde* this luther* knight	smiteth alle	*shouted / wicked*
to gronde.[31]		

But the vivid description of Becket's wounding has little to do with jurisdictional claims, for it intensifies the moment's pity by a method absolutely typical of saint's life (where the horror of undeserved injury is almost always central), and it is this more traditional sort of intensity that doubtless accounts for the massive success of the collection as a whole. The *South English Legendary* survives in fifty-one different manuscripts, a truly extraordinary number relative to its early date (only the *Prick of Conscience* [c.1350], *The Canterbury Tales* [1391–1400] and the various versions of *Piers Plowman* [1370–91], among Middle English texts, survive with more witnesses).[32]

Jacobus de Voragine's *Legenda Aurea* (1255–66) slightly preceded the *South English Legendary*, and by the end of the fifteenth century it had been translated into English three separate times,[33] but the *South English Legendary* owes nothing to this text, and so it is therefore also significant for introducing the notion of a cycle of linked narratives into English. This idea became particularly significant when Chaucer made it the structuring device of *The Canterbury Tales*, and, while it is customary to look to Continental literature for his inspiration (particularly the linked narratives of Boccaccio's *Decameron* [1349–51]), Chaucer's first attempt at a framed cycle of narratives was in fact the text we now call *The Legend of Good Women* (1388–92), a sequence of stories of martyrdom that Chaucer clearly understood as a variation on these earlier collections of saints' lives, since the name he gave this text when he referred to it at a later point was the 'Seintes Legende of Cupide'.[34] In the *Prologue* to the *Legend of Good Women* Chaucer also refers to a 'lyf . . . of Seynt Cecile' (F 426, G 416) which he had already written, and in time, this text became The Second Nun's Tale when it was incorporated into *The Canterbury Tales*. This life draws heavily on the *Legenda* as well as other Latin accounts of St Cecilia, but it is worth pausing over in relation to the *South English Legendary* because its very presence in the canon of Chaucer's work offers a substantial (and generally ignored) testimony not so much to the success of the *Legendary* as to its jurisdictional claims. Although it is common enough to emphasize Chaucer's debt to Middle English romance (as I did in chapter 1), Chaucer's romances are serious only where he draws heavily on Continental sources (The Knight's Tale, *Troilus and Criseyde*), while his most self-conscious emulation of Middle English romance style is sheer burlesque (The Tale of Sir Thopas). It is therefore possible to say that saint's life was the only traditional English genre that Chaucer embraced without apology.

Saint's life maintained this quiet centrality in English writing well into the fifteenth century. Lydgate is necessarily a key figure here, since, like Chaucer, his literary ambitions were large, but he also wrote a large number of saints' lives, both short (the *Legend of St Petronilla*, the *Legend of St George*, the *Legend of Seynt Gyle,* the *Legend of Seynt Margaret*) and quite long (*St Albon and St Amphabell* and *St Edmund and Fremund*).[35] In the most ambitious of these, *St Edmund and Fremund*, Lydgate's prayer for an adequate 'stile'[36] also shows particularly well how saint's life had become central to a truly literary ambition:

> O amatist* with peynes purpureat*   *amethyst / purple*
> Emeraud trewe of chastite most cleene,

Which nat-withstandyng thi kyngli hih estat
For Cristis feith suffredist peynes keene:
Wherfore of mercy, my dulnesse to susteene,
Into my brest sende a confortatiff*   *comfort*
Of sum fair language, tenbelisshe* with thi liff!   *to embellish*
(ll. 214–20)

The elaborate diction Lydgate employs here ('purpureat', 'confortatiff'),
the rime royal of this stanza, as well as his complex – even tortured – syntax
('which nat-withstandyng'), all are typical of Lydgate's style generally, but
more important than these marks of elevation is Lydgate's sense that 'sum
fair language' is required for the proper telling of a pious 'liff'. This is to
marry 'Cristis feith' with a new self-consciousness about the potential for
ornament and elevation in English. Saint's life is not just massively central,
in other words, it is being entered into those high valuations that created
'literature' as such (what mankind cannot do without); and, soon enough,
the essential next step was taken by Osbern Bokenham, who associates
the thirteen saints' lives of his *Legendys of Hooly Wummen* (1443–7) with the
emergent lineage of 'eloquent' writers ('Gower, Chauncers . . . lytgate'),[37]
proving the adequacy of his verse to such comparisons, as had become
customary, by employing an elaborate and wholly Lydgatian style ('Thus
for this sexefold propyrte [property] / Of the margaryte [pearl] wych deuly
longe [duly belongs] / To seynt Margarete be congruyte [congruence] /
Of symylitude', ll. 313–16).

Religious writing still made important claims in its own right of course,
and this is also well proved by Lydgate, who seems to demonstrate such
purity of purpose in the style he uses in his *Life of Our Lady* (1421–2).
This is not a saint's life in the traditional sense but, rather, a linked series
of paeans to Mary organized around the events that most compellingly
demonstrate her virtue. This formal originality is doubtless one reason for
this poem's success (it survives in forty-seven manuscripts and a Caxton
printing, and is still often praised),[38] but its most compelling quality is the
simplicity of language Lydgate employs as a kind of constant correlative
for the simplicity he praises in Mary ('For this is the flour, that god hym
self behelde / The white lylye of the chosyn vale / The swete Roose, of
the fayre felde / Which of colour wexyth [grows] neuer pale').[39] John Capgrave is the inheritor of this purer religious strain, and while his *Life of St
Katharine* (*c*.1445) is a lengthy work (in five books of several thousand lines
each), and it offers, among other set pieces, a careful portrait of learned
argument ('And on your grounde a-geyn I thus replye: / I wulde [would
like to] knowe to me hoo worthy ware [would be]'),[40] Capgrave generally

makes good on his initial promise to 'set' his 'story . . . more pleyn' than in his source (Pro. 233).

Religious writing also bulked large throughout the Middle English period because of its cultural agility: the set of principles it had to hand, inherent in Christian doctrine itself, which could wrest doctrinal truth from even the most irreligious text or event. In what is actually the more modest of these principles, the whole genre of historical writing could be rendered sacred wherever it was agreed, as Augustine of Hippo taught in his *De doctrina Christiana* [On Christian Doctrine], that 'whatever evidence of past times that which is called history gives us' [quidquid . . . de ordine temporum transactorum indicat ea quae appellatur historia], it is relevant only in so far as it 'helps us a great deal in the understandings of the sacred books' [plurimum nos adjuvat ad sanctos libros intelligendos].[41] For Augustine this meant that the history of the world could be divided into six ages in which every event since the coming of Christ could be tucked, inconsequentially, into the very end of the sixth age ('there is no sacred history *of* the last age: there is only a gap for it *in* the sacred history').[42] The view is most influential in Middle English in the text called the *Cursor Mundi* (c.1325), whose 30,000 line account of 'quatking curs this world es past' [what course the world has taken][43] spends almost all of these lines on the events between Creation and the Crucifixion and allots precisely four lines to everything that has happened since:

Sex eildes* ha we broght in place,	*ages*
The sext es tald* the time o grace,	*called*
That began at cristes come,*	*coming*
And lastes to the dai o dome.*	*judgment*

(ll. 21,847–50)

Doctrinal purity is hardly equivalent to dullness, however, and this text is often wrongly assimilated to the category of religious instruction simply because it makes biblical events so clear.[44] As can be seen in its version of the story of Abraham and Isaac, for example, its octosyllabic couplets unfold with a kind of jaunty concision that tends to boil down a biblical story to a quick sequence of compelling events:

Wit this he stod the child nerhand,*	*near*
And dernlik* he drou the brand*	*undetected / sword*
That the child was not parceveid	
Ar* the suerd him hade deceveid;	*before*
He liftd his hand him to smyte,	
Bot godds help him come ful tite.*	*very quickly*
Ar that he moght have given the dint;*	*blow*

His suerd be-hind the angel hint*   *took hold of*
And bade him thar biside him tak
A scepe* his sacrifice to mak.   *sheep*

(ll. 3169–78)

The *Cursor Mundi* also sets out, with profound simplicity, the biblical injunction that makes such interest in, and clarity about, scriptural event so important:

All that written es in writt*   *writing*
Wroght* es for to lere* us wiit,*   *written / teach / wisdom*
Hu we agh* to lede ur liif,   *ought*
Cristen folk, bath* man and wiif.   *both*

(ll. 23,863–6)

These lines are simply a translation of Romans 15: 4 ('Quaecumque enim scripta sunt ad nostram doctrinam scripta sunt' [For what things soever were written, were written for our learning]), but even as they explain the importance of the kind of history the *Cursor* provides, they reveal the astonishingly absorptive power of any such view: where 'all that written is' is understood to mean '*everything* that is written' (for this is all the Latin version of the verse says) then *every* writing is doctrine.

This attitude was underwritten by the interpretative relationship scripture created between the Old and New Testaments, with the latter, as Christ put it in the Sermon on the Mount, coming to 'fulfil' (Matthew 5: 17), or give meaning to, the former. Such relationships also underwrote a reading strategy outlined, again, by Augustine in the *De doctrina Christiana*, whereby any text could be brought to yield sacred meanings, simply because it did not, at first, seem to do so:

> A method of determining whether a locution is literal or figurative must be established. And generally this method consists in this: that whatever appears in the divine Word that does not literally pertain to virtuous behaviour or to the truth of faith you must take to be figurative. Virtuous behaviour pertains to the love of God and of one's neighbour; the truth of faith pertains to a knowledge of God and of one's neighbour.

> [Demonstrandus est igitur prius modus inveniendae locutionis, propriane an figurata sit. Et iste omnino modus est, ut quidquid in sermone divino neque ad morum honestatem neque ad fidei veritatem proprie referri potest, figuratum esse cognoscas. Morum honestas ad diligendum deum et proximum, fidei veritas ad cognoscendum deum et proximum pertinet.][45]

Once set in motion such a method knew no bounds ('a work of art is true insofar as it is false'), and medieval commentators were therefore able to find Christian meanings in an enormous variety of secular writings (e.g.

Horace's satires, Aesop's fables, Virgil's *Aeneid*).[46] It has even been alleged that no medieval Christian writer would attempt to write in a way that did not both invite and expect such interpretation,[47] and it is, oddly enough, Chaucer who has seemed to provide the greatest ballast for this view in what is usually called his *Retractions*, a very short text, usually appended in manuscripts to The Parson's Tale (and therefore customarily edited with it), in which Chaucer lists many of the texts we know him to have written ('The Book of Troilus, The Book also of Fame . . . The Book of the Duchesse . . . 'The Tales of Caunterbury, thilke that sownen into sinne [those which conduce to sin]', X.1086) among his 'giltes' (X.1084) and 'revoke[s]' them (X.1085). It is easy to take this view to the *Tales* themselves, to note, first, just how many of the pilgrims are 'exegetes' who tend to convert the 'literal' into the 'figurative' (the Wife of Bath, the friar in The Summoner's Tale, the Pardoner, and the Parson, in particular), and to suggest that Chaucer was very keen for his readers to evaluate each figure based on the quality of their reading ('the first is hopelessly carnal and literal, the second is an arrant hypocrite, the third is aware of the spirit but defies it, and the last is . . . altogether admirable').[48] But it is equally clear that Chaucer could not allow himself such simplicity, for at precisely the moment that he professes his complete faith in the exegetical method of reading described in Romans 15: 4 ('For oure book seyth, "Al that is writen, is writen for oure doctrine"', X.1083), he neutralizes it by simultaneously listing all the works he has written for some reason other than 'doctrine'.[49] That is, if it was really the case that 'all' that is ever written conduces to doctrine then neither Chaucer (nor any writer) of any writing (of any kind) would ever have anything to revoke or retract.

Laughter

The *Retractions* are complex in their exposure of the difficulties of adhering simply and precisely to doctrine, but Chaucer also frequently employed the laughter that a number of theories of culture have identified as the mode of thought and action that customarily resisted the church's jurisdiction. In the broadest form of this view, laughter is always (in every period) a 'social gesture', designed to censure or eradicate orthodoxy, a reaction to any 'rigidity' or 'mechanical elasticity' that seeks to relax it.[50] Laughter in this sense is not an emotion so much as a species of 'intelligence'; what it wants from orthodoxy, by the same token, is the thoughtfulness whose obvious or extravagant absence has rendered that orthodoxy so ridiculous.[51] A more culturally specific version of such a theory understands laughter in the Middle Ages as that which opposed 'official' culture in 'therapeutic' rather than corrective ways.[52] In this theory, laughter is a 'positive, regenerating, creative' force, that began to disrupt the church's dogmatism as the barrier between Latin and the vernacular also dissolved (and Boccaccio's *Decameron* is a key example).[53] Although this view tends to romanticize the 'folk' or 'the people', and allies laughter not just with populism but with cultural change ('medieval laughter [has an] indissoluble and essential relation to freedom'),[54] in acknowledging that certain sorts of laughter were authorized by the church, brought under its jurisdiction 'as a parallel' for officialdom, what such a cultural theory also notices is that laughter was *the* 'legitimate' mechanism for regenerating orthodoxy from within.[55]

This positive and exuberant sort of laughter is represented with particular clarity by the poem usually called *The Land of Cockaygne* (c.1325). That laughter is certainly satiric in a more traditional sense, particularly in so far as monastic life is equated with opulence ('Ther beth [are] rivers gret and fine / Of oile, melk, honi, and wine')[56] and sexual licence ('And euch monke him taketh on . . . And techith the nunnes an oreisun [prayer]', ll. 162; 165). But the poem's vision of monastic excess is in some places *so* unbridled that the vision takes on a life of its own, becoming a kind of celebration of its own imaginative extravagance:

The yung* monkes euch dai	*young*
Aftir met* goth to plai:	*mealtime*
Nis* ther hauk no fule so swifte	*is not*
Bettir fleing bi the lifte*	*air*
Than the monkes, heigh of	
mode,*	*spirit*
With har* slevis and har hode.	*their*
Whan the abbot seeth ham* flee,	*them*
That he holt* for moch glee;*	*considers / sport*
Ak* natheles, al theramang,	*but*
He biddith ham light* to	*alight*
evesang.	
The monkes lightith noght adun,	
Ac furre* fleeth* in o randun.*	*further / run away / with great speed*
Whan the abbot him isseeth*	*sees*
That is* monkes fram him fleeth,	*his*
He taketh maidin of the route*	*troop*
And turnith up hir white toute*	*bottom*
And betith the taburs* with is hond	*drums*

To make is monkes light to lond.
(ll. 121–38)

There is a madcap perfection in the way the monks' refusal to live by any rule extends to gravity, but the poem is not in fact unique: it has a host of analogues in Old French and Middle Dutch, and reaches deeply, in both spirit and manner, into what is usually called 'goliardic' poetry, a mode of Latin verse produced in the twelfth and thirteenth centuries, almost exclusively by clerics, generating a great deal of its humour by turning the world (or the language of the Bible, the liturgy, the most respected learning) upside down (the manuscript containing *The Land of Cockaygne* also contains a typical instance of such verse, the *Missa de Potatoribus* or 'Mass of the Drunkards').[57] But the laughter in *The Land of Cockaygne* offers a particularly good instance of that mode of literary laughter which is therapeutic because it is so independently generative, so free of even the jurisdiction that authorizes it, that it is finally separate from official culture, as if a law unto itself.

The texts that most consistently and easily carved out a space for such therapeutic laughter were, however, those stories of animals or beast fables that seemed to proclaim their lack of seriousness in their choice of subject. Beast fables were a staple schoolroom text (particularly the *Fables* attributed to Avianus and the *Romulus vulgaris* often attributed to 'Aesop'),[58] and they therefore tended to teach lessons about the importance of hard work (a calf who skips along mocking an ox while he ploughs is in turn mocked by the ox as he is led to the sacrificial altar: 'such is the death given you by the forbearance that leaves you free from my yoke' ['hanc tibi', testis ait, 'dedit indulgentia mortem, / expertem nostri quae facit, esse iugi']).[59] Such a tendency to expose the cruelty of natural events, and a concomitant tendency to punish the least naivety, could make such stories distinctly unfunny, and yet, because they are hard on animals rather than people, beast fables always engage laughter's capacity to move past particular targets or problems toward a more general sense of play. This movement is particularly clear in the earliest surviving beast fable in English, *The Fox and the Wolf* (c.1275), a short poem (only 295 lines long) in a grand manner (for it derives, at root, from the French beast epic the *Roman de Renard* [1171–1250]). It tells the story of a fox who foolishly leaps into one of two buckets hanging over a well, and must then dupe a passing wolf into jumping into the other bucket so that he will be lifted back out of the well:

The wolf gon sinke,* the vox arise –	*sank*
Tho gon the wolf sore agrise!*	*was very afraid*
Tho* he com amidde* the putte,*	*then / in the middle of / well*
The wolf thene vox* opward* mette.[60]	*fox / on the way up*

Like much beast fable the purpose of this text really begins and ends with the pleasure it provides: it may show that stupidity is roundly punished (the wolf is savagely beaten when discovered in the well by a friar), but satisfaction comes not from this pitiable result, but from watching the trick that exposes this stupidity unfold. Of course, beast fables were understood (and understood themselves) as fundamentally didactic, and, as in Lydgate's collection called *Isopes Fabulles*, every story not only ends with a moral but tends to proceed with an abundance of proverbs and sententious sayings ('Vertu gynneth [begins] at occupacion, / Vyces all procede of [from] idelnesse').[61] But the often ostentatious inconsequence of the lessons so taught is also well proved by Lydgate's free-standing beast fable *The Churl and the Bird*, in which the bird who promises 'three greete wisdames'[62] to the churl, if he lets her go, offers, as chief among these 'wisdames', that the churl should never have released her!

Lydgate's interest in beast narrative was doubtless both provoked and schooled by Chaucer's unusual skill in exploiting its capacity to celebrate the very penchants, practices and attitudes that it simultaneously mocks, and Chaucer's most extraordinary achievement in this genre is another poem about birds, The Nun's Priest's Tale. This story of a rooster, Chauntecleer, and his close brush with death at the hands of a fox, also reaches back to beast epic, particularly in its first half, which mercilessly mocks rhetorical pretension as Chauntecleer tries at length to prove to his doubting wife, Pertelote, that the frightening dream he has just had may be prophetic (as, indeed, it is) only to ignore every word he has uttered:

For whan I feele a-night* your softe side	*at night*
– Al be it that I may nat on yow ride,	
For that oure perche is maad so narwe,* allas! –	*narrow*
I am so ful of joye and of solas,	
That I deffye* bothe swevene* and dreem.	*defy / dream*

(VII.3167–71)

That words will never alter certain natural facts is very much the lesson of the first part of this tale, but such views both complicate and focus the lesson of its second half, in which Chauntecleer, once he is caught, talks his way out of his predicament by persuading the fox to taunt those who chase him (thereby opening his mouth and freeing Chauntecleer).

Laughter of an even deeper sort lurks behind this contradiction (the poem may seem to be consuming itself), although it is possible to gather the strands of these different views of language into the general claim that words *matter*, precisely because they *can* alter action through persuasion. This is a view that the *telling* of the tale tends everywhere to prove, as Chaucer employs his own considerable rhetorical skills in marrying the ostentatiously minor and domestic subject with the grandest of styles (laughter lurks here in the often sublime extravagance of this marriage). Here, for example, is his heady amalgam of the colloquial and the tragic, swirled up into a vision of monumental, but domestic, chaos:

This sely* widwe and eek hir doghtres two,	*poor*
Herden* thise hennes crie and maken wo,	*heard*
And out at dores stirten* they anon,	*rushed*
And syen* the fox toward the grove gon,	*saw*
And bar* upon his bak the cok away,	*bore*
And cryden, 'Out! Harrow!' and'Weylaway!'*	*alas*
Ha, ha, the fox!' – and after hym they ran,	
And eek* with staves* many another man.	*also / staffs*
Ran Colle our dogge, and Talbot, and Gerland,	
And Malkin, with a distaf* in hire hand;	*spinning staff*
Ran cow and calf, and eek the verray hogges,	
So fered* for the berkyng* of the dogges,	*afraid / barking*
And shoutinge of the men and wommen eek	
They ronne* so, hem thoughte hir	*ran*
herte breek.*	*their hearts would break*

(VII.3375–88)

This is also a text which demonstrates an unusual degree of self-consciousness about the jurisdiction such laughter is challenging, for, in conclusion, its narrator not only insists that it is edifying ('Taketh the moralitee, goode men', VII.3440), but, at precisely this point, he cites Romans 15: 4 ('For Seint Paul seyth that al that writen is, / To oure doctrine it is ywrite [written], iwys', VII.3441–2). Although the frivolous context of this citation may make it seem comic, the meaning of the verse is activated by such circumstances in ways it could never be in the *Retractions*; for, here, in a poem whose value seems to reside so much in the pleasures it gives, the serious point must be that writing that seems to teach so little is still doctrinally valuable (*'al* that is written . . .').

Such pleasures are close to purely structural in The Nun's Priest's Tale – resident in the relationship between parts rather than in any one part as such – but the broader category of texts in which this was true in the Middle Ages was not beast fable, but the kind of narrative usually described as *fabliau*. These are traditionally defined as 'humorous stories in verse' ('contes à rire en vers'), and, since stories of this kind exist in most cultures (and stretch back to antiquity), it is also possible to say that they originate in 'the East' (India, say, or even China), although the body of such writing that most influenced English writers was French.[63] These narratives are not unlike beast fable in their mockery of stupidity or appetite or greed, but since they tend to push such failings to the extreme, and work toward the supremely fitting punishment rather than any sort of correction, the life of these stories lies in no teaching, but almost wholly in the interlocking events that comprise them: as stories they are unusually but fundamentally invested in *plot*. The one early *fabliau* that survives in English is called *Dame Sirith* (*c.*1274), a poem in both tail-rhyme stanzas and couplets (the shift to the latter seems to ease the representation of dialogue), which describes a lecherous clerk who is helped in his attempt to woo a married woman by 'Dame Sirith', who lies and tells the wife that her own daughter once spurned the clerk with disastrous results:

Thenne bigon the clerc to wiche,*	*use sorcery*
And shop* mi douter til a biche,*	*transformed / bitch*
This is mi douter that Ich of speke:	
For del of* hire min herte breketh.[64]	*grief over*

This poem's interest in event is most purely signalled by its narration of the wife's complete about-face at this juncture, without any registration of the coercion that has caused it or the emotional or ethical costs: all the wife is allowed to worry about is the disaster that could never, really, have befallen her ('Louerd Crist, that me is wo, / That the clarc [clerk] me hede fro [went away from me] / Ar [before] he me hevede [had] biwonne!', ll. 379–81). There is, to be sure, a certain bitterness inherent in any laughter at such stupidity, but it is the common stock of *fabliau*, and there was also clearly a serious appetite for such stories (there are at least 147 *fabliaux* extant in Old French, and seven survive in the Anglo-Norman dialect).[65] The only other early example of the genre in English is a fourteenth-century fragment of a play or 'interlude' which takes its plot from *Dame Sirith*, the *Interludium de Clerico et Puella*.[66] But the *fabliau* was made a crucial part of Middle English literature by Chaucer, who not only incorporated three such texts into *The Canterbury Tales* (The Miller's Tale, The Reeve's Tale, The Shipman's Tale) but also absorbed the genre's investment in consequences and events to a variety of narratives that could equally be placed in other genres (i.e. The Friar's Tale, The Summoner's Tale, The Merchant's Tale and the fragmentary Cook's Tale).

Each of Chaucer's three *fabliaux* demonstrates something important about the genre, but the most intricate structurally is The Miller's Tale, in which plot is 'virtually made philosophical' as the careful interconnection of parts becomes its own 'assertion of the binding, practical sequentiality of all events'.[67] In fact, The Miller's Tale consists of not one but two plots, elegantly and meaningfully woven together: in the first of these, a clerk, Nicholas, tricks the carpenter, John, who has given him lodging, into believing that an enormous flood is imminent, and while John is cowering in a 'kneading tub' hung from the roof to escape the coming waters, Nicholas has sex with Alisoun, the carpenter's wife; in the second plot, Alisoun decides to play a trick on the parish clerk, Absolon, who just happens to come courting while she and Nicholas are in bed together, and, having promised him a kiss, she instead puts her arse out of the window. It is the 'sudden union of these two plots' that is truly 'sublime', however, and this occurs when Absolon returns to avenge his humiliation armed with a hot 'cultour' (the freshly forged blade of a ploughshare), and Nicholas makes the mistake of trying to repeat Alisoun's joke, sticking his arse out of the window:[68]

This Nicholas anoon leet fle* a fart,	*fly*
As greet as it hadde been a thonder-dent,*	*thunder-clap*
That with the strook he was almoost yblent;*	*blinded*
And he was redy with his iren* hoot,*	*iron / hot*
And Nicholas amidde the ers* he smoot,*	*arse / struck*
Of gooth the skin, an hande-brede aboute;*	*hand's breadth all round*
The hoote cultour brende* so his toute,*	*burnt / arse*
That for the smert* he wende for to die,*	*pain / thought he would die*
As he were wood,* for wo he gan to crye:	*mad*
'Help! Water, water, help, for Goddes herte!'	
This carpenter out of his slomber sterte,*	*started*
And herde oon* cryen 'Water!' as he were wood,	*someone*
And thoghte, 'Allas, now comth* Nowelis* flood!'	*comes / Noah's*
He sette him up* withouten wordes mo,	*sat up*
And with his ax he smoot the corde atwo,*	*in two*
And doun gooth al – he fond* neitherto selle*	*found / sell*

Ne breed* ne ale, til he came to the celle*   *bread / cellar*
Upon the floor, and there aswowne* he lay.   *in a swoon*
(I.3806–23)

The skill with which these plots are interwoven is demonstrated best in
the way that Nicholas's cry for water not only takes up the whole of a
line, but that line is, at once, the conclusion of one plot and the trigger for
the conclusion of the other. The two parallel plots also acquire meaning
as they are drawn so completely together: in the sexual idyll Nicholas and
Alisoun have constructed for themselves, both the hot cultour and the
explosion of John on to the scene represent the world of consequences they
have tried to banish; for John, that idyll represents all the practical facts he
has ignored while worrying about problems that never could arise. There
is a great deal of bitterness here too (John breaks his arm in his fall and
his explanations are scorned by the whole of the town: 'no man his reson
herde', I.3844), but the laughter released by the poem's dramatic, surprising and neat conclusion must respond to more purely poetic energies, to
a structure so perfectly realized that we may smile simply to witness the
perfection of its completion.[69]

Meaning is not always so purely structural in Chaucer's *fabliau*, but the
elevation of plot to meaning is fundamental to his other two *fabliaux* as
well. In The Shipman's Tale, for example, this elevation occurs by means
of a less extravagant double plot whereby a story about sex (a monk wants
to sleep with a married woman) is shadowed by a financial transaction (the
wife asks the monk for money in exchange for this 'servise' [VII.191], and
the monk borrows that money from the woman's husband). The interweaving of the various kinds of favour tends to equate the different sorts
of appetite they satisfy, and the conclusion of the tale presses the point
home with a pun, for, when asked to repay the money to the husband,
the monk says he has actually given it back to the wife, and, when she is
in turn asked for the money by her husband, she conflates both sorts of
debt by telling her husband to 'score it upon my taille' (VII.416), relying
on the fact that 'taille' meant 'tally' (an amount of money owed) but was
also a euphemism for genitals ('tail').[70]

The plot of The Reeve's Tale is freighted with meaning by the Canterbury frame narrative, in which it emerges as a direct consequence of The
Miller's Tale (the Reeve has promised to 'quite' [I.3864] or 'pay back' the
Miller for a tale he feels makes fun of carpenters like himself), for, as a
story about the wages of revenge, it both illustrates and describes the cycle

of violence vengefulness can produce (in the tale itself, a trick played by a miller on two clerks leads to a sequence of increasingly savage tricks played by the clerks on the miller and, then, on all his family). The tale concludes with a proverb that is at once the tale's moral and a particularly dark description of *fabliau*: if 'a gilour shal himself bigiled be' [a trickster shall himself be tricked] (I.4321), as the Reeve insists, if every consequence is but the trigger for a different sort of comeuppance, then there is no 'guile' sufficient to escape such tricks unscathed ('Him thar nat wene wel that ivele dooth' [He who does evil need not expect any good], I.4320). Here, we are no longer in the territory of 'laughter' in the humorous sense, but rather in the jurisdiction of 'pleasure' or 'enjoyment' in a tale excellently told, or a meaningful structure beautifully executed, and we are therefore also in the position to see half of those qualities that Bradshaw later used to define *litterature* slowly lodging themselves into the purposes of Middle English writing along with the implicit claim that such writing might exist – might be written – for no other purpose than to delight. The process occurs in texts other than *fabliau* of course; we could certainly trace something like this movement in romance, where the appeal to pleasure is there in the first lines of the earliest Middle English such text we have ('Alle beon hi blithe [everyone be happy] / That to my song lithe [listens]!').[71] However, what is at issue here is not just the expectation that texts provide pleasure, but a general self-consciousness about that fact.

I have laid such emphasis on *The Canterbury Tales* in these last paragraphs because I think this self-consciousness first emerges into clear view in English writing not only in this collection but by means of it. It is particularly significant I think that in the conclusion to The General Prologue the Host continually returns to synonyms for pleasure as he sets out the scheme of the tale-telling contest that will structure the whole of the *Tales* (he describes himself as 'right a murye [merry] man' [I.757]; he speaks 'of mirthe' [I.759]; he finds the company of pilgrims particularly 'murye' [I.764]; he offers them 'mirthe' [I.766 and I.767], then 'disport' [I.775], then 'confort' [I.776], insisting that they will certainly be 'murye' [I.782] if they follow his advice). The contest the Host designs makes diversion or entertainment a fundamental function of each of the tales the pilgrims tell ('to shorte [shorten] with oure weye', I. 791). The Host also requires these tales to be edifying (that they will be 'tales of best sentence [serious meaning] and moost solaas [pleasure]', I.798), but, as this framing narrative unfolds, it becomes clear that edification is a function allied rather than opposed to pleasure. The Tale of Melibee, for example, as serious a work as the pilgrimage produces, is presented, above all, as a 'mirye tale', VII.964). And even the Parson, who prefaces his treatise on the Seven Sins by citing Paul's injunctions to Timothy against the falsehoods of 'fables' (X.31–4) (I Timothy 1: 4, 4: 7 and 2 Timothy 4: 4) and promises 'moralitee and vertuous matere' (X.38), characterizes his effort as 'a mirye tale in prose' (X.46), and recommends it to the pilgrims for the pleasure it will give:

And thanne that* ye wol yeve*	*if / give*
me audience,*	*a hearing*
I wole ful fain,* at Cristes reverence,*	*very gladly / in Christ's honour*
Do yow plesaunce* leefful,* as I kan.	*pleasure / lawful*
(X.39–41)	

This is as modest a claim for pleasure as any of the others I have cited, but the repetition is as decisive as its location in the preface to the tale meant 'to knitte up al this feste [entertainment] and make an ende' (X.47). The jurisdictional argument of the *Tales* proceeds neither strenuously nor with any precision, but by presumption, with the importance of literature's capacity merely to divert entered so often, as such a fundamental criterion of value that is, finally, transformed into a literary fact.

The aesthetic

There is a further step away from other cultural areas and purposes that literature can take, and it was by a more severe gathering *in* of jurisdiction – a kind of acute self-consciousness akin to narcissism – that Middle English writing also began to adopt the second quality that Bradshaw used to define *litterature*, conceiving of itself now as a positive good, worthy and excellent as such, and not in relation to any other quality or function. Since the eighteenth century we have tended to describe such an inwardness with the word 'aesthetic', a term borrowed from German (via two volumes called the *Aesthetica* by Alexander Baumgarten), ultimately derived from the Greek (*aisthetikos*, 'of or pertaining to things perceptible by the senses').[72] Taken in its original meaning 'the aesthetic' ought to mean something like 'the sensuous', and it ought to refer to all of those ways in which a text activates the senses as a sort of re-enactment of lived experience. The way such meanings might lead simply and directly in the ethical direction of 'the good' or 'excellence' can be seen if we look carefully at a poem such as 'Sumer is icumen in', one of the earliest of Middle English lyrics we have, and one of the more purely sensual poems in Middle English:

Sumer is icumen* in,	*has come*
Lhude* sing, cuccu!*	*loud / cuckoo*
Groweth sed* and bloweth* med*	*seed / blooms / meadow*
And springth the wude* nu.*	*forest / now*
Sing, cuccu!	
Awe* bleteth* after lomb,	*ewe / bleats*
Lhouth* after calve* cu,*	*lows / calf / cow*
Bulluc sterteth,* bucke ferteth.*	*leaps / farts*
Murie* sing, cuccu!	*merrily*
Cuccu, cuccu,	
Wel singes thu,* cuccu.	*you*
Ne swik* thu naver* nu!	*cease / never*
Sing cuccu nu, sing cuccu!	
Sing cuccu, sing cuccu nu![73]	

These verses implicate every sense – we are asked to hear the cuckoo singing, feel the wind blowing, see the bullock start and, most astonishingly, smell the buck fart – and both their meaning and their impact lie in the compression of such a broad sensory world into so small a space: the fecundity of spring is modelled in the exuberance with which these varied images unfold. But 'the aesthetic' comes to refer to a certain inwardness and self-possession (to texts that seem to carry their own justification within them because they never justify themselves) because of the *purity* of the sensuality on view in a poem such as this. This resolute phenomenality – a poem written by some person for other people, but so uninterested in that world that it evokes a world without people – has also, often, seemed to speak of the culture that produced it precisely 'by remaining silent' about it.[74] It may seem both perverse and joyless to insist that such an exuberant and innocuous poem as 'Sumer is icumen in' exists to leave something out, but the poem is usefully exemplary of all the qualities of 'the aesthetic' since this is verifiably the case: this poem is, in fact, a *contrafactum*, a secular set of words for a part song, written as an alternative to the pieties of the Latin verses that were originally sung with the music to which these English words were also set.[75] And the very improbability of this fact – the resistance this poem might produce in any reader to the notion that it is 'about' or 'for the purpose of' something else – is also the mark of 'the aesthetic', which we may also define as the extent to which a text embarrasses any attempt to re-embed it in cultural facts. A poem can be said to inhabit the realm of 'the aesthetic' in this important and extended sense, then, to the extent that we want to read it simply 'as it is', in so far as our most substantive reactions to it seem but a reflex ('just something I happen to feel').[76]

The aesthetic is never purely autonomous (one might press, for example, on 'Sumer is icumen in's demand that someone *'sing'* as an acknowledgement of the liturgical context it supplants), and before any Middle English text was able to mark out the aesthetic as a realm English writing inhabited as of right, this space was claimed by the extravagance or richness with which texts did not so much deny as blot out any obvious context. This is dramatically true of the very precocious *The Owl and the Nightingale* (c.1216) and the varied and fascinating meanings which proliferate in and from it. This poem begins, not incidentally, in pure phenomenality, as the description of a natural scene ('Ich was in one sumere dale, / In one suthe digele hale' [I was in a summer valley, in a very remote retreat])[77] from which an owl and nightingale emerge as if naturally (the nightingale 'piping' from behind a 'vaste thicke hegge' [secure, dense hedge] [l. 17], the owl sitting, imperturbably, on 'on old stoc' or stump [l. 25]). The poem has a clear literary context: its jaunty octosyllabic couplets are an early adaptation of the staple form of contemporaneous French and Anglo-Norman verse; the debate in which the birds engage is a parodic version of the 'dialectic' common in medieval schools and universities, and there was also a tradition of poetry employing this form (both extant manuscripts of *The Owl and the Nightingale* also collect the Anglo-Norman *Le Petit Plet*, a debate between 'youth' and 'age').[78] But *The Owl and the Nightingale* also tends to neutralize the broad traditions and cultural connections on which it relies even as it partakes of them, less by mocking them than by revelling in them, usually in the form of an extended and knowing joke. A small but representative example here is the way that the poem works what may be known of an owl's natural behaviour (from observation, or from encyclopaedias) into the owl's initial response to the nightingale, who has attacked her for the sound of her voice. The owl is bursting with fury, but this only becomes clear belatedly, since she simply *waits* to reply – until that hour when owls naturally sing:

> Thos Hule abod fort hit was eve:
> Ho ne mighte no leng bileve,

Vor hire horte was so gret
That wel-negh hire fnast atschet,
And warp a word tharafter longe:
'Hu thincthe nu bi mine songe?
West thu that ich ne cunne singe
Thegh ich ne cunne of writelinge?'

[The owl waited until it was evening, but she could hardly stand it any longer, for her heart was so swollen that her breath nearly burst out of her, and then she threw out a word after a while: 'How does my song seem to you now? Do you think that I do not know how to sing because I know nothing about warbling?']

(ll. 41–8)

The dissonance between what is 'natural' for each bird is often the basis of their disagreement (the nightingale says the owl is an 'unwight' [unnatural creature] [l. 90] because it flies at night; the owl accuses the nightingale of being small, 'lutel an unstrong' [l. 561]), but fun is always had at the expense of these presumptions (of an ethics based in the 'natural') because the birds almost always insist on using human ethics to evaluate avian behaviour ('Wat dostu godes among monne? [What good do you do among men?]', l. 563). The birds' every argument – and debate and dialectic as a structure – is itself consumed by their madcap capacity to contradict both themselves and each other, thereby eroding not only every position they adopt but any larger position from which either of them might be judged (there is hardly a poem in English literature whose basic subject has produced such a variety of critical views).[79] The birds certainly take on serious subjects – both have an unusually feminist view of women and their oppression by men[80] – and it has been argued that the very erosion of a secure point of view means that the poem as a whole is about the difficulties of finding secure ground for 'judgment'.[81] But the poem's powers of erosion may be even more severe than this, for among its more extended and repeated jokes is the capacity of the birds to agree about argument, or, conversely, to argue 'without fighting', as the nightingale defines their task near the beginning of the poem:[82]

We mughe bet mid fayre worde,
Witute cheste and bute fighte,
Plaidi mid foghe and mid righte;
And mai hure either wat hi wile,
Mid righte segge and mid sckile.

[We might better make our case in decorous language, without strife and without fighting, with propriety and justice, and each of us can justly and with reason say what we want to.]
(ll. 182–6)

The birds also seem to fall over themselves in agreement at the poem's end ('"Certes", cwath the Hule, "that is soth"' ['Certainly', said the owl, 'that is true'], l. 1769), '"Do we", the Nightegale seide' ['Let's do that', the Nightingale said], l. 1781), even as they also agree to restage the argument before 'Nicholas of Guildford' (the owl says that he can recite their argument word by word, subject to the nightingale's correction – '"Telle ich con word after worde: / an yef the thincth that ich misrempe [go astray] / Thu stond ayein and do me crempe [stop me]"' [ll. 1786–8] – and the nightingale agrees). The poem transforms all this agreeable disagreement into the emphatic gesture that concludes the poem, as the birds fly off not just out of the reach of any judgement but out of the reach of the poem and its narrator:

An hu heo spedde of heore dome
Ne chan ich eu na more telle –
Her nis na more of this spelle.

[But how they fared in their judgement, I can say no more, since there is no more of this story.]
(ll. 1792–4)

This gesture is just one more joke which uses the very need for a conclusion as its material (the narrator's excuse somehow presumes that a poem such as this did not *need* to stop at some point), but it is also a grand acknowledgement that no conclusion *can* be reached in a poem so fundamentally governed by the proliferation – rather than the regulation – of meaning.

Because *The Owl and the Nightingale* makes this proliferation so pleasurable – because it everywhere frustrates specification with a wit we must admire – it also brings us squarely into that area of 'the aesthetic' which is sometimes described with the phrase 'art for art's sake', a concealment of worldly determinants so complete that, in classic Marxist accounts, it is associated with 'an insoluble contradiction . . . between the artist and his social environment', but a 'contradiction' that also 'exercises a favourable effect on the work of the artist to the extent that it enables him to rise above [that] environment'.[83] No such argument has ever been made about

The Owl and the Nightingale, but something of the sort has been said about a poem both similarly elaborate in its artfulness and similarly pleasurable, the allegorical dream vision by the *Gawain*-poet usually called *Pearl* (*c*.1380). All of the *Gawain* poet's poems could be described in terms of elaborate artfulness, but *Pearl* is unique in parlaying such elaboration into a generative principle, beginning at the level of the letter (as words in each line alliterate), interlinking lines (which rhyme in the pattern *abababab-bcbc*), yoking stanzas (which form twenty different sections, each sharing a particular refrain and a particular word or phrase picked up from that refrain in each stanza's first line) and, finally, governing the poem as a whole (whose last line is also its first line). The linking of every layer of signification is deeply connected to the poem's fascination with ornament, as well as to the particular ornament it favours, the 'pearl', even as the linking of every level of the poem and the poem's end with its beginning gives the *poem* something of the round and perfected shape of that pearl. In addition the 'pearl' signifies everything *Pearl* seems designed to say, since it is also employed as the poem's most common and active metaphor, not only as a figure for beauty, richness and – through its perfection – spiritual grace, but as a figure for the 'maiden' the poem's narrator has lost and 'meets' again in his dream. *Pearl* cannot be dated with certainty, but there is general agreement that it was written some time in the reign of Richard II (1378–99), and convincing evidence links the *Gawain*-poet with Richard's court.[84] It is in this light that the poem's elaborate artfulness has been described as a 'defence' against a political world in 'crisis', a 'perfection' in which the problems of the realm are completely 'absorbed in[to] . . . art'.[85] This is certainly a point that the narrator of *Pearl* makes when he first surveys the dream landscape and describes how its richness helps him to forget his grief:

The adubbement* of tho	*adornment*
downes* dere	*hills*
Garten* my goste* al grefe foryet.*	*made / spirit / forget*
So frech* flavores* of frytes* were,	*such refreshing / fragrance / fruits*
As fode* hit con me fayre refete.*	*as if it were food / refresh*
Fowles ther flowen in fryth*	*woodland*
in fere,*	*together*
Of flaumbande* hwes,* bothe	*flaming / colours*
smale and grete.	
Bot sytole-stryng* and gyternere*	*citole-string / cithern*
Her reken* myrthe* moght not	*beautiful / music*
retrete;*	*imitate*

> For quen* those bryddes her   *when*
>   wynges bete,
> Thay songen* wyth a swete asent.*   *sang / concord*
> So gracios gle* couthe* no   *charming / joy*
>   mon gete*   *obtain*
> As here and se her adubbement.[86]   *to hear*

The poem consists of much more than either such effects or description, however, and most of its lines are filled with a debate between the dreamer and the 'Pearl-maiden' (as she is usually referred to in criticism), in which the general issue is how to accommodate the human tendency to 'measure' with a Christian grace that is infinite (the poem insists upon the difficulty by defining grace with the language of measure: 'The grace of God is gret innogh', ll. 612, 624, 636, 660). Underlying this general exploration there is a more particular search for consolation in the face of a monumental personal loss. The 'Pearl-maiden' is clearly the dreamer's young daughter ('Thou lyfed not two yer in oure thede [land]', l. 484), and what he desperately wants to know is that she is not, in heaven, as grief-stricken as he is on earth:

> Bot kythes* me kyndely* your coumforde,*   *show / kindly / comfort*
> Pytosly* thenkande* upon thysse: *piteously / thinking*
> Of care and me ye made acorde,*   *companions*
> That er* was grounde of alle my blysse.   *formerly*
>   (ll. 369–72)

Because of the intensity of such concerns, and the richness in which they are couched, what is generally *not* noticed by most readers is the way that all the complexity of Christian doctrine as well as all those practical problems involved in fitting that doctrine to equally complex lives – that is, the concerns that everywhere troubled the confessional and instructional literature of this period – are planed completely flat. To an eye and ear also aware of the difficulties faced by the institutional church in this period, and in particular to the kinds of incendiary debate pursued with vigour by Wyclif and his followers, this 'silent marginalization of the Church' is as striking as it is complete.[87]

The various techniques of art used for their 'own sake' in *Pearl* (metre, versification, dream vision, allegory, debate) are also inherited, and when the aesthetic emerges in a more permanent form in English – when 'art for art's sake' is self-consciously embraced as an aspiration – it is, as I suggested at the beginning of this chapter, also an inheritance, the importation into English of a set of jurisdictional claims that had long been available in Latin writing and its French translations. The decisive moment occurs, it is probably time to be clear, when an English writer is prepared to claim that his own efforts have a value equivalent to those venerated classics which had been valued in and of themselves, when, in short, Chaucer is prepared to enter his masterpiece, *Troilus and Criseyde* (1381–6), into the pantheon occupied by 'Virgile, Ovide, Omer, Lucan and Stace [Virgil, Ovid, Homer, Lucan and Statius]' (V.1792), although he is hardly the first Middle English writer to draw from the stories or mythography of these classical texts, or to write as if from or about their ancient world. In fact, Middle English had long owed a great deal to the clutch of twelfth-century French poems sometimes called the *romans antiques* which retell much of the significant event of the classical epics, the *Roman de Thèbes* (c.1150), the *Roman d'Eneas* (c.1155–60) and Benoît de Sainte-Maure's *Roman de Troie* (1155–70).[88] The *Seege of Troye* (1300–25), based on Benoît, is an early example of such a Middle English poem;[89] the *Gest Historiale of the Destruction of Troy* (c.1350–1400), based on Guido delle Colonne's Latin prose version of Benoît, the *Historia destructionis Troiae* (1287), takes the measure of English ambitions in this sphere, for it stretches to 14,044 alliterative lines.[90] The use of antiquity in Geoffrey of Monmouth's *Historia Britanniae*, as it passed (via Wace) into Lagamon's *Brut*, provides ample proof that such art need not represent a withdrawal from the political, for these texts tend to exploit the past to legitimize a contemporaneous politics.[91] But *Sir Orfeo* (c.1300), an early romance, offers a strong intimation of what is to come, for it draws on the story of Orpheus as told in Ovid's *Metamorphoses* (probably via some intermediate text) to place 'a king / In Inglond'[92] as well as in a decidedly mythographic world ('His fader was comen of King Pluto / And his moder of King Juno', ll. 5–6), a move that enables a surprisingly gripping allegory in which the death of 'Dame Herodis', Orfeo's wife, can be figured as a kidnapping by fairies ('The Quen was oway y-twight [snatched away], With fairy [magic] forth y-nome [taken]', ll. 168–9) from which, in an equally enchanting revision of the classical story, she can be successfully rescued. In such a poem, social and political facts are not so much ignored as rendered wholly irrelevant, but it was Chaucer who first recognized the potential of such distancing – in particular, the scope it gave for writing about human thought and action free even from the necessities of Christian doctrine. The conclusion of Chaucer's Knight's Tale – which derives, ultimately, from the *Thebaid* of Statius (AD 45–96) via Giovanni Boccaccio's *Teseida* (1339–41) – illustrates the potential of such abstraction particularly well, for when 'Arcite', one of two knights competing in battle for the noble Emily, is mortally injured, just at the point of victory, the poem is released into a searching exploration of what can only be termed the meaning of life in a world unmoored from any secure theology (as Arcite poses the astonishingly naked question 'What is this world? What axeth [ask] men to have?', I.2777). In a concluding speech that attempts to make sense of this tragedy in such terms, Theseus understands human achievement as providing its own measure, praising the life well lived as its own reward:

Thanne is it wisdom, as it thinketh me,*	*it seems to me*
To maken vertu of necessitee,	
And take it wel* that we may nat eschue,*	*as good / avoid*
And nameliche* that to us alle is due.	*especially*
And whoso gruccheth oght,* he dooth	*grumbles at all*
folye,*	*acts foolishly*
And rebel is to hym that al may gye.*	*rule*
And certeinly, a man hath moost honour	
To dien in his excellence and flour,	
Whan he is siker* of his goode name.	*sure*

(I.3041–9)

Chaucer drew deeply in this passage on a philosophical work of late antiquity which he had recently translated, Boethius' *Consolation of Philosophy* (AD 522–4), a treatise in the form of a debate between 'Boethius' (a figure for the author who was himself, at that point, in prison and condemned to death) and the personification 'Philosophy'. Boethius was himself a Christian, but the *Consolation* sets itself the task of exploring the nature of the good, happiness and the potential for free will in a world created and governed by an omnipotent being who does not, however, give meaning to human endeavour (in ways that the Christian god always does). As it is adapted to the pagan narrative of The Knight's Tale, this vision can be bleak ('this world nys [is not] but a thurghfare ful of wo', I.2847), but one of its more powerful side-effects is to make the world begin and end at the limits of the poem and, in that way, to throw a certain emphasis on the *poem* as an achievement ('Whan that the Knight had thus his tale ytold, / In al the route [company] ne was ther yong ne old / That he ne seide [did not say] it was a noble storye', I.3109–11).

What we are talking about here, it is important to be clear, is not Chaucer's 'originality', which has always been overestimated, partly because it has suited modern scholarship to have a singular origin, partly because it suited Chaucer's immediate *successors* to have an origin they could praise (and, in that way, praise themselves).[93] What is at issue here is really a certain sort of daring or, perhaps (as Chaucer might well have thought of it), a simple bid for latter-day estimation which was successful in ways that

Chaucer himself could never have predicted or known. The bid was also made, not in any one poem, but over the course of a large body of work, so that, if something important seems to be occurring in The Knight's Tale, this is in part because Chaucer had prepared the ground, from a slightly different direction, in *The House of Fame* (c.1380), a dream vision that employs a great deal of classicizing machinery (divisions into books, each with a proem and invocation) but which is not so much set in pagan antiquity as a series of encounters with antiquity's treasures – treasures that are then used to map out an aesthetic space that can be emphatically claimed. Book I of this poem offers a condensed version of the story of Aeneas and Dido as it appears in Ovid's *Heroides* (5 BC), but Chaucer begins, boldly, with a direct translation of the first lines of Virgil's *Aeneid* (29–19 BC), which his narrator has found 'on a wall . . . writen on a table of bras' (ll. 141–2):

I wol* now synge, yif I kan,	*will*
The armes and also the man	
That first cam, thurgh his destinee,	
Fugityf of* Troy contree,	*fleeing from*
In Itayle, with ful moche pyne*	*very great pain*
Unto the strondes* of Lavyne.[94]	*shores*
(ll. 143–8)	

Book II describes how this narrator, 'Geoffrey', is snatched up by an unusually garrulous eagle, who carries him through the cosmos toward the 'House of Fame' and quietly, but steadily, raises the issue of just where 'Geoffrey', or any individual, might fit into this vastness:

'Now turn upward,' quod* he, 'thy face,	*said*
And behold this large space	
This eyr,* but loke* thou ne be	*air / take care*
Adrad* of hem that thou shalt se'.	*afraid*
(ll. 925–8)	

It is the layout of the House of Fame, as described in Book III, that dramatically imagines such a fit in aesthetic terms, with the earthly world now emphatically banished (to 'no more . . . than a prikke', l. 907) and 'fame', for 'Geoffrey', finally figured as serried ranks of the most well-known and praised writers of antiquity, frozen as statues, fit for nothing but admiration:

Tho saugh I stonde on a piler,*	*pillar*
That was of tynned* yren* cler,	*tin-plated / iron*
The Latyn poete Virgile,	
That bore hath up* a longe while	*has borne up*
The fame of Pius Eneas.	

And next him on a piler was,
Of coper,* Venus clerk Ovide,   *copper*
That hath ysowen* wonder wide   *spread*
The grete god of Loves name.

. . .

  Thoo* saugh I on a piler by,   *then*
Of yren wroght ful sternely*   *sturdily*
The grete poete daun Lucan.
      (ll. 1481–9; 1497–9)

Other sorts of authority are mixed in with the classical poets on these
pillars (particularly historians such as Josephus, Guido delle Colonne,
Geoffrey of Monmouth), and many other classical poets are mentioned
(Statius, Homer, Claudian). Such citation of august poetic forebears
had also become traditional in the French and Italian literature on which
Chaucer generally relied (particularly in Jean de Meun's portion of the
Romance of the Rose [1275], Dante's *Inferno* [1308–21] and Boccaccio's *Filo-
colo* [1336–9]).[95] But Chaucer is the first English writer to attempt anything
like the associations implicit in this scene, to put himself forward as such
a 'grete poete', to measure his ambition on a plane where – like those
august poets of the pagan past – human action is its own reward, where
'excellence' and 'honour' (to hark back to Theseus's phrasing) become
qualities synonymous with such a 'name'. Fame's house is itself a precise
portrait of the aesthetic realm, a place of indescribable 'beaute' (l. 1172)
on a 'hygh . . . roche' (l. 1116) and intricately wrought 'of ston' (l. 1184), a
place both of the world but apart from it, a product of earthly endeavour
but capable of shaping that endeavour through its powerful influence.
It is doubtless a mark of Chaucer's uncertainty before such momentous
judgements that *The House of Fame* goes on to consider the unpredictable
nature of the renown it bestows (that a person will receive it undeserv-
edly, that the deserving will languish in obscurity), and, as the poem turns
to the more unsettling house of 'rounynges' [whisperings] and 'jangles'
[gossip] (l. 1960), or rumour, it breaks off (Chaucer seems to have left it
unfinished).

Such a vision might have been no more than comic – a self-mocking
account of aspirations rather than an important cultural articulation – had
Chaucer not written *Troilus and Criseyde* soon afterward, a poem that also
employs an elaborate classical machinery (proems and books), with a story
taken from pagan antiquity (about events in Troy just before its fall), but
which also claims equality with these classics on the grounds of its own
excellence. The poem is characterized as much by its delicacy as by its

epic ambitions: much of its power derives, as I suggested in the previous chapter, from the juxtaposition of monumentality and intimacy, the siege of Troy and its storied figures (Hector, Priam, Helen) as against the complex but private unfolding of the tragic affair of two reluctant lovers, Troilus and Criseyde. The pressures that large political movements may bring to bear on the fragile individual are themselves dramatized – made both acutely moving and central to the poem's explorations – in the fragility of Criseyde's situation ('for of hire lif she was ful sore in drede', I.95), for however keenly she may love Troilus both she and he are acutely aware of just how little freedom she has to make her own choices (as she puts it at a key moment, ' "Ne hadde I er now [if I had not, before now], my swete herte deere, / Ben yolde [been yielded], ywis, I were now nought heere!" ', III.1210–11). So important is the interaction between these levels that Chaucer allows Criseyde to imagine the way her most private decisions must have implications on the larger stage, even after she seems to have been shuffled off it, when, once entrusted to the Greeks, she chooses to entrust herself to another lover and realizes that she will now become infamous, as a 'betrayer':

Allas, of me, unto the worldes ende,	
Shal neyther ben ywriten* nor ysonge*	*written / sung*
No good word, for thise bokes wol	
me shende.*	*ruin*
O, rolled shal I ben on many a tonge!	
Thorughout the world my belle shal	
be ronge!*	*[i.e. my story shall be told]*
And wommen moost wol haten me of all.	
Allas, that swich a cas* me sholde falle!*	*occurrence / befall*
(V.1058–64)	

Chaucer can be seen to recoil from the purity of this logic, throwing up a kind of Christian screen between himself and these pagan proceedings in the poem's last stanzas, condemning these 'payens corsed olde rites [pagans' accursed practices]!' (V.1849), and fervently dedicating his efforts in *Troilus* to the service of 'that sothfast [true] Crist, that starf on rode [died on the cross]' (V.1860). But before erecting this screen Chaucer locates his own poem among the 'bokes' that Criseyde has already imagined, in this irretrievable sense extending the bounds of his own achievement outward to the 'worldes ende'. The bid for fame could hardly be clearer in this instance, for Chaucer emphatically enters his own 'book' into that pantheon of famous poets that he had already so carefully mapped out in *The House of Fame*:

Go, litel bok, go, litel myn tragedye,
Ther God thi makere yet, er* that he dye,   *before*
So sende myght* to make* in som   *the power / compose*
   comedye!
But litel book, no makyng* thow n'envie,*   *composition / do not envy*
But subgit* be to alle poesye;*   *subject / poetry*
And kis the steppes wher as thow seest
   pace*   *pass*
Virgile, Ovide, Omer, Lucan and Stace.

(V.1786–92)

The modesty here is as unnecessary as it is false, and when Chaucer says
that *Troilus and Criseyde* should be 'subgit . . . to alle poesye', it is by means
of the august examples he then gives – the most prestigious he could name
really – that we may recognize the boldness of the claim he is making for
his efforts as much as for himself. Here, English literature opens itself into
the aesthetic so fully that poetry (or 'poesye', as it is here called) is now a
realm unto itself, the source of its own reward, and its only measure.

Few bids for fame have been so successful, but one might say that the
claims Chaucer makes for the jurisdiction of English writing were realized
only as such claims were believed, acted upon and then repeated by his successors. When later English writers wanted to insist on the self-sufficiency
of the aesthetic, then, they tended to write the kind of poems Chaucer
wrote: so Lydgate wrote his own *Troy Book* (c.1412–20) and the *Siege of
Thebes* (1420–2), also repeating, in these poems, exactly the sorts of gestures
of fealty Chaucer had employed, but now to the lodestar of 'poesye' that
Chaucer had himself become:

My maister Galfride, as for chefe poete
That evere was yit* in oure langage;   *yet*
The name of whom shal passen* in noon age,   *die*
But every ylyche, with-oute eclipsinge, shyne.
And for my part, I wil never fine,*   *cease*
So as I can, hym to magnifie
In my writynge, plainly, til I dye;
And God, I praye, his soule bring in Ioy.[96]

My maister Chaucer, that founde ful many spot
. . .
To hym I make a direccioun
Of this boke to han inspeccioun.

(5.3521; 3535–6)

At this point, the claims of the aesthetic are so secure that they are no longer
pagan or even exclusively secular, as is clear enough in the *Life of Our Lady*,

where Lydgate makes his 'makyng' (l. 1642) subject to 'Chauser . . . poete of Brytayne' (ll. 1628–9). The merging of the strongest strains of religious literature and such aesthetic ambitions continue in the *Legendys of Hooly Wummen*, where Bokenham not only associates himself with 'Gower, Chauncers' and 'lytgate' (l. 417), as I have already mentioned, but with 'Homer, Ouvde, or ellys Virgyle' (l. 410). It is a mark of a different sort of arrival that the modesty that had become traditional in connection with such gestures has completely vanished by John Skelton's *The Garlande or Chapelet of Laurell* (1495–1523) where Gower, Chaucer and Lydgate can be found *urging* 'poeta Skelton' to join them in their 'collage [college] above the sterry [starry] sky',[97] and 'Skelton' can be found giving grudging assent:

. . . but if my warkes* therto be agreable,	*works*
I am elles* rebukyd of that I intende,	*also*
Which glad am to please, and lothe* to offende.	*loath*

(ll. 439–41)

But the claims of this lineage and English literature reach their culmination in the work with which I began this chapter, Bradshaw's *Life of St Werburge*, where, in addition to the definition of *litterature*, Bradshaw enters his own efforts into this aesthetic realm with all the usual fanfare, but, now also, given the well-established tradition of such gestures, as a self-evident fact:

To all auncient poetes, litell boke, submytte* the,	*submit*
Whilom flouryng in eloquence facundious,*	*elegant*
And to all other whiche present nowe be,	
Fyrst to maister Chaucer and Ludgate	
sentencious*	*sententious, meaningful*
Also to preignaunt* Barkley nowe beyng religious,	*meaningful*
To inventive Skelton and poet laureate;	
Praye them all of pardon both erly and late.	

(2.2020–6)

In picking out the writers in whose company he wishes to be seen, Bradshaw is also tracing the history of the category of which his poem is now part, from Chaucer to Lydgate, adding a new figure (Alexander Barclay [1484–1552], author of a *Life of St George*, five *Eclogues* and *The Ship of Fools*), as is always possible, endorsing more recent claims, such as those of Skelton, simply by repeating them. This is not all that English literature had been in the Middle English period, nor all that later periods would insist that literature is and ought to be, but such writing has acquired for itself that sense of self-importance, that purposeful insistence on a freedom from other cultural constraints, that so many English writers and readers after the sixteenth century came to mean when they referred to 'literature'.

Resources for the Study of Middle English Literature

The World Wide Web has made the study of Middle English literature much easier by putting most of this writing only a few clicks of the mouse away from any reader. An enormous number of texts are now available in on-line editions from TEAMS (the Consortium for the Teaching of the Middle Ages), in association with the University of Rochester, at www.lib. rochester.edu/camelot/teams/tmsmenu.htm. In those institutions that subscribe to the service, a wide variety of older, scholarly editions are also available in the Chadwyck-Healey archive *English Poetry (600–1900)*, http://collections.chadwyck.co.uk/home/home_ep.jsp. Other useful collections of texts can be found at the electronic archive at the University of Virginia (http://etext.lib.virginia.edu/collections/languages/english/mideng.browse.html), the 'Labyrinth' at Georgetown University (http://etext.lib.virginia.edu/collections/languages/english/mideng.browse.html) and the Corpus of Middle English Verse and Prose (http://www.hti.umich.edu/c/cme/), a part of the *Middle English Compendium* at the University of Michigan.

The *Compendium* also contains an electronic version of the *Middle English Dictionary* (http://ets.umdl.umich.edu/m/med/), which puts this extraordinary tool on any desktop linked to the web. The detail of this dictionary can make it daunting for the beginner or the casual reader, and a wide variety of Middle English forms can also be deciphered with the assistance of the *Oxford English Dictionary*, also available on line in any institution with a subscription to the service (www.oed.com/). But the sophistication of the search tools available in the electronic version of the *Middle English Dictionary* also makes it possible for both the newest user and the expert to generate a ready-made glossary entry for any Middle English word, common or obscure, in its more usual or most eccentric spelling. A particular word may be sought by the dictionary headword under 'MED Lookups' (http://ets.umdl.umich.edu/m/med/lookup.html), although it is always prudent in such cases to select 'Headword and forms' before clicking the search button (rather than accepting the default setting, which is 'Headword' only), since headwords in the *Middle English Dictionary* are not always predictable (and a search may be thrown off by the simple omission of a final –e). The most powerful search tools in this electronic dictionary, however, are to be found on the 'Search the MED entries' page, http://ets.umdl.umich.edu/m/med/med_ent_search.html, for it is here that you may simply type in any spelling of any Middle English word in virtually any Middle English text into the field for 'Boolean search', specify 'within quotation' for the range of that search, and you will receive back, almost instantaneously, a list of all the possible headwords under which that spelling occurs. Such a search can also be narrowed – and the range of headwords returned reduced – by pairing the form of the word you are interested in with any other word in the given clause or phrase (the more unusual that word or form is, the fewer 'hits' the search is likely to return).

For those who require a more basic introduction to Middle English as a language, the best place to begin is the introductory discussion in either *The Riverside Chaucer* (pp. xxix–xli) or *A Book of Middle English*, ed. Burrow and Turville-Petre (§5). A more comprehensive introduction is provided in *An Introduction to Middle English*, ed. Horobin and Smith. There are a number of web sites that offer simple tuition (often with the assistance of audio files to aid in pronunciation), and, at this writing, the best summary of these can be found at the Chaucer Metapage, www.unc.edu/depts/chaucer/index.html. Among the sites listed there, the most comprehensive guide to Middle English is (again, at this writing) the Harvard Chaucer page, www.courses.fas.harvard.edu/~chaucer/, and, in particular, the 'Teach Yourself Middle English' section of this site: www.courses.fas.harvard.edu/~chaucer/teachslf/less-0.htm.

The key studies and texts describing the broader cultural contexts in which I have tried to situate Middle English literature are, I hope, recorded with some care in the notes to each chapter. A wide net through cultural facts and contexts can also be cast by searching the rich entries for key personages (both writers and otherwise) in the *Oxford Dictionary of National Biography*, ed. Matthew and Harrison. For institutions with a subscription, its sixty-one volumes are also available, and searchable, on line at www.oxforddnb.com/. The most comprehensive interdisciplinary bibliography for the study of the Middle Ages is the *International Medieval Bibliography* (Leeds, 1967–), now also provided on line, for subscribing institutions, by Brepols (www.brepolis.net/login/overview.cfm).

Perhaps the most important strand of literary scholarship in which cultural contexts feature broadly is the burgeoning fund of 'companions' to various authors and literary kinds. *A Companion to Middle English Literature and Culture, c.1350–1500*, ed. Brown, stakes the broadest claim to this territory. Although it has now been issued in a revised edition, the oldest of any of these companions is the *Cambridge Companion to Chaucer*, ed. Mann and Boitani, and its early arrival on the scene as well as the centrality of its subject make it unusually comprehensive. Also invaluable in the particular area of Chaucer are *A Companion to Chaucer*, ed. Brown, *A Concise Companion to Chaucer*, ed. Saunders, and *The Yale Companion to Chaucer*, ed. Lerer. Other key authors are attended to in *A Companion to Piers Plowman*, ed. Alford, *A Companion to the Gawain-poet*, ed. Brewer and Gibson, *A Companion to Malory*, ed. Archibald and Edwards, and *A Companion to the Book of Margery Kempe*, ed. Arnold and Lewis. More broadly thematic companions include *The Cambridge Companion to Medieval English Theatre*, ed. Beadle, *The Cambridge Companion to Medieval Romance*, ed. Krueger, and *The Cambridge Companion to Medieval Women's Writing*, ed. Dinshaw and Wallace.

The resource on which I have relied most deeply in the writing of this book, and which yet holds a vast and untapped store of information about Middle English literature and its contexts, is *A Manual of the Writings in Middle English*, a collaborative survey of all Middle English, in production since 1967 and still in progress at this writing. Its volumes parcel up the literature of the period into broad, usually innovative (if occasionally awkward) categories, and each one offers both a concise, text-by-text survey of all the known texts within that category and an itemized bibliography (in a second section, at the back of each volume, keyed to the earlier descriptions by item numbers), which includes a summary of all extant medieval witnesses (both manuscript and printed) of that text, all published editions including selections, and references to all the key works of scholarship that treat both that text and its contexts. Since the subjects of individual volumes are often omitted in library catalogues, and included in summary form on the fly-leaves of the *Manual* itself only from volume 8 onwards, I list them here:

Vol. 1:   Romances
Vol. 2:   The *Pearl*-Poet, Wyclyf and his Followers; Translations and Paraphrases of the Bible; Saints' Legends; Instructions for Religious
Vol. 3:   Dialogues, Debates and Catechisms; Thomas Hoccleve; Malory and Caxton
Vol. 4:   Middle Scots Writers; The Chaucerian Apocrypha

Vol. 5:   Dramatic Pieces; Poems Dealing with Contemporary Conditions

Vol. 6:   Carols; Ballads; John Lydgate

Vol. 7:   John Gower; Piers Plowman; Travel and Geographical Writings; Works of Religious and Philosophical Instruction

Vol. 8:   Chronicles and Other Historical Writing

Vol. 9:   Proverbs, Precepts and Monitory Pieces; English Mystical Writings; Tales

Vol. 10:   Works of Science and Information

Vol. 11:   Sermons and Homilies; The Lyrics of MS Harley 2253

The *Manual* expressly excludes Chaucer, properly enough, since a separate series of bibliographies is devoted to him, including a regularly updated on-line bibliography (maintained by Mark Allen), http://uchaucer.utsa.edu/cgi-bin/Pwebrecon.cgi?DB=local&PAGE=First, and the annotated bibliography published yearly in volumes of *Studies in the Age of Chaucer*. What the *Manual* therefore provides, both in its emphasis and the detail of its attention, is a host of unusual and little-trodden pathways, each uniting the obscure with the more canonical, through the whole of this rich period of our literary history. The *Manual* does not understand itself as a tool of cultural study, but the combination of its breadth and its studious attention to the particular concerns and emphases of Middle English writing necessarily makes it one of our key resources.

Chronology

1066	Edward the Confessor dies; Harold Godwineson defeated at Hastings by William of Normandy; 'Abingdon' version of the *Anglo-Saxon Chronicle* breaks off
1079	'Worcester' version of the *Anglo-Saxon Chronicle* ends
1086	*Domesday Book*
1087	William I dies; accession of William II, 'Rufus'
1095	Wulfstan, Bishop of Worcester, last Anglo-Saxon bishop, dies
1096–9	The First Crusade; Jerusalem captured
1100	William II dies; accession of Henry I; *First Worcester Fragment*
c.1125	William of Malmesbury, *Gesta regum Anglorum*; *Gesta pontificum Anglorum*
1135	Henry I dies; accession of Stephen
1138	Geoffrey of Monmouth, *Historia Regum Britanniae*
1146–8	Second Crusade
c.1150	*The Proverbs of Alfred*
1152	Henry of Anjou (future Henry II) marries Eleanor of Aquitaine
1154	Stephen dies; accession of Henry II; last entry in *Peterborough Chronicle*
1155	Wace, *Roman de Brut*
1160–80	Chrétien de Troyes flourishes (*Yvain*); 'Oxford' (Bodleian Library, MS Digby 23) version of the *Song of Roland* copied
1170	Thomas Becket murdered
1187–92	Third Crusade
1189	Henry II dies; accession of Richard I
1190	Richard I joins Third Crusade
c.1190–1220	*Katherine*-group
1193	Murder and mass suicide of Jews in York

1198–1204	Fourth Crusade
1199	Richard I dies; accession of John
*c.***1200**	Lagamon's *Brut*
1204	Normandy lost to Philip II of France
1208	England under papal interdict
1214	Interdict lifted
1215	Magna Carta; Fourth Lateran Council
*c.***1215–24**	*Ancrene Wisse*
1216	John dies; accession of Henry III (age nine)
*c.***1216**	*The Owl and the Nightingale*
1221	Dominican friars arrive in England
1224	Franciscan friars arrive in England
1227–9	Fifth Crusade
*c.***1230**	Guillaume de Lorris begins *Roman de la Rose*
*c.***1230–5**	*La Mort le Roi Artu*
1236	Henry III marries Eleanor of Provence
*c.***1240–50**	*King Horn*; *Floris and Blancheflour*
1258	Provisions of Oxford limit royal power; first official proclamation in English
*c.***1260**	*Manuel des pechiez*
1264	Battle of Lewes: victory for Simon de Montfort
*c.***1264**	*A Song of Lewes*
1265	Battle of Evesham; Simon de Montfort killed
*c.***1270**	*A Luve-Ron*
1272	Henry III dies; accession of Edward I, 'Longshanks'
*c.***1274**	*Dame Sirith*
1275	First legislation allowing imprisonment of those who defame 'great men'
*c.***1275**	Jean de Meun completes *Roman de la Rose*; *Proverbs of Hendyng*; *The Fox and the Wolf*
*c.***1280**	*Havelok the Dane*
1290	Jews expelled from England
*c.***1290**	*The Stacions of Rome*; *South English Legendary*
*c.***1300**	*Song of the Husbandman*; Robert of Gloucester's *Chronicle*; *Northern Passion*; *Lay Folks Mass Book*; *Sir Orfeo*
*c.***1303**	Robert Mannyng's *Handlyng Synne*; *The Flemish Insurrection*
1306	*Execution of Simon Fraser*
1307	Edward I dies; accession of Edward II; *Satire on the Retinues of the Great*

1314	Scots defeat the English at Bannockburn
1315–16	Famine in England
c.1325	*The Simonie*; *The Land of Cockaygne*
1326	Queen Isabella invades England (in opposition to Edward II)
1327	Edward II deposed and killed; accession of Edward III
c.1330	Edinburgh, National Library of Scotland, MS 19.2.1, the 'Auchinleck MS' (*Arthur and Merlin, Bevis of Hampton, Guy of Warwick, Horn Child, Kyng Alisaunder, Richard Coeur de Lion, Lai le Freine, Tristrem*); Harley MS 2253 (*Annot and Johon, Alysoun*)
1333	Battle of Halidon Hill (English defeat Scots)
1337	War with France; beginning of the 'Hundred Years' War'
1338	Robert Mannyng's *Chronicle*
c.1340	*Ayenbite of Inwit*
1346	Overwhelming English victory over French at battle of Crécy
1347	Capture of Calais
1348–50	Black Plague throughout Europe
1349	Ordinance of Labourers; Richard Rolle dies
c.1350	*Prick of Conscience*; *Tale of Gamelyn*
c.1352–70	*Winner and Waster*
c.1356	'John Mandeville' writes the account of his 'travels'
1357	*Lay Folks Catechism*
1360	Treaty of Brétigny ceding large territories in Southwest France to England
1361–2	Severe outbreak of plague in England
1369	Chaucer's *The Book of the Duchess*
c.1375	*Northern Homily Cycle*
1373	Julian of Norwich experiences her 'revelations'
1376	Death of Edward, the Black Prince; earliest surviving reference to the York Cycle; 'Good Parliament'
1377	Edward III dies; accession of Richard II; first poll tax; Pope Gregory XI issues bulls attacking Wyclif's writings
c.1378	B-text of *Piers Plowman*
c.1380	Chaucer's *The House of Fame, Parliament of Fowles*; *Pearl*
1381	Rebels march on London
c.1381–6	Chaucer's *Troilus and Criseyde*
1382	*The Insurrection and Earthquake*

*c.*1382–90	Mirk's *Festial*
1384	John Wyclif dies
1386	'Wonderful Parliament'
*c.*1385–6	Usk's *Testament of Love*
1386–7	Chaucer's *Legend of Good Women*
1387–8	Lords Appellant challenge Richard II
*c.*1387	Chaucer begins *The Canterbury Tales*
1388	'Merciless Parliament'; Thomas Usk executed
*c.*1390	*Sir Gawain and the Green Knight*; version of Gower's *Confessio Amantis* dedicated to Richard II; tail-rhyme *Ipomedon*
*c.*1393	*Confessio Amantis* dedicated to Henry of Derby; *Pierce the Ploughman's Crede*
1394	Death of Queen Anne
1396	Walter Hilton dies; truce with France
1397	Arrest and execution of Richard, fourth Earl of Arundel
1398	Henry of Derby banished for ten years
1399	Death of John of Gaunt, Duke of Lancaster; Henry of Derby's banishment extended to life and Lancastrian estates confiscated; Richard II deposed; accession of Henry of Derby as Henry IV; *The Complaint of Chaucer to His Purse*; Gower's *In Praise of Peace*
1400	Richard II dies; Chaucer dies
*c.*1400	Alliterative *Morte Arthur*; *Jack Upland*; *Friar Daw's Reply*; *Richard the Redeless*
1401	*De heretico comburendo*, statute permitting burning of heretics; William Sawtre executed
1407	*Testimony of William Thorpe*
1408	John Gower dies
1409	Archbishop Arundel's *Constitutions* promulgated
*c.*1409	*Mum and the Sothsegger*
*c.*1409–11	Lydgate's *Life of Our Lady*
1410	Lollard John Badby burnt
*c.*1411	Nicholas Love's *Mirror of the Blessed Life of Jesus Christ*
1412	Hoccleve's *Regiment of Princes*; Siege of Bourges brings English forces back into extensive campaign in France
*c.*1412–20	Lydgate's *Troy Book*
1413	Henry IV dies; accession of Henry V; trial of John Oldcastle as a Lollard; Richard II's bones brought to

	Westminster; Margery Kempe visits Julian of Norwich and sails for the Holy Land
1415	English defeat French at Agincourt; Charles d'Orléans imprisoned in England; Brigittine order established at Syon Abbey; Hoccleve's *In Remonstrance to John Oldcastle*
1417	Oldcastle captured and executed
1418	Siege of Rouen
1420	Treaty of Troyes (Henry V's heir to be King of England and France); Henry V marries Catherine of Valois
1420–2	*Siege of Thebes*
1422	Henry V dies; accession of Henry VI (age nine months) to thrones of England and France; Humphrey of Gloucester becomes 'Protector' of England; earliest surviving reference to the Chester Cycle
1427	Lydgate's *Title and Pedigree of Henry VI*
1429	Lydgate's *Ballade to King Henry VI upon his Coronation*
*c.*1430	*Life of Alexander*
1431	Henry VI crowned King of France in Paris
*c.*1431–8	Lydgate's *Fall of Princes*
*c.*1433–8	*The Book of Margery Kempe*
1436	*Libelle of English Polycye*
1437	End of Henry VI's minority
*c.*1440	Gutenberg perfects movable metal type; *Partonope of Blois*
1443–7	Bokenham's *Legendys of Hooly Wummen*
1445	Henry VI marries Margaret of Anjou
*c.*1445	Capgrave's *Life of St Katharine*
1447	Humphrey of Gloucester arrested and dies
1448	John Lydgate dies
1449	Rouen, Harfleur and most of Normandy fall to French forces
1450	Jack Cade's rebellion; Reginald Pecock forced to recant his 'heresies'
*c.*1450	*Pseudo-Turpin Chronicle*; prose *Siege of Thebes*; prose *Merlin*; *King Ponthus and the Fair Sidone*; *Robin Hood and the Monk*
1451	French overrun Gascony
1453	End of Hundred Years' War; Turks take Constantinople
1455	First battle of St Albans begins 'Wars of the Roses'

1459	Reginald Pecock dies; decisive defeat of Yorkist forces by royal army
*c.***1460**	Prose *Ipomedon*; *A Trade Policy*
1461	Defeat of Lancastrian forces at battle of Towton; Henry VI deposed; Edward IV declared king
1463	Ashby's *A Prisoner's Reflections, Active Policy of a Prince*
*c.***1463–77**	Earliest surviving text of the York Cycle
*c.***1468–70**	Malory writes *Morte Darthur*
*c.***1468–71**	Fortescue's *De Laudibus Legum Anglie*
1470	Henry VI reinstated
1471	Henry VI deposed and killed; Edward IV restored to throne
1476	Caxton sets up a printing press in Westminster
1483	Edward IV dies; Richard of Gloucester acts as Protector for Edward V, then usurps throne as Richard III
1485	Battle of Bosworth Field; Richard III killed; accession of Henry VII
1485	Caxton prints Malory's *Morte Darthur*
*c.***1490**	*The Floure and the Leafe*; *The Assembly of Ladies*
*c.***1490–1510**	Towneley collection
*c.***1495–1523**	Skelton's *Garlande or Chapelet of Laurell*
1498	Skelton's *Bowge of Court*
*c.***1500**	N-Town collection; *Valentine and Orson*; *The Squyr of Lowe Degree*; *A Gest of Robyn Hood*
1509	Henry VII dies; accession of Henry VIII
*c.***1513**	Bradshaw's *Life of Saint Werburge*
1519	Skelton's *Magnyfycence*
1521–2	*Collyn Clout*
1529	Skelton dies

Notes

Introduction

1 Marx, Preface to *A Critique of Political Economy*, 389.
2 Ibid., 389–90.
3 Arnold, *Culture and Anarchy*, 94 ('individual') and 123 ('right reason').
4 Ibid., 95.
5 The term is still in use, although the most modern instance cited in the *OED* (s.v. 'galantine') is dated 1870.
6 *Two Fifteenth-Century Cookery Books*, 101.
7 *Curye on Inglysch*, 75–6.
8 Marx, *Capital*, 1: 284.
9 Volosinov, 'Concerning the Relationship of the Basis and Superstructures', 65.
10 Ibid.
11 Althusser, 'Ideology and Ideological State Apparatuses', 36.
12 Ibid., 17 (for a list of 'ideological state apparatuses'), 43 ('practices', 'rituals').
13 Ibid., 8.
14 Ibid., 9 ('great'), and 10 ('questions').
15 A number of these are printed in *Curye on Inglysch*, 39–41, and *Two Fifteenth-Century Cookery Books*, 57–64.
16 *Two Fifteenth-Century Cookery Books*, 61.
17 *Curye on Inglysch*, 215.
18 *Two Fifteenth-Century Cookery Books*, 68.
19 Marx, 'Eighteenth Brumaire', 300. For Williams's criticism of this position in others, see, in particular, *Culture and Society*, 272–4.
20 Williams, *Long Revolution*, 69.
21 Williams, 'Base and Superstructure in Marxist Cultural Theory', 35.
22 Williams, *Long Revolution*, 46–7.
23 Salter, *Fourteenth-Century English Poetry*, 9.

Chapter 1 Technology

1 Adams, *Education of Henry Adams*, 361. Further citations identified by page number in the text.
2 For these general points, see White, 'Dynamo and Virgin Reconsidered'.
3 Gimpel, *Medieval Machine*, p. viii. Gimpel includes a valuable chronology of the various mechanical inventions of the Middle Ages (pp. xiii–xviii).
4 White, *Medieval Technology*, 24–8 (stirrup) and 44 (plough).
5 Ibid., 59–60 (harness) and 69–71 (three-field system and yields); Gimpel, *Medieval Machine*, 32–3 (harness) and 39–40 (three-field system).
6 White, *Medieval Technology*, 110.

7 Ibid., 83. See also Gimpel, *Medieval Machine*, 14–15 (on the cam) and 15–28 (on mills).

8 White, *Medieval Technology*, 87.

9 Ibid., 119.

10 Geddes, 'Iron', 179. On the history of the mechanical clock, see also Gimpel, *Medieval Machine*, 147–70, and Frugoni, *Books, Banks, Buttons*, 85–90.

11 Hellinga, 'Printing', 65–6.

12 White, *Medieval Technology*, 42.

13 Cipolla, *Clocks and Culture*, 39, and White, *Medieval Technology*, 103.

14 White, *Medieval Technology*, 79.

15 Ibid., 14.

16 Ibid., 104.

17 Febvre and Martin, *Coming of the Book*, 74.

18 Stock, 'Science, Technology, and Economic Progress', 26.

19 White, 'Dynamo and the Virgin Reconsidered', 63–4.

20 *Rule of Saint Benedict*, 110–11. On the *opus dei*, see 102–3.

21 Theophilus, *De Diversis Artibus*, III.pro (p. 62).

22 This tradition is described in White, 'Iconography of *Temperantia*'.

23 William of Malmesbury, *Gesta Regum Anglorum*, ii.225.6. Cited in White, 'Eilmer of Malmesbury', 60.

24 Auerbach, *Mimesis*, 131.

25 See, for example, the extracts from the 'Rights and Ranks of People' [Rectitudines Singularum Personarum], and its insistence that 'the thegn . . . contribute three things in respect of his land: armed service, and the repairing of fortresses, and work on bridges' [he threo thinc of his lande do: fyrdfæreld and burhbote and brycgeweorc], *English Historical Documents*, 2: 875; *Die Gesetze der Angelsachsen*, 1: 444. For this standard view, see Stephenson, *Mediaeval Feudalism*.

26 Reynolds, *Fiefs and Vassals*, 362 ('allowed') and 394 ('fugitive'). On the complexity of feudalism in England and its law, see ibid., 323–95.

27 Bumke, *Concept of Knighthood*, esp. 115–20.

28 White, *Medieval Technology*, 2.

29 Keen, *Chivalry*, 23.

30 See *Carmen de Hastingae Proelio*, ll. 289–407.

31 *Chanson de Roland*, cxli, ll. 1877–8.

32 White, *Medieval Technology*, 36–7.

33 *Gesta Normannorum Ducum*, vii.14 (166).

34 William of Poitiers, *Histoire de Guillaume le Conquérant*, II.16 (186).

35 *Two of the Saxon Chronicles*, 1: 199 ('D'); *Anglo-Saxon Chronicle*, 199.

36 The *Abingdon Chronicle* breaks off, poignantly, just after describing Harold's victory at Stamford Bridge, as if the Norman Conquest, in this case at least, so quickly overwhelmed Anglo-Saxon culture that it could not describe its own demise. See *Norman Conquest*, 70–1, and *Two of the Saxon Chronicles*, 1: 198.

37 Poole, *From Domesday Book to Magna Carta*, 253.

38 It is as such writing that these continuations are anthologized in *Early Middle English*, ed. Bennett and Smithers, 201–12.

39 Strohm, 'Origin and Meaning'.

40 See Kay, *Chansons de geste in the Age of Romance*.

41 Auerbach, *Mimesis*, 121.

42 See Hanning, *Individual in Twelfth-Century Romance*.

43 Chrétien de Troyes, *Chevalier au lion*, ll. 809–21, *Yvain*, 291–2. Further quotations are identified by line number in the text.

44 Hanning, *Individual in Twelfth-Century Romance*, 53. On love in *Yvain*, see ibid., 118–22.

45 Lagamon, *Brut*, ll. 10669–79. Further citations identified by line number in the text.

46 Kay, Chansons de geste *in the Age of Romance*, 5–6.

47 Crane, *Insular Romance*, 6.

48 For the date, see *Ywain and Gawain*, p. lviii.

49 White, *Medieval Technology*, 78.

50 *King Horn*, ll. 227–30, 243–50.

51 *MED*, s.vv. 'knighthode n.', 'worshipe n.'.

52 White, *Medieval Technology*, 57–69 (for quoted phrase, see 57).

53 Ibid., 64–5.

54 Ibid., 69–78.

55 On the importance of largesse to the 'lesser knighthood', see Keen, *Chivalry*, 28–30.

56 Duby advances the argument that the 'etiquette that governed court life' was an elaborate 'game' designed to 'control' knights, *The Three Orders*, 302–4.

57 *Floris and Blancheflour*, l. 1047.

58 *Havelok the Dane*, 2795–7; 2798–801; 2808–9.

59 Jameson, *Political Unconscious*, 118–19.

60 Pearsall and Cunningham, 'Introduction' to *Auchinleck Manuscript* (facsimile).

61 Loomis, 'Chaucer and the Auchinleck MS', 111.

62 On the *Tale of Melibee*, see chapter 5, 113–14.

63 Pearsall, *Canterbury Tales*, 165.

64 Kean, *Chaucer and the Making of English Poetry*, 1: 9 ('plain and easy') and, more generally, 1: 1–23; Brewer, 'English and European Traditions', 15 ('tap-root') and 1–15 more generally; Spearing, *Medieval to Renaissance Poetry*, 35 ('biting the hand').

65 Brewer, 'English and European Traditions', 16–30.

66 Gower, *Confessio Amantis*, 1.288. Further citations identified by book and line number in the text.

67 On the 'vital role' played by those romances told within the poems' confessional frame in 'holding the work together', see Dimmick, ' "Reding of Romance" ', 128.

68 Schlauch, *English Medieval Literature and its Social Foundations*, 102.

69 Jameson, *Political Unconscious*, 118.

70 On the various explanations for the fourteenth-century efflorescence of alliterative poetry, see Chism, *Alliterative Revivals*, esp. 16–40. On the extent to which the poems of the 'alliterative revival' are inherently part of a larger continuum of alliterative practice (much of it in prose), see Hanna, 'Alliterative Poetry', esp. 489–97, and Salter, 'Alliterative Modes and Affiliations in the Fourteenth Century'.

71 See *Sir Gawain and the Green Knight*, ll. 1105–21. Further citations identified by line number in the text.

72 A subtle but still representative defence of Gawain's 'integrity' is Burrow, 'Honour and Shame'.

73 *Alliterative Morte Arthur*, ll. 4260–1. Further citations identified by line number in the text.

74 On the 'tragic' mode of this text, see Simpson, *Reform and Cultural Revolution*, 106–10.

75 For an incisive discussion of Malory's manipulation of his sources, see Benson, *Malory's Morte Darthur*. On the precision and importance of Malory's language, see Lambert, *Malory: Style and Vision*, and Mann, *Narrative of Distance*.

76 Malory, *Works*, 3: 1259. Further citations identified by volume and page number in the text.

77 For a more extensive account of Malory's worries about chivalric ethics, and the more positive prospects he wrings from these doubts, see Cannon, 'Malory's Crime'.

78 White, 'Cultural Climates and Technological Advance', 226.

79 Lyall, 'Materials: The Paper Revolution', 12.

80 Pearsall, 'English Romance in the Fifteenth Century', 74–5.

81 Ibid., 58; emphasis mine.

82 For a discussion of these romances, see Cooper, 'Counter-Romance'. On the complexity of political affiliation in this period, see MacFarlane, 'The Wars of the Roses'. On Malory, in particular, in relation to civil war, see Riddy, 'Contextualizing *Le Morte Darthur*', and Cannon, 'Malory's Crime', 163–70.

83 Pearsall, 'English Romance in the Fifteenth Century', 66 ('nostalgia'), 71 ('obsolescence').

84 See *OED*, s.v. 'technology'.

85 See Hopkins, *Sinful Knights*.

86 Foucault, *Technologies of the Self*, 27.

87 Augustine, *Confessions*, X.iii; *Confessions*, trans. Chadwick, 180–1 (I have slightly altered Chadwick's translation here).

88 Foucault understands confession as 'one of the West's most highly valued techniques for producing truth', *History of Sexuality*, Vol. 1, 59.

89 'Fourth Lateran Council, Constitutions', 245.

90 The earlier rule for anchorites on which *Ancrene Wisse* draws heavily, the *De Institutione Inclusarum* (1160–2), offers no such instruction. For this text, see Aelred of Rievaulx, 'A Rule of Life for a Recluse'. There are also two Middle English translations of this text, one of the fourteenth, the other of the fifteenth century (see *Aelred of Rievaulx's De Institutione Inclusarum*).

91 A good summary of the text's dissemination is given in *Anchoritic Spirituality*, 41–2. The definitive treatment is in Dobson, *Origins*, 286–301.

92 *Ancrene Wisse*, 1: 129; *Ancrene Wisse*, trans. White, 157–8. Further quotations will be cited from the page numbers of this edition and this translation in the text.

93 Foucault, *History of Sexuality*, Vol. 1, 60.

94 The definitive work on the self in *Ancrene Wisse* is Georgianna, *Solitary Self*. See also chapter 4 ('The Place of the Self') in Cannon, *Grounds of English Literature*, 139–71.

95 Augustine, *Confessions*, X.iii; *Confessions*, trans. Chadwick, 180.

96 Nietzsche, *On the Genealogy of Morals*, 517 ('sting of conscience') and 520 ('internalization').

97 *Ayenbite of Inwyt*, 5.

98 For these tabulations, see Lewis and McIntosh, *Descriptive Guide*, 1, and Pearsall, *Canterbury Tales*, 8.

99 *MWME* 7: 2269.

100 *Pricke of Conscience*, ll. 330–5; 340–5.

101 The *Manuel des pechiez* is printed as a parallel text in Mannyng, *Handlyng Synne*, ed. Furnivall.

102 All Mannyng's narratives are listed (and those original to him identified) in Appendix II (381–7) of Mannyng, *Handlyng Synne*, ed. Sullens.

103 Mannyng, *Handlyng Synne*, ed. Sullens, ll. 8951–8. Further citations will be taken from this edition and identified by line number in the text.

104 On the complex use to which Mannyng puts narrative, see Miller, 'Displaced Souls, Idle Talk, Spectacular Scenes'.

105 See chapter 3, 98–9.

106 Mann, *Chaucer and Medieval Estates Satire*, 16; emphasis Mann's. See also 3–7 (on estates satire as a literary form) and 7–10 (on 'social stereotypes').

107 Patterson, *Chaucer and the Subject of History*, 368. On the Pardoner as the 'subject of confession', see ibid., 374–86 and 397–406. On the literature of misogyny or anti-feminism, see Mann, *Feminizing Chaucer*, 39–45. On Chaucer's use of that literature in a variety of

texts (including the Wife of Bath's Prologue), see ibid., 45–69. For a convenient collection of these texts in translation, see *Women Defamed, Women Defended*.

108 This point is Jill Mann's in *Feminizing Chaucer*, 63–4.
109 Patterson, *Chaucer and the Subject of History*, 313.
110 Dinshaw, *Chaucer's Sexual Poetics*, 126.
111 The famous claim for printing's importance is Elizabeth L. Eisenstein's: 'My thesis, briefly stated, is that the advent of printing was, quite literally, an *epoch-making* event', 'The Advent of Printing', 19; emphasis Eisenstein's.
112 For a representative instance of such pronouncement, see Blake, 'Manuscript to Print', 403.
113 Febvre and Martin, *Coming of the Book*, 46–7 and 74.
114 Ibid., 75–6.
115 Hellinga, 'Printing', 69.
116 Ibid., 73–4.
117 For a cogent summary of the complexities of early modern printing practice, see the seminal essay by McKenzie, 'Printers of the Mind'.
118 On these details, see Meale, ' "The Hoole Book" ' (esp. 7).
119 Blake, *Caxton and his World*, 46–7.
120 On the chronology of Caxton's early printings (and the difficulties involved in establishing the priority and sequence of extant books), see Hellinga, *Caxton in Focus*, 80–3.
121 Blake, 'Spread of Printing in English', 73, and Blake, *Caxton and his World*, 76.
122 For a comprehensive list, see Blake, *Caxton and his World*, 224–39.
123 Ibid., 35.
124 Blake, 'Spread of Printing in English', 67.
125 *Prologues and Epilogues of William Caxton*, 107.
126 Ibid., 109.
127 Ibid., 90.
128 Ibid., 91.
129 The discovery of the manuscript of the *Morte* led to a comprehensive edition, by Eugène Vinaver, which insisted that Malory did not write a unified work but 'eight separate romances', gathered together by Caxton as the *Morte* (1: xxxix). This view no longer holds sway and was dealt its keenest blows by Brewer, ' "The Hoole Book" ', and Benson, *Malory's Morte Darthur*.
130 Benjamin, 'Work of Art in the Age of Mechanical Reproduction', 236.
131 Blake, *Caxton and his World*, 70.
132 See Eisenstein, *Printing Press as an Agent of Change*, 114–16.
133 The story of this reclamation is well told in Matthews, *Making of Middle English*.

Chapter 2 Insurgency

1 For a gripping account of the Rising, in much more detail, see Justice, *Writing and Rebellion*, 1–4. See also Keen, *England in the Later Middle Ages*, 266–73, Harriss, *Shaping the Nation*, 229–34, and the helpful 'chronology of the revolt' in *Peasants' Revolt of 1381*, 36–44.
2 Walsingham, *Historia Anglicana*, 1: 454; *Peasants' Revolt of 1381*, 132.
3 Keen, *England in the Later Middle Ages*, 272.
4 Walsingham, *Historia Anglicana*, 2: 32; *Peasants' Revolt of 1381*, 374.
5 Five of these letters are preserved in *Knighton's Chronicle*, 222–5. A sixth is preserved in Walsingham, *Historia Anglicana*, 2: 33–4. All six are re-edited in Justice, *Writing and Rebellion*, 13–15, as well as Green, 'John Ball's Letters', 193–5, but they are most readily accessible in *Peasants' Revolt of 1381*, 380–3.

6 *Peasants' Revolt of 1381*, 380–1.

7 Justice, *Writing and Rebellion*, 29–30. On *schedulae* more generally, see Hudson, 'Lollard Book Production', 134–5, and Scase, '"Strange and Wonderful Bills"'. On the vogue of such bills in the fifteenth century, see Scattergood, *Politics and Poetry in the Fifteenth Century*, 25.

8 Marx, *Capital*, 1: 382–3. For the statute itself, and a translation, see *Statutes of the Realm*, 1: 307–9.

9 See Keen, *England in the Later Middle Ages*, 265–7. Keen describes the revolt of 1381 as 'the climax of a crisis of confidence in government which was largely generated by failures in war' (259).

10 Hudson, *Premature Reformation*, 383.

11 On 'Wyclif in the Rising', see Justice, *Writing and Rebellion*, 75–101 (for the quoted phrase see 90).

12 Kane, 'Some Fourteenth-Century "Political" Poems', 82 ('unhistorical', 'anachronistic'), 83 ('general principle'), 84 ('protest', 'dissent'), 89 ('revolutionary'), 91 ('inadequacy').

13 See Robbins, 'Middle English Poems of Protest', his 'Dissent in Middle English Literature', and his section on 'Poems Dealing with Contemporary Conditions' in *MWME* 5: 1385–536.

14 Kane, 'Some Fourteenth-Century "Political" Poems', 84.

15 On 'Piers Plowman in the Rising', see Justice, *Writing and Rebellion*, 102–39. See also this chapter, 65.

16 *Historical Poems of the XIVth and XVth Centuries*, 328. The text can be found in Cambridge, Trinity College, MS 108. A lengthier version of such a poem from about the same period is the 'Ten Abuses'; see *An Old English Miscellany*, 185.

17 See Markus, *Saeculum*, esp. 22–44.

18 On 'social and spiritual complaints' more generally, with particular attention to the 'abuses of the age genre', see Coleman, *English Literature in History*, 60–7.

19 *Historical Poems of the XIVth and XVth Centuries*, 144. This poem appears in Cambridge, St John's College, MS 37, preceded by eight lines of Latin verse which the Middle English I have quoted may be said to paraphrase. There are then two more lines of Latin and five more lines of Middle English attacking 'holy church'. On this 'complaint tradition in lyrics', see Wenzel, *Preachers, Poets and the Early English Lyric*, 174–208. For comments on a version of the poem I quote, see ibid., 189.

20 *MWME* 5: 1432.

21 Moffat, 'The Recovery of Worcester Cathedral MS F.174'.

22 I quote this text and its translation from Brehe, 'Reassembling the First Worcester Fragment', 530–1.

23 For a representative and careful reading in this vein, see Lerer, 'Old English and its Afterlife', 22–6.

24 For a more extensive version of this reading, see Cannon, *Grounds of English Literature*, 34–40.

25 On the 'reality of the grievances the poet isolates for comment', see Scattergood, *Politics and Poetry in the Fifteenth Century*, 351–2. See also Scattergood, 'Authority and Resistance', 188–9.

26 On the poem's tendency towards 'abstraction', see Newhauser, 'Historicity and Complaint', esp. 216.

27 *Song of the Husbandman*, ll. 9–12. For this poem, see also *Historical Poems of the XIVth and XVth Centuries*, 7–9.

28 *Punctuation Poem*, II. For two other such poems, see *Secular Lyrics of the XIVth and XVth Centuries*, 101–2.

29 *Jack Upland*, ll. 191–3. Further citations will be identified by line number in the text.

30 *Friar Daw's Reply*, ll. 71–2. Further citations from this poem will be identified by line number in the text.

31 *Upland's Rejoinder*, l. 217.

32 *The Insurrection and Earthquake*, ll. 13–14. Further citations identified by line number in the text.

33 The earthquake was also reported in the *Fasciculi Zizaniorum* (where it is linked directly to Lollardy). See *Peasants' Revolt of 1381*, 376–7. *Knighton's Chronicle* reports an earthquake, not in 1381, but in 'xii Kalendas Iunii' [21 May 1382] (242–3).

34 The text I print here is a hybrid of the normalized edition in *The Peasants' Revolt of 1381* (383) and Green's edition ('John Ball's Letters', 194), which, rightly to my mind, sets out the rhyming lines of this 'letter' as verse.

35 *Historical Poems of the XIVth and XVth Centuries*, p. xlii. Robbins here compares the poem in the letter to another 'abuses' poem which uses 'now' repeatedly ('Now pride ys yn pris, / Now covetyse ys wyse, / Now lechery ys schameles', etc.).

36 The phrase 'critical realism' is associated with Georg Lukács, who opposed it, negatively, to 'socialist realism'. I use it here to pick up Lukács's more general observation, that 'good realistic detail often in itself implies a judgment'; *The Meaning of Contemporary Realism*, 75. For a trenchant discussion of the 'realism of complaint' in late Middle English literature, see Coleman, *English Literature in History*, 67–71.

37 For an important account of some of these conventions in medieval literature, see, in particular, Muscatine, *Chaucer and the French Tradition*, 58–67.

38 See *The Simonie*, ll. 373–420 (on the famine) and 421–44 (on the insurgencies). Further citations identified by line number in the text. See McKisack, *Fourteenth Century*, 49–50 (on the famine) and 64–7 (on the insurgency).

39 Pearsall, 'The Timelessness of *The Simonie*', 63.

40 See Salter, '*Piers Plowman* and *The Simonie*'.

41 See especially Langland, *Piers Plowman*, 6.199–273, 13.422–60, 14.97–332, 20.1–50. On the general issue, see Pearsall, 'Poverty and Poor People in *Piers Plowman*'.

42 Aers, *Community, Gender, and Individual Identity*, 67. See, also, the whole of this chapter in this same volume on '*Piers Plowman*: Poverty, Work, and Community' (20–72).

43 A great deal of commentary has collected around this passage, but see, in particular, Shepherd, 'Poverty in *Piers Plowman*', 175; Justice, *Writing and Rebellion*, 242–4; Kim, 'Hunger, Need, and the Politics of Poverty', 147–50.

44 On 'need' in *Piers* and its complications, see Mann, 'Nature of Need Revisited'.

45 Muscatine, *Poetry and Crisis in the Age of Chaucer*, 82. The passage Muscatine specifies here is 4.47–109.

46 See Kinney, 'Temper of Fourteenth-Century English Verse of Complaint' (esp. 89).

47 Aers, '*Vox Populi* and the Literature of 1381', 438–9. The letters react to the B-text (usually dated *c*.1378), that is, a version of the text that does not include the particular passage I have focused on. For the relevant passages in the letters, see *The Peasants' Revolt of 1381*, 381 and 382.

48 'Lollard Disendowment Bill', ll. 20–1.

49 Lawton, 'Lollardy and the *Piers Plowman* Tradition', 793.

50 *Pierce the Ploughman's Crede*, l. 473. Further citations identified by line number in the text.

51 For a fuller discussion of the cultural context of these plays see chapter 4, 141–2.

52 On the Lollard implications of the form of the mystery plays, see Simpson, *Reform and Cultural Revolution*, 538. On 'priesthood of all believers', see Hudson, *Premature Reformation*, 276 and 325.

53 The Towneley collection is named for the family who owned the manuscript containing these plays from the seventeenth to the nineteenth centuries, but the plays are thought to have been originally connected with Wakefield, in Yorkshire. See Meredith, 'Towneley Cycle', esp. 142–5.

54 'The First Shepherds' Play', ll. 10–11. Further citations from this play will be by line number in the text.

55 'The Second Shepherds' Play', ll. 16–18. Further citations identified by line number in the text.

56 See Keen, *England in the Later Middle Ages*, 19–21 and 500–1 (on 'maintenance'), and 9 and 158 (on 'purveyance').

57 On the subversive tendencies of this substitution, see Beckwith, *Signifying God*, 64–5.

58 For the general category, see Keen, *Outlaws of Medieval Legend*, esp. 1–11.

59 Hilton, 'Origins of Robin Hood', 208.

60 See chapter 1, 18–20.

61 *Gamelyn*, l. 895. Further citations identified by line number in the text.

62 On *Gamelyn* and the Robin Hood tradition, see Gray, 'The Robin Hood Poems', 12, and Holt, 'Origins and Audience of the Ballads', 223.

63 For the phrase 'funhouse mirror', see Chism, 'Robin Hood', 16. On the probability that the Robin Hood stories were fundamentally aristocratic in origin, see Holt, 'Origins and Audience of the Ballads'.

64 *A Gest of Robyn Hode*, ll. 53–6. Further citations identified by line number in the text.

65 *Robin Hood and the Monk*, l. 203.

66 *Robin Hood and the Potter*, ll. 135–6. Further citations identified by line number in the text.

67 On the length and complexity of the whole of this tradition, see Knight, *Robin Hood*.

68 *A Trade Policy*, l. 79. Further citations identified by line number in the text.

69 Scattergood, *Politics and Poetry*, 90–5 (on the *Libelle*) and 370–1 (on *Trade Policy*). On the *Libelle*, see also chapter 3, 95–6.

70 See *Statutes of the Realm* 2, 403–7 (Anno 3° Edwardi IV, AD 1463, c.1–4). Robbins, 'On Dating a Middle English Moral Poem'. Cited in Scattergood, *Politics and Poetry*, 377 n. 17.

71 For this poem, see *English Lyrics of the XIIIth Century*, 133–4.

72 For the contents of this manuscript, usually dated *c.*1330–40, and a description, see Ker, *Facsimile of British Museum MS. Harley 2253*, pp. ix–xvi and xxi–xxiii, and Revard, 'Scribe and Provenance'.

73 Scattergood, 'Authority and Resistance', 194.

74 *Satire on the Retinues of the Great*, ll. 33–5. Further citations identified by line number in the text.

75 Scattergood, 'Authority and Resistance', 197.

76 *Satire on the Consistory Courts*, l. 61. Further citations identified by line number in the text.

77 Skelton, *Collyn Clout*, ll. 1 and 5. Further citations identified by line number in the text.

78 For a history of the genre in the form of a bibliography, see Mann, *Chaucer and Medieval Estates Satire*, 297–312. On *The Simonie*, see this volume, 310.

79 The influential text here was Manly, *Some New Light on Chaucer*.

80 See Mann, *Chaucer and Medieval Estates Satire*, 86–105.

81 Ibid., 197 ('consistent') and 198 ('the presentation'). For this last point Mann also cites Woolf, 'Chaucer as a Satirist', 152.

82 Patterson, *Chaucer and the Subject of History*, 246.

83 *Wynnere and Wastoure*, l. 36. Further citations identified by line number in the text.

84 On the influence of *Winner and Waster* on *Piers Plowman*, see Hussey, 'Langland's Reading of Alliterative Poetry', and Turville-Petre, *Alliterative Revival*, 4–5 and 32–3.

85 On the way this passage convenes a potentially insurgent class, see Justice, *Writing and Rebellion*, 137–8. In the C-text Langland substitutes 'tho men' for the first use of 'communes' and 'knighthood' for the second ('Thenne cam ther a kyng, knyghthede hym ladde, / Myght of tho men made hym to regne. / And thenn cam Kynde Wytt and clerkus he made / And Conscience and Kynde Wit and knyghthed togedres . . .', C Pro. 139–42). On this change as a possible response to the rising of 1381, 'suppressing the agency of commoners', see Crane, 'Writing Lesson', 211–13.

86 See Mann, *Chaucer and Medieval Estates Satire*, 68–73. See also Kirk, 'Langland's Plowman and the Recreation of Fourteenth-Century Religious Metaphor'.

87 Middleton, 'William Langland's "Kynde Name" ', 16.

88 Green, 'John Ball's Letters', 193–4.

89 Justice, *Writing and Rebellion*, 137. See, more generally on this point, Justice's whole chapter on '*Piers Plowman* in the Rising', 102–39.

90 See n. 85 above and, also, Kerby-Fulton, 'Langland and the Bibliographic Ego', 86–8, and Middleton, 'Acts of Vagrancy', 286–8.

91 See Hudson, 'A Lollard Sect Vocabulary?', esp. 16–17.

92 *The Plowman's Tale*, l. 48. Further citations by line number in the text.

93 *Statutes of the Realm*, 2: 126 (Anno 2° Henrici IV AD 1400–1, *c*.15).

94 Strohm, *Empty Throne*, 43. For a nuanced and detailed reading of this action see this same volume, 40–5.

95 Simpson, *Reform and Cultural Revolution*, 246–7.

96 Justice, *Writing and Rebellion*, 24.

97 Ibid., 30. For a thorough account of the 'languages of record' in England from 1066 to 1307 (and still largely applicable until the fifteenth century), see Clanchy, *From Memory to Written Record*, 197–223.

98 *Selections from English Wycliffite Writings*, 107.

99 Hudson, *Premature Reformation*, 383. See also Hudson, 'Wyclif and the English Language'.

100 Hudson, 'Lollardy', 142 n. 5. Cited in Watson, 'Censorship and Cultural Change', 831 n. 22.

101 Hudson, *Premature Reformation*, 57.

102 Watson, 'Censorship and Cultural Change', 831 ('self-censorship') and 832 ('sharp decline').

103 Berndt, 'Linguistic Situation in England', esp. 370–1.

104 Berndt, 'Period of the Final Decline of French', 342–3.

105 Robert of Gloucester, *Metrical Chronicle*, ll. 7537–43.

106 Berndt, 'Period of the Final Decline of French', 355. See also Fisher, 'Chancery and the Emergence of Standard Written English'.

107 Berndt, 'Period of the Final Decline of French', 351.

108 For the English text of the proclamation, see *Early Middle English Texts*, 7–9.

109 On the complex politics of the use of English in this proclamation, see Machan, *English in the Middle Ages*, 21–69.

110 Mannyng, *Handlyng Synne*, ed. Sullens, l. 10804.

111 Usk, *Testament of Love*, Pro. 5–27.

112 For these borrowings, see *Chaucer's Dream Poetry*, 3–70.

113 Hoccleve, *Regiment of Princes*, l. 4978.

114 Lydgate, *Life of Our Lady*, 2.1635–6.

115 Lydgate, *Troy Book*, 3.4242–3.

Chapter 3 Statecraft

1 Weber, 'The Profession and Vocation of Politics', 310–11.
2 See D'Entrèves, *Notion of the State*, esp. 9–10.
3 *OED*, s.vv. 'statecraft' and 'craft n1.', I, 2a.
4 Langland's allegory grows thin at this point, since the mice and rats harm men (rather than cats or each other): mice eat 'men's grain' and rats destroy their clothes ('For many mennes malt we mees wolde destruye, / And also ye route of ratons rende mennes clothes', Pro. 198–9).
5 Saul, *Richard II*, 20 (for the phrase I quote and a general version of this political scene). For these readings, see Langland, *Vision of Piers Plowman: A Complete Edition of the B-text*, ed. Schmidt, 412–13, and Langland, *Piers Plowman: An Edition of the C-text*, ed. Pearsall, 38 (n. to Pro. 165–215).
6 For a general account of this volatile period, see Harriss, *Shaping the Nation*, 441–4.
7 For this legislation, see *Statutes of the Realm*, 1: 35 (Anno 3 Ed.I [1275], *c*.34); 2: 9 (Anno 2 Ric.II [1378], Stat.1, *c*.5); 2: 59 (Anno 12 Ric.II [1388], *c*.11). Cited in Simpson, 'Constraints of Satire', 17 (nn. 14–16).
8 For the relevant passages of the *Constitutions*, see Watson, 'Censorship and Cultural Change', 827–9, nn. 13–15 (I quote from 828 n. 15). Watson takes his translation from Foxe, *Acts and Monuments*, 3: 242–9.
9 On the 'failure' of the *Constitutions*, see Kerby-Fulton, *Books Under Suspicion*, 15–20 and 397–401. In this same volume Kerby-Fulton also describes the ways in which an exploratory theology flourished in 'revelatory writing' in England, even after the *Constitutions*.
10 On William's claim, see *English Historical Documents*, 2: 228–9 (for the account of William of Jumièges) and 231 (for the account of William of Poitiers).
11 See chapter 1, 15.
12 On the method and cultural force of this 'Norman plantation', see Knowles, *Monastic Order*, 100–27 (for the phrase 'overseas culture', see 124).
13 For the classical poems, see *Anglo-Saxon Minor Poems*, 16–26. For the incipits of the passages in rhythmic prose, see ibid., p. xxxiii n. 1. For the texts themselves, see *Two of the Saxon Chronicles*, 1: 114–15, 119–21, 123, 143, 187, 201, 210, 212, 220–1, 239.
14 *Anglo-Saxon Minor Poems*, 25.
15 *Two of the Saxon Chronicles*, 1: 201.
16 *Early Middle English Verse and Prose*, p. xii. For an analysis of this early period along these general lines, see Shepherd, 'Early Middle English'.
17 Strauss, *Persecution and the Art of Writing*, 25. Strohm, *Politique*, 147.
18 For the text of the appeal, see *A Book of London English*, 22–31.
19 Strohm, 'Politics and Poetics', 84. For a detailed account of Usk's factional involvements and London politics in this period, see ibid., 85–90.
20 Usk, *Testament of Love*, I.i.18. Further citations will be identified by book, chapter and line number in Shoaf's edition of this text.
21 Boethius, *Consolation of Philosophy*, 45 (I.pr4); *Philosophiae Consolationis Libri Quinque*, 13. The complexities of this factionalism are sketched out by Boethius in this prose section of book 1 (*Consolation*, 40–6, *Philosophiae Consolationis Libri Quinque*, 10–14). On Boethius and the importance of the *Consolation* more generally, see Chadwick, *Boethius*.
22 This passage is singled out for praise by C.S. Lewis in, perhaps, the most appreciative assessment Usk ever received (Lewis, *Allegory of Love*, 230). In this one instance, I have followed the punctuation in Skeat's edition (see I.iii.40–3) rather than Shoaf's.
23 Strohm, 'Politics and Poetics', 103.
24 Patterson, *Censorship and Interpretation*, 18.
25 Lewis, *Allegory of Love*, 223.

26 Simpson, 'Ethics and Interpretation', 83–4.

27 On these proverbs in the key passage, see Mann, ' "He Knew Nat Catoun" ', 55–8.

28 For a discussion of this relationship as a version of 'the court', see Fradenburg, 'The Manciple's Servant Tongue'.

29 *MED*, s.v. 'fals adj.', 1a and 4.

30 *Testimony of William Thorpe*, ll. 623–32. Further citations will be identified by line number in the text.

31 *Two Wycliffite Texts*, pp. xlv–liii.

32 Steiner has shown how Thorpe's manipulation of the techniques of legal record allows his testament to become a 'written transcript . . . of the sermon for which he was arrested!'; *Documentary Culture and the Making of Medieval English Literature*, 237. On the text's relationship to teaching and, more broadly, the intellectual work of the universities, see Copeland, *Pedagogy, Intellectuals, and Dissent in the Later Middle Ages*, 191–219.

33 *Two Wycliffite Texts*, p. lvi.

34 *Richard the Redeless*, I.38. Further citations will be identified by passus number and line number in the text.

35 *Mum and the Sothsegger*, l. 868. Further citations will be identified by line number in the text.

36 For more detailed comments on this poem's 'strategy', see Simpson, 'Constraints of Satire', 21–4.

37 Strohm, *Politique*, 206.

38 On this period, see, in particular, Keen, *England in the Later Middle Ages*, 464–74. On the difficulty of identifying 'Yorkists' and 'Lancastrians', see MacFarlane, 'The Wars of the Roses'.

39 On Fortescue's political troubles and its relation to his writings, see especially Strohm, *Politique*, 134–54.

40 See Field, *Life and Times*, 105–25 (on the 1450s) and 146–7 (on the turbulent years 1468–70). The 'Winchester Manuscript' of the *Morte* concludes: 'For this book was ended the ninth yere of the reygne of Kyng Edward the Fourth [that is, 1469–70], by Syr Thomas Maleoré, Knyght, as Jesu helpe hym for Hys grete myght, as he is the servaunt of Jesu bothe day and nyght'; Malory, *Works*, 3: 1260. Further citations identified by volume and page number in the text.

41 Charles d'Orléans, *Fortunes Stabilnes*, ll. 5632–3. Further citations identified by line number in the text.

42 On the circumstances of his imprisonment and how it may have shaped his 'intellectual work and his poetry' (44), see Askins, 'The Brothers Orléans and their Keepers'.

43 Ashby, *A Prisoner's Reflections*, ll. 123–5. Further citations identified by line number in the text.

44 Brentano, 'Western Civilization: The Middle Ages', 552.

45 Kantorowicz, *King's Two Bodies*, 249.

46 *The Luve-Ron*, l. 4. Further citations identified by line number in the text. The poem can also be found in *English Lyrics of the XIIIth Century*, 68–74.

47 See Woolf, 'The Theme of Christ the Lover-Knight in Medieval English Literature'.

48 *The Early English Carols*, p. cxxiv. For a definition of the carol, see p. xxiii. On the role of the Franciscans in helping to develop the genre of the religious 'carol', see pp. cxxi–cxxviii.

49 Kantorowicz, *King's Two Bodies*, 255.

50 *Poems of Laurence Minot*, IV.49–50. Further citations will be identified by poem number and line number in the text.

51 See *MWME* 5: 1412–13, and Moore, 'Lawrence Minot'.

52 *A Song of Lewes*, ll. 25–9 (the last two lines are abbreviated for this and all but the first two stanzas). On the political context of the poem, see Scattergood, 'Authority and Resistance', 182–3.

53 On the historical background here, see ibid., 171–4.

54 *The Flemish Insurrection*, ll. 25–32.

55 *The Execution of Simon Fraser*, ll. 2–3. Further citations identified by line number in the text.

56 On the poem's historical context, but also on the way it 'concentrates unremittingly on the degrading details of . . . punishment', as well as the kinds of 'anxiety' such 'triumphalism' may generate, see Scattergood, 'Authority and Resistance', 174–7 (quoted phrases at 175 ['concentrates'] and 177 ['anxiety']).

57 On the songs or 'tags', see *MWME* 5: 1400–1.

58 *Chronicle of Pierre de Langtoft*, 2: 236. Further citations identified by volume and page number in the text.

59 See Turville-Petre, 'Politics and Poetry', 8–9; *Chronicle of Pierre de Langtoft*, 2: viii–ix.

60 *Chronicle of Pierre de Langtoft*, 2: 250–1.

61 For the songs, see Mannyng, *Chronicle*, II.6423–8, 6599–604, 6683–8, 6711–16, 6735–6, 6765–78, 6813–26, 8063–8. These are also discussed by Sullens in this edition, 58–60.

62 Turville-Petre, 'Politics and Poetry', 8.

63 Ibid., 9.

64 Gower, *In Praise of Peace*, l. 12. Further citations identified by line number in the text.

65 For descriptions of the poems, see *MWME* 5: 1426–7. The second is not available in modern editions, but for the first, see *Historical Poems of the XIVth and XVth Centuries*, 74–7.

66 *Early English Carols*, 289. Greene calls this poem the 'Agincourt Carol' (439).

67 *The Five Dogs of London*, ll. 13–14.

68 The description of the poem's display comes from Bale's *Chronicle* [1544], as cited in *Historical Poems of the XIVth and XVth Centuries*, 355. On the poem's dissemination, see also Scattergood, *Politics and Poetry*, 26.

69 For a detailed decoding of the complicated symbolism of this poem, see Scattergood, *Politics and Poetry*, 184–6. For the poem, see *Historical Poetry of the XIVth and XVth Centuries*, 210–15. Other poems in this volume celebrating Yorkist victories include *The Battle of Towton* (215–18) and *The Battle of Barnet* (226–7).

70 *Early English Carols*, 290–1.

71 For these poems, see Lydgate, *Minor Poems, Part 2*, 613–22 (*Title and Pedigree*) and 624–30 (*Ballade*).

72 *Early English Carols*, 291–2.

73 *On the Recovery of the Throne by Edward IV*, 272. This poem has no line numbers in Wright's edition, so this and all further citations from this poem are identified by page number.

74 See Scase, *Reginald Pecock*, esp. 80–95. On the progressive interweaving of Lollard concerns and orthodox writings in both Latin and English, see Ghosh, *Wycliffite Heresy*.

75 Love, *Mirror of the Blessed Life of Jesus Christ*, p. xv (for translation and discussion of this note) and 7 (for the note).

76 Ibid., 90–4 (on confession) and 150–4 (on the Eucharist). Further citations will be identified by page number in the text.

77 See Knapp, *Bureaucratic Muse*, esp. 12–13 and chapters 1 (17–43) and 3 (77–106).

78 Hoccleve, *Regiment of Princes*, ll. 1023–8. Further citations identified by line number in the text.

79 See Burrow, 'Autobiographical Poetry in the Middle Ages'.

80 For such an analysis of the *Regiment*, see Perkins, *Hoccleve's Regiment of Princes*, esp. 126–50.

81 Simpson, *Reform and Cultural Revolution*, 212.

82 Pearsall, 'Hoccleve's *Regement of Princes*', 410.

83 Hoccleve, *Remonstrance to John Oldcastle*, ll. 319–20. Further citations identified by line number in the text.

84 Hoccleve, *Balade, After King Richard II's Bones Were Brought to Westminster*, ll. 33–4.

85 See, especially, Hoccleve, *Thomas Hoccleve's Complaint*, ll. 36–210.

86 Hoccleve, *Dialogue with a Friend*, ll. 554–7.

87 *Libelle of Englyshe Polycye*, l. 1144. Further citations identified by line number in the text.

88 On the poem's authorship, see ibid., pp. xxxviii–xlvi.

89 For a detailed discussion of the historical context of this poem, see Scattergood, *Politics and Poetry*, 90–5.

90 Bracton, *De Legibus et Consuetudinibus Angliae*, 2: 305. For the original, see *Institutes of Justinian*, 8 (I. 2. 6). A version of this commonplace introduces the beast fable in the Prologue to *Piers Plowman*: 'Precepta Regis sunt nobis vincula legis!' (the precepts of the king are for us the law's fetters), Pro. 145. On the concept of the Prince as the 'animate law' and its evolution, see Kantorowicz, *King's Two Bodies*, 127–58.

91 *Secretum Secretorum*, 74.

92 Ibid., p. ix. On this text and its importance to English literature, see especially Ferster, *Fictions of Advice*, 39–54.

93 For the various dedications, see Gower, *Confessio Amantis*, Pro. 24*–33* (Richard II) and Pro. 83–92. Further citations will be identified by book and line number in the text. See also Simpson, *Sciences and the Self*, 280 and 289–96.

94 Simpson, *Sciences and the Self*, 284.

95 Ibid., 281.

96 Lydgate, *Fall of Princes*, 1.426–7. Further citations identified by book and line number in the text.

97 On Lydgate's 'monastic background', see Pearsall, *John Lydgate*, 22–48.

98 Lawton, 'Dullness and the Fifteenth Century', 762.

99 Ibid., 771.

100 Pearsall, *John Lydgate*, 7 ('no poet'), 11 ('uncurious' and 'unselective'), and 241 ('which can easily').

101 Lydgate, *Siege of Thebes*, ll. 160–1. Further citations identified by line number in the text.

102 Pearsall, *John Lydgate*, 156.

103 Patterson, 'Making Identities in Fifteenth-Century England', 89. On the efforts which allowed the French 'to turn the tables on the English' quickly, see Keen, *England in the Later Middle Ages*, 382–93 (phrase quoted from 385).

104 Simpson, *Reform and Cultural Revolution*, 57.

105 Lydgate, *Reson and Sensuallyte*, l. 801. Further citations identified by line number in the text.

106 Lewis, *Allegory of Love*, 277.

107 Fortescue, *Governance of England*, 112. Further citations identified by page number in the text.

108 Ashby, *Active Policy of a Prince*, ll. 417–19. Further citations identified by line number in the text.

109 For this prologue see ibid., 12–13.

110 Greenblatt, *Renaissance Self-Fashioning*, 228. On the increasing importance of such self-interest to politics and political behaviour in the fifteenth century, see Strohm, *Politique*, esp. 4–6, and 116–27.

111 Skelton also wrote a more traditional work of counsel in Latin, the *Speculum Principis* (1501).

112 Skelton, *Magnyfycence*, l. 166. Further citations identified by line number in the text.

Chapter 4 Place

1 Higden, *Polychronicon*, I. lix (2: 158–9).

2 For a convenient summary of these dialects and their features, see Milroy, 'Middle English Dialectology', 172–7.

3 On the relationship between variation and standardization, see ibid., 157–9.

4 *Prologues and Epilogues of William Caxton*, 108.

5 For such a map, see *Fourteenth Century Verse and Prose*, p. viii. For a more nuanced discussion of such 'mappings', see Salter, *Fourteenth-Century English Poetry*, 52–85.

6 *Dan Michel's Ayenbite of Inwyt*, 1.

7 A large number of 'regional texts', including the Minot manuscript, are identified in the 'Plan and Bibliography', *MED*, 10–12.

8 *York Plays*, 10–13 and 39.

9 See Mannyng, *Chronicle*, ed. Sullens, 45–51.

10 For these shelfmarks, see *MWME* 9: 3415–20; for their localization, see 'Plan and Bibliography', *MED*, 12.

11 Dobson, *Origins of Ancrene Wisse*, 154.

12 Tolkien was the first to describe 'AB language', in '*Ancrene Wisse* and *Hali Meithhad*'. Dobson provides a searching account of the implications of Tolkien's description in *Origins of Ancrene Wisse*, 114–26.

13 See Peterson, 'The *Pearl*-poet and John Massey of Cotton, Cheshire', 260–1 and 261 n. 1.

14 I derive this example from Milroy, 'Middle English Dialectology', 189. See also *The Owl and the Nightingale*, ed. Cartlidge, pp. xv–xvi and xl–xliii, and Cartlidge, 'The Linguistic Evidence for the Provenance of *The Owl and the Nightingale*'.

15 Samuels, 'Langland's Dialect', 232–3.

16 Orme, *Medieval Schools*, 53.

17 On monastic schools, see ibid., 266–77; Knowles, *Monastic Order*, 487–92; Knowles, *Religious Orders*, 1: 294–8.

18 Orme, *Medieval Schools*, 55.

19 Ibid., 63–4.

20 Ibid., 68–73.

21 Ibid., 88–97. See also Curtius, *European Literature and the Latin Middle Ages*, 42–5.

22 Although Murphy is describing an earlier period, the curriculum of the grammar school was extraordinarily conservative, and the most detailed account of such exercises is his 'Roman Writing Instruction as Described by Quintilian', esp. 44–53.

23 Curtius, *European Literature and the Latin Middle Ages*, 48–54.

24 On these core texts, and for more detailed summaries, see Mann, ' "He Knew Nat Catoun" ', 44–9. For an English translation of the *Distichs of Cato*, see the parallel text in *Minor Latin Poets*, 585–639, and for the *Fables* of Avianus, see the same volume, 669–749. For the *Eclogue of Theodulus*, see *Ten Latin Schooltexts*, 110–57. For Claudian's *On the Rape of Proserpina*, see *Claudian*, 2: 293–377. For the *Achilleis*, see *Statius*, 2: 508–95.

25 Mann, ' "He Knew Nat Catoun" ', 55.

26 Ibid., 64–6.

27 Ibid., 53. This article details Chaucer's most important uses of these school texts (53–64).

28 On six of the extant versions, see *MWME* 9: 2972–3; on the seventh, a prose translation by Caxton, see *MWME* 3: 787–8.

29 'Great Cato', ll. 149–52 (Latin and Anglo-Norman lines are unnumbered in this edition). Translations of the 'prologue' and short maxims at the beginning of the *Distichs* precede 'Great Cato'.

30 *Dicta Catonis*, 593 (I give a page reference here as this prologue is not lineated). For the Middle English version of these lines, see 'Little Cato', ll. 7–8 ('Little Cato' translates the fifty or so short maxims that precede the distichs themselves).

31 Mann, ' "He Knew Nat Catoun" ', 41.

32 On these connections, see Cannon, *Grounds of English Literature*, 127–35.

33 *The Owl and the Nightingale*, ed. Cartlidge, ll. 295–7. For the proverbs, see the convenient summary in *The Owl and the Nightingale*, ed. Stanley, 160–3.

34 Alfred's practice is described by his contemporary biographer. See Asser, 'Life of Alfred', 75 and 99–100.

35 There are a few tantalizing, late witnesses to the survival of Alfred's commonplace book, but they may refer to *The Proverbs of Alfred*. See *Proverbs of Alfred*, 4–5.

36 *Proverbs of Alfred* [Text J], ll. 1–16. Further citations will be identified by line number, from 'Text J', in the text. I have silently added modern punctuation in all of these passages.

37 For a discussion of this transition, with *The Proverbs of Alfred* as a key example, see Pearsall, *Old English and Middle English Poetry*, 76–9.

38 For a summary account of the relationship between these manuscripts and their implications, see *Proverbs of Alfred*, 47–9.

39 See *MED*, s.v. 'hende adj.', 3; *MWME* 9: 2975.

40 *The Proverbs of Hendyng*, ll. 79–86.

41 For political interpretations, see Patterson, ' "What Man Artow?" ', esp. 135–60, and Ferster, *Fictions of Advice*, 89–107.

42 For *Publilius Syrus* itself, see *Minor Latin Poets*, 3–111.

43 Patterson, ' "What Man Artow" ', 141.

44 Ferster, *Fictions of Advice*, 118.

45 *Chaucer's Poetry*, ed. Donaldson, 1101.

46 On this text, see *MWME* 9: 2977–8.

47 Ashby, *Dicta Philosophorum*, ll. 281–3.

48 *MWME* 9: 3361.

49 On these versions and their manuscripts, see *Dicts and Sayings of the Philosophers*, pp. xix–xxix. See also *MWME* 9: 2978.

50 *Dicts and Sayings of the Philosophers*, 54 ('Scrope MS').

51 On the genre generally, see Nicholls, *Matter of Courtesy*, 7–21 and 57–78, and Sponsler, *Drama and Resistance*, 50–74 ('Conduct Books and Good Governance').

52 *How the Good Wife Taught her Daughter*, ll. 40–5. Further citations by line number in the text. This edition includes a valuable summary of texts offering 'parental instruction' in the Middle Ages (29–78).

53 Orme, *Medieval Schools*, 129.

54 *Stans Puer ad Mensam*, ll. 86–92. On this poem (easily confused with a poem by Lydgate of the same name), see *MWME* 9: 3004.

55 On these texts, see *MWME* 9: 2966–9.

56 *The Book of Curtesy*, ll. 39–42. On the textual history of this poem, see *MWME* 9: 3002–3.

57 *Rule of Saint Benedict*, 24–5. Further citations will be given by page number in the text.

58 See chapter 1, p. 15.

59 Pearsall, *John Lydgate*, 4.

60 Knowles, *Monastic Order in England*, 145–58 (on the Cluniacs), 208–66 (on the Cistercians), 375–91 (on the Carthusians).

61 See Dickinson, *Origins of the Austin Canons*, 7–58 (on the slow emergence of the order) and 98–131 (on the order in England).

62 This can be particularly well observed in the *Map of Monastic Britain* published by the Ordnance Survey.

63 For a survey of that variety, see Cannon, 'Monastic Productions'.

64 *Ancrene Wisse*, 1: 1; *Ancrene Wisse*, trans. White, 1. Further quotations will be identified by page number in this edition as well as page number in this translation in the text. On this particular aspect of *Ancrene Wisse*, see Beckwith, 'Passionate Regulation' (esp. 806–7).

65 On the paradoxes inherent in the anchoritic life, see Cannon, 'The Form of the Self', esp. 47–8, 53–6.

66 For a translation of this text, see Aelred of Rievaulx, 'A Rule of Life for a Recluse'.

67 Southern, *Making of the Middle Ages*, 218. On the nature of Cistercian spirituality see ibid., 227–40.

68 On the revisions, see Dobson, *Origins of Ancrene Wisse*, 259–71.

69 Ibid., 286.

70 On this textual history, see ibid., 286–304.

71 The phrase 'vernacular theology' was coined for this purpose by Watson. See his 'Middle English Mystics', esp. 544–5 and 559–65.

72 Rolle, *Form of Living*, 89. Further citations will be identified by page number in the text.

73 For other such lyrics see ibid., 104, and Rolle, *Ego Dormio*, 67–9, 70–2.

74 Rolle, *Meditations on the Passion*, 35. Further citations will be identified by page number in the text.

75 Julian of Norwich, *A Revelation of Love*, 127. Further citations will be identified by page number in the text.

76 On that luxury, see Harvey, *Living and Dying in England*, 34–71 (on diet), 77–81 (on the monastic 'way of life') and 154–63 (on the generosity of the 'monastic day').

77 Kempe, *Book of Margery Kempe*, 119–20.

78 Hilton, *Scale of Perfection*, 31. Further citations by page number in the text.

79 *The Cloud of Unknowing*, 33.

80 *MWME* 2: 460–1.

81 *MWME* 2: 463–4. These translations have been edited as *Aelred of Rievaulx's de Institutione Inclusarum*.

82 *MWME* 2: 467–9.

83 *MWME* 2: 470–2.

84 *MWME* 9: 3430–1.

85 *MWME* 9: 3426.

86 Herlihy, *Medieval Households*, 62.

87 Ibid., 3.

88 See ibid., 56–78, and Starkey, 'The Age of the Household'.

89 Green, *Poets and Princepleasers*, 103.

90 On romance as a household art, see Smith, *Arts of Possession*, 4–21.

91 *Havelok the Dane*, ll. 1–4. For another example, see *King Horn*, ll. 1–2.

92 Green, *Poets and Princepleasers*, 37.

93 Ibid., 105–6.

94 On the importance of intimate spaces in the poem, see Windeatt, *Troilus and Criseyde*, 192–7.

95 *Sir Gawain and the Green Knight*, l. 1108. Further citations by line number in the text.

96 On the later elaboration of the 'game of love', see especially Stevens, *Music and Poetry*, 154–202.

97 The classic study of such lyrics is Topsfield, *Troubadours and Love*. See also the chapters on 'courtly culture' by Ruth Harvey (8–27) and '*fin amour*' by Linda Paterson (28–46) in *The Troubadours: An Introduction*.

98 *Annot and Johon*, ll. 1–10. For this poem, see also *Middle English Lyrics*, 21–2.

99 *Alysoun*, ll. 9–12. For this poem, see also *Middle English Lyrics*, 23.

100 Guillaume de Lorris and Jean de Meun, *Le roman de la rose*, ll. 23–5, and *The Romance of the Rose*, 31. Further citations will be identified by line number (for the original) and page number (for the translation) in the text.

101 The translation is usually divided into three sections, 'A', 'B', and 'C', each probably by a different author, and only 'A' is thought to be by Chaucer.

102 For an extremely helpful set of translations of this material, carefully aligned with its use in Chaucer, see *Chaucer's Dream Poetry*.

103 Lewis, *Allegory of Love*, 2.

104 Ibid., 36.

105 Lydgate, *The Complaint of the Black Knight*, ll. 510–11. Further citations identified by line number in the text.

106 Lydgate, *The Temple of Glass*, ll. 349–55. Further citations identified by line number in the text.

107 *The Floure and the Leafe*, ll. 64–5. Further citations identified by line number in the text.

108 *The Assembly of Ladies*, ll. 722–8.

109 On the authorship of both of these poems, see *The Floure and the Leafe*, ed. Pearsall, 14–15.

110 For a description of the manuscript and editions of some of its key texts, see Robbins, 'The Findern Anthology'.

111 'A Woman's Lament', ll. 16–18, in McNamer, 'Female Authors', 305. For an analysis of this poem in relation to the Sarum rite for marriage, see ibid., 297. McNamer includes a complete edition of those Findern lyrics most likely to be by women (303–10).

112 'A Woman Affirms her Marriage Vows', ll. 1–7 in McNamer, 'Female Authors', 303.

113 *Paston Letters*, 1: 662 (no. 415). For discussion of this letter, see McNamer, 'Female Authors', 288.

114 See *Paston Letters*, 1: lxxi.

115 Hilton, 'Towns in English Medieval Society', 20.

116 Platt, *English Medieval Town*, 21–6. See also Reynolds, *Introduction to the History of English Medieval Towns*, 16–65.

117 Hilton, 'Towns in English Medieval Society', 21.

118 Ibid., 22.

119 Ibid., 24.

120 Ibid., 22.

121 Dyer, *Standards of Living in the Later Middle Ages*, 140 and 188.

122 For the *Chronicle*'s self-attribution to 'roberd', see Robert of Gloucester, *Metrical Chronicle*, ll. 11748–9. For mentions of 'gloucestre' or the 'earl of gloucestre', see lines 8028, 8037, 8044, 8901, 8904, 8913, 9134, 9257, 9279, 9294, 9485, 9536, 9832, 10569, 10729.

123 Mannyng, *Handlyng Synne*, ll. 61–7. For another such signature, see Robert Mannyng, *Chronicle*, I.135–6 ('Of Brunne I am if any me blame, Robert Mannyng is my name').

124 *The Owl and the Nightingale*, ll. 191 ('Maister'), 1752–3 ('at Porteshom'). On 'the feint' as the characteristic gesture of the form of *The Owl and the Nightingale*, see Cannon, *Grounds of English Literature*, 112.

125 'St Edmund the King', ll. 89–96.

126 'St Kenelm', ll. 227 ('holy'), 231–2 ('fat and rond'). Further citations identified by line number in the text.

127 *Saint Erkenwald*, ll. 26–7. Further citations identified by line number in the text.

128 Thrupp, 'The City as the Idea of Social Order'.

129 *Pearl*, ll. 985–96. Further citations by line number in the text.

130 On the parallels between the procession in *Pearl* and the London pageants, as well as the importance of the New Jerusalem to those pageants, see Bowers, *Politics of Pearl*, 108–20.

131 On the 'absent city', see Wallace, *Chaucerian Polity*, 156–81.

132 'Finally, the relationships between the producers, within which the social characteristics of their labours are manifested, take on the form of a social relation between the products of labour'; Marx, *Capital*, 1: 164.

133 *London Lickpenny*, l. 8, etc. Further citations identified by line number in the text. On the way *London Lickpenny* 'shows a community that the person without goods to trade cannot enter', see Farber, *Anatomy of Trade*, 174–9 (quotation from 176).

134 Black, *Guilds and Civil Society*, 31.

135 Barron, *London in the Later Middle Ages*, 199–200.

136 Ibid., 231. See also Simpson, ' "After Craftes Conseil" ', 115–20, and Farber, *Anatomy of Trade*, 164–9.

137 See Nightingale, 'Capitalists, Crafts, and Constitutional Change', esp. 4–5, and Simpson, ' "After Craftes Conseil" ', 120–6.

138 On the 'role of work' in the *General Prologue*, see Mann, *Chaucer and Medieval Estates Satire*, 10–16.

139 See *MED*, s.v. 'compaignie n.', 1e.

140 'Craft' is also represented as a gift of 'Grace' in passus 19 of *Piers Plowman* (19.229a–59), and the importance this accords urban social structures in the vision of a larger Christian community is carefully addressed in Simpson, ' "After Craftes Conseil" ', esp. 111–14 and 120–7.

141 Lydgate, *Henry VI's Triumphal Entry into London*, l. 66. Further citations identified by line number in the text.

142 Lydgate, *A Mumming at London*, ll. 1–3. For the other mummings, see Lydgate, *Minor Poems, Part 2*, 668–82 and 691–701. On the larger political importance of these texts, see Nolan, *John Lydgate and the Making of Public Culture*, 71–119.

143 See *MED*, s.v. 'misterie n2.', b and c. For the date, see Twycross, 'Theatricality of Medieval English Plays', 38.

144 On the performance of the plays, see Twycross, 'The Theatricality of Medieval English Plays', esp. 38–55. For a detailed description of the staging of the York cycle, see Stevens, *Four Middle English Mystery Cycles*, 17–87.

145 For a concise account of the extant manuscripts of the plays, see *English Mystery Plays*, 10–18.

146 See Justice, 'Trade Symbolism in the York Cycle'.

147 *York Plays*, VIII ['The Building of the Ark'], ll. 73–6.

148 On this structuring as a 'principle of selection', see Kolve, *Play Called Corpus Christi*, 63–100.

149 Homan, 'Ritual Aspects of the York Cycle', esp. 306–7. See also James, 'Ritual, Drama and the Social Body in the Late Medieval English Town'.

150 *York Plays*, XXXV ['The Crucifixion'], ll. 101–8.

151 Homan, 'Ritual Aspects', 313.

152 Beckwith, *Signifying God*, 49–52.

153 Ibid., 33–7.

154 Reynolds, *Introduction to the History of English Medieval Towns*, 69–74, and Dyer, *Standards of Living in the Later Middle Ages*, 133–4.

155 Dyer, *Standards of Living in the Later Middle Ages*, 188–91.

156 Ibid., 223 and 230–1. On the various modes of travel (by the 'ordinary traveller', the 'messenger', the 'outlaw', 'preachers and friars', and 'pardoners'), see Jusserand, *English Wayfaring Life in the Middle Ages*.

157 See Pearsall, 'Origins of the Alliterative Revival'.

158 *Wynnere and Wastoure*, ll. 7–9. Cited in Putter, *Introduction to the Gawain-poet* (33), which also includes a helpful discussion of the kinds of geographical mobility written into the alliterative poetry of this period (28–37). I translate these lines rather than gloss them because they are so difficult.

159 *Statutes of the Realm*, 2: 56 (Anno 12° Ricardi II, AD 1388, c.3). On this clause and its implication for *Piers Plowman* in particular, see Middleton, 'Acts of Vagrancy', esp. 216–46.

160 On the pilgrims as representative of the variety of English economic life, see Wallace, *Chaucerian Polity*, 82–103.

161 *Statutes of the Realm*, 2: 56.

162 On the 'eighth conclusion' of the Lollards denouncing pilgrimage, see Hudson, *Premature Reformation*, 307–9. For the text of that 'conclusion', see *Selections from English Wycliffite Writings*, 27. For a lengthier denunciation of pilgrimage printed from a fifteenth-century manuscript anthology, see ibid., 83–8.

163 On the first displacement (of pilgrimage into labour), see Simpson, *Piers Plowman*, 67–71. On the structuring role of the search for truth in the poem, see Carruthers, *Search for St Truth*, 19–33.

164 See Dyas, *Pilgrimage in Medieval English Literature*, 56–63; Webb, *Pilgrimage in Medieval England*, 63–91; Hall, *English Mediaeval Pilgrimage*, 6–10.

165 'St Edmund the King', ll. 99–100.

166 On the practice and history of the *hajj*, see Robinson, *Islam*, 127–44.

167 Momen, *An Introduction to Shi'i Islam*, 181–2.

168 Webb includes a helpful map showing just how many resting-places of saints were important by the end of the Anglo-Saxon period (*Pilgrimage in Medieval England*, 15).

169 On the importance of the crusades to pilgrimage, see Zacher, *Curiosity and Pilgrimage*, 46–7.

170 *The Stacions of Rome*, ll. 102–18.

171 All of these texts are described by Zacher in *MWME* 7: 2235–54.

172 See *MWME* 7: 2241–2 (on *Advice*) and 7: 2249 (on *Information*).

173 See *MWME* 7: 2243 (*Rome*) and 7: 2250–1 (*Italy*).

174 For descriptions of both texts, see *MWME* 7: 2244–5.

175 *Mandeville's Travels*, 229. Further citations identified by page number in the text.

176 For this textual history (and a description and summary of the text), see *MWME* 7: 2239–41.

177 On Mandeville's embrace of cultural diversity, see Zacher, *Curiosity and Pilgrimage*, 147–50, and (as cited in Zacher) Bloomfield, 'Chaucer's Sense of History', 310–11.

178 On Mandeville's motivating curiosity, see Zacher, *Curiosity and Pilgrimage*, 130–41.

179 On Kempe's 'queerness', her capacity to 'sho[w] something disjunctive within unities', see Dinshaw, *Getting Medieval*, 143–82 (for the phrases I quote, see 151).

180 Kempe, *Book of Margery Kempe*, 46. Further citations identified by page number in the text.

Chapter 5 Jurisdiction

1 Bradshaw, *Life of Saint Werburge*, 2.15–21. Further citations identified by book and line number in the text.

2 The *OED* records two earlier uses of the term (s.v. 'literature', 1) and the *MED* adds a few more, while eliminating the first cited by the *OED* because it occurs in Middle Scots (*MED*, s.v. 'litterature n.').

3 The *OED* defines 'literature', as Bradshaw uses it (wrongly to my mind), as 'acquaintance with "letters" or books' (s.v. 'literature', 1). The *MED* does not cite Bradshaw's uses under its entry for 'literature' (because it only covers the period to 1475), but it understands every use of the term it does cite to mean 'knowledge from books, book learning' (*MED*, s.v. 'litterature n.').

4 Williams, *Keywords*, 183–4.

5 This transformation from material to abstraction is well described in Williams, *Marxism and Literature*, 45–52.

6 See *OED*, s.v. 'jurisdiction'.

7 Simpson, *Reform and Cultural Revolution*, 1–2.

8 I quote here from Raymond Williams's more general description of the role of 'creative practice' in cultural change (*Marxism and Literature*, 209).

9 For a more detailed discussion of the way Chaucer's successors created his importance, see Cannon, *Making of Chaucer's English*, 179–220.

10 On the connections between *Ancrene Wisse* and the *Katherine*-group, see chapter 4, 107. For a summary of the way early manuscripts gather these texts together, see *Ancrene Wisse*, ed. Shepherd, pp. ix–xiv.

11 *Northern Passion*, ll. 11*–17* (quotation from London, British Library, Harley MS 4196, or the 'expanded version'). Further citations identified by line number in the text.

12 *Northern Passion*, ll. 799–800 (Cambridge, UL MS Dd.1.1, or the 'original version').

13 For the text of this French source, see *Northern Passion*, 2: 102–25.

14 For a description of the original (and unpublished text), see *MWME* 11: 4024–6.

15 *Northern Homily Cycle*, ll. 3943–8. Further citations identified by line number in the text.

16 *Lay Folks Mass Book*, ll. 484–94 ('Text B').

17 *MWME* 7: 2350 (on the texts and their dialectical variation) and 2555–6 (for the shelf marks and dates of the manuscripts themselves).

18 *MWME* 7: 2270–1 (for a description of the text) and 2492–4 (for surviving manuscripts).

19 *Lay Folks Catechism*, 59–61. Further citations identified by page number in the text. On the text's alliteration, see also Salter, 'Alliterative Modes and Affiliations in the Fourteenth Century', 29, and Lawton, 'Gaytryge's Sermon, Dictamen and Middle English Alliterative Verse'.

20 See, for example, the description 'Later Middle English Sermons and Homilies' in *MWME* 11: 4057–167, most of which remain unedited.

21 Mirk, *Instructions for Parish Priests*, ll. 12–14. Further citations identified by line number in the text. On this text generally, see *MWME* 7: 2369–71.

22 *MWME* 7: 2575.

23 Mirk, *Festial*, 86 (for the whole of this 'Sermon for De Dominica Prima Quadragesime', see 86–96). Further citations identified by page number in the text.

24 *MWME* 7: 4059–60 and 4271–2.

25 *Patience*, l. 346. Further citations identified by line number in the text.

26 *Cleanness*, l. 27. Further citations identified by line number in the text.

27 For example, the life of St Oswald, *Northern Homily Cycle*, ll. 17,277–512.

28 For an edition based on this manuscript, see *Early South-English Legendary*. For a list of the contents of many of the early manuscripts, see ibid., pp. xiii–xxiv. On the text generally, see *MWME* 2: 413–18.

29 On the Harley MS, see *South English Legendary*, 3: 3–4. The *Southern Passion* has been edited separately (see my 'references' below).

30 'Prologue' (*South English Legendary*, 1: 1–3), l. 12. Further citations to this prologue identified by line number in the text.

31 'St Thomas Becket', ll. 2137–44.

32 For a table of these survivals, see Brown and Robbins, *Index of Middle English Verse*, 737 (although the tables are not repeated there, it is important to note that this index has been wholly updated in *A New Index of Middle English Verse*). On the number of manuscripts of the *South English Legendary*, see *MWME* 2: 413.

33 See *MWME* 2: 430–9.

34 The reference comes in an autobiographical passage inserted into The Introduction to The Man of Law's Tale (II.61).

35 The shorter lives can be found in Lydgate, *Minor Poems*, 145–54 (*St George*), 154–9 (*St Petronilla*), 161–73 (*St Gyle*), 173–92 (*St Margarete*). The longer poems are edited separately (see my 'references' below).

36 Lydgate, *St Edmund and Fremund*, l. 212. Further citations identified by line number in the text.

37 Bokenham, *Legendys of Hooly Wummen*, l. 417. Further citations identified by line number in the text. The association here is ostensibly negative ('I dwellyd nevere with the fresh rethoryens / Gower, Chauncers, ner with lytgate', ll. 416–17) but both the modesty and its insincerity are traditional – in their way, typically Chaucerian.

38 On the poem's manuscripts, see *MWME* 6: 2128–9. Pearsall says the poem 'stuns expectation' and judges it 'one of the finest pieces of religious poetry in English'; *John Lydgate*, 285.

39 Lydgate, *Life of Our Lady*, I. 106–9.

40 Capgrave, *Life of St Katharine*, II.1389–90. Further citations by book and line number in the text and will be taken, as here, from the text Furnivall prints from London, British Library MS Arundel MS 396.

41 Augustine, *On Christian Doctrine*, II. 28 (63); *De doctrina Christiana*, II.8. I have slightly adapted Robertson's translation here.

42 Markus, *Saeculum*, 23. On the six ages, see ibid., 17–18, and for a discussion of Augustine's theory of history at length, 22–44.

43 *Cursor Mundi*, l. 230. Further citations identified by line number in the text and will be taken, as here, from the text Morris prints from London, British Library, MS Cotton Vespasian A.iii.

44 On such assimilation and its problems, see Thompson, *Cursor Mundi*, 4–5 (and n. 10).

45 Augustine, *On Christian Doctrine*, 3.10 (87–8); *De doctrina Christiana*, III.33–4 (88).

46 Robertson, *Preface to Chaucer*, 337. My examples of allegorized secular texts are derived from Robertson (337–8).

47 The view is advanced most strongly in Robertson, 'Historical Criticism'.

48 Robertson, *Preface to Chaucer*, 317. For a detailed discussion of these exegetes, see 317–36. For a reading which shows how the Pardoner's status as an exegete models a complex and deeply fetishistic psychology, see Dinshaw, *Chaucer's Sexual Poetics*, 156–84.

49 Strong resistance to 'exegetics' as a modern mode of reading is offered in Donaldson, 'Patristic Exegesis in the Criticism of Medieval Literature: The Opposition'.

50 Bergson, *Laughter*, 73–4.

51 Ibid., 62–4.

52 Bakhtin, *Rabelais and his World*, 67.

53 Ibid., 71–2. Bakhtin also locates this movement in what he continually calls the 'Renaissance', even though he includes Boccaccio in this period. For him, 'Renaissance' is less a

moment in time than a particular transformation, which necessarily takes in the Middle English centuries, even if he does not turn his attention in that direction.

54 Ibid., 88–9.

55 Ibid., 74.

56 *The Land of Cokaygne*, ll. 45–6. Further citations identified by line number in the text.

57 On the analogues of *The Land of Cokaygne*, see *Early Middle English Verse and Prose*, 136–8. For a helpful characterization of goliardic literature, see Mann, 'Chaucer and the Medieval Latin Poets', esp. 172–83.

58 See Mann, 'Beast Epic and Fable'.

59 Avianus, *Fables*, XXXVI ('The Calf and the Ox' [*De Vitulo et Bove*]), ll. 13–14.

60 *The Fox and the Wolf*, ll. 239–42.

61 Lydgate, *Isopes Fabulles*, ll. 134–5.

62 Lydgate, *The Churl and the Bird*, l. 159.

63 Bédier, *Les Fabliaux*, 37. On their possible Eastern origin, see ibid., 67–9.

64 *Dame Sirith*, ll. 353–6. Further citations identified by line number in the text.

65 See Bédier, *Fabliaux*, 37–8, and Hines, *Fabliau in English*, 38–42.

66 For this text, see my 'references' below.

67 Muscatine, *Chaucer and the French Tradition*, 224.

68 Tillyard, *Poetry Direct and Oblique*, 90.

69 For readings of the tale that lay emphasis on the bitterness, see Patterson, *Chaucer and the Subject of History*, 244–79, and Miller, *Philosophical Chaucer*, 36–81.

70 See *MED*, s.vv. 'talie n.' ('a scored wooden stick used for financial recordkeeping') and 'tail n.', 1b c ('pudendum').

71 *King Horn*, ll. 1–2.

72 For this lexical history and its implications, see Williams, *Keywords*, 31–2. See also Eagleton, *Ideology of the Aesthetic*, 13.

73 For the poem (which I quote in its entirety), see *Middle English Lyrics*, 4–6.

74 Eagleton, *Criticism and Ideology*, 177.

75 For the alternative Latin verses as they appear below the English (along with their musical setting) on the relevant page of London, British Library, MS Harley 978, see *Middle English Lyrics*, 5.

76 Eagleton, 'The Ideology of the Aesthetic', 25.

77 *The Owl and the Nightingale*, ed. Cartlidge, ll. 1–2. Further citations identified by line number in the text.

78 For a history of the genre, see *Middle English Debate Poetry*, pp. xiii–xx. On its relation to dialectic, see Cannon, *Grounds of English Literature*, 114–27. On the contents of the two manuscripts in which the poem survives, London, British Library, MS Cotton Caligula A.ix, and Oxford, Jesus College, MS 29, see *The Owl and the Nightingale*, ed. Cartlidge, p. xxvii.

79 For an excellent summary of these views, see *The Owl and the Nightingale*, ed. Cartlidge, pp. xvi–xxvii.

80 On this feminism and how it might have arisen, see Cannon, *Grounds of English Literature*, 127–38.

81 See Schleusener, 'The Owl and the Nightingale'.

82 On the essentially legal nature of this plan and the way that it raises issues of jurisdiction, see Holsinger, 'Vernacular Legality'.

83 Plekhanov, 'On Art for Art's Sake', 88.

84 For a neat summary of the evidence about the poem's date, see Putter, *Introduction to the Gawain-poet*, 2–3. For a strong argument about the connection of *Pearl* to Richard's court, see Bowers, *The Politics of Pearl*. On the 'historical context' for alliterative poetry more generally, see Putter's volume, 28–37.

85 Muscatine, *Poetry and Crisis in the Age of Chaucer*, 69. This is a point that Muscatine makes about the *Gawain*-poet generally with his interest in 'purity', both ethical and spiritual, another form this defensiveness takes. See ibid., 37–69.

86 *Pearl*, ll. 85–96. Further citations identified by line number in the text.

87 Aers, 'The Self Mourning: Reflections on *Pearl*', 73. On this Wycliffism and its incendiary views, see chapter 2, above, esp. 42.

88 See Nolan, *Chaucer and the Tradition of the 'Roman Antique'*.

89 *MWME* 1: 116–17.

90 *MWME* 1: 115–16.

91 On this process for Geoffrey, see Ingledew, 'The Book of Troy and the Genealogical Construction of History'. On this process for Lagamon, see Cannon, *Grounds of English Literature*, 55–68.

92 *Sir Orfeo*, ll. 1–2. Further citations identified by line number in the text.

93 For sustained attention to the ways that Chaucer is 'traditional' when thought not to be, see Cannon, *Making of Chaucer's English*, 48–90. On the circularity by which latter-day opinion creates the origin it seeks to find in Chaucer, see ibid., 179–220.

94 'Arma virumque cano, Troiae qui primus ab oris / Italiam fato profugus Laviniaque venit / litora – multum ille et terris iactatus et alto / vi superum.' [Arms and the man I sing, who first from the coasts of Troy, exiled by fate, came to Italy and Lavine shores; much buffeted on sea and land by violence from above.], Virgil, *Aeneid*, Book 1, ll. 1–4.

95 Wallace, 'Chaucer's Italian Inheritance', 48 and 56 n. 33.

96 Lydgate, *Troy Book*, Book 3, ll. 4256–63. Further citations identified by book and line number in the text.

97 Skelton, *Garlande or Chapelet of Laurell*, l. 403. Further citations identified by line number in the text.

References

Adams, Henry, *The Education of Henry Adams: An Autobiography*, ed. Jean Gooder, London: Penguin Books, 1995.

Aelred of Rievaulx, 'A Rule of Life for a Recluse', trans. Mary Paul Macpherson, 41–102 in *Treatises and the Pastoral Prayer*, Cistercian Fathers Series 2, Kalamazoo, MI, 1971; 2nd printing, 1982.

Aelred of Rievaulx's De Institutione Inclusarum: Two English Versions, ed. John Ayto and Alexandra Barratt, EETS o. s. 287 (1984).

Aers, David, *Community, Gender, and Individual Identity: English Writing 1360–1430*, London: Routledge, 1988.

——, 'The Self Mourning: Reflections on *Pearl*', *Speculum* 68 (1993), 54–73.

——, '*Vox Populi* and the Literature of 1381', 432–53 in *Cambridge History of Medieval English Literature*, ed. David Wallace, Cambridge: Cambridge University Press, 1999.

Alliterative Morte Arthur, 115–238 in *King Arthur's Death*, ed. Larry D. Benson, Exeter: University of Exeter Press, 1986 [first pubd 1974].

Althusser, Louis, 'Ideology and Ideological State Apparatuses', 1–60 in his *Essays on Ideology*, London: Verso, 1984 [first pubd 1970].

Alysoun, 138–9 in *English Lyrics of the XIIIth Century*, ed. Carleton Brown, Oxford: Clarendon Press, 1932.

Anchoritic Spirituality: Ancrene Wisse and Associated Works, trans. and intro. Anne Savage and Nicholas Watson, New York: Paulist Press, 1991.

Ancrene Wisse, 2 vols, ed. Bella Millett with Richard Dance, EETS o. s. 325 and 326 (2005).

Ancrene Wisse: Guide for Anchoresses, trans. Hugh White, Harmondsworth: Penguin, 1993.

Ancrene Wisse: Parts Six and Seven, ed. Geoffrey Shepherd, Exeter: Short Run Press, 1985 [first pubd 1959].

The Anglo-Saxon Chronicle, trans. G. N. Garmonsway, rev. edn, London: Dent, 1962 [first pubd 1954].

The Anglo-Saxon Minor Poems, ed. Elliott Van Kirk Dobbie, Vol. 6 of *The Anglo-Saxon Poetic Records: A Collective Edition*, New York: Columbia University Press, 1942.

Annot and Johon, 136–8 in *English Lyrics of the XIIIth Century*, ed. Carleton Brown, Oxford: Clarendon Press, 1932.

Arnold, Matthew, *Culture and Anarchy* with *Friendship's Garland and Some Literary Essays*, Vol. 5 in *Complete Prose Works*, ed. R. H. Super, Ann Arbor: University of Michigan Press, 1960–77.

Ashby, George, *Dicta Philosophorum*, 42–100 in *Poems*, ed. Mary Bateson, EETS e. s. 76 (1899).

——, *A Prisoner's Reflections*, 1–12 in *Poems*, ed. Mary Bateson, EETS e. s. 76 (1899).

——, *Active Policy of a Prince*, 12–41 in *Poems*, ed. Mary Bateson, EETS e. s. 76 (1899).

Askins, William, 'The Brothers Orléans and their Keepers', 27–45 in *Charles d'Orléans in England*, ed. Mary-Jo Arn, Cambridge: D. S. Brewer, 2000.

The Assembly of Ladies, 105–26 in *The Floure and the Leafe and The Assembly of Ladies*, ed. D. A. Pearsall, Manchester: Manchester University Press, 1980.

Asser, 'Life of Alfred', 67–110 in *Alfred the Great: Asser's Life of King Alfred and other Contemporary Sources*, trans. Simon Keynes and Michael Lapidge, Harmondsworth: Penguin, 1983.

Auerbach, Erich, *Mimesis: The Representation of Reality in Western Literature*, trans. Willard R. Trask, Princeton, NJ: Princeton University Press, 1953 [originally pubd in German 1946].

Augustine, *Confessions*, trans. Henry Chadwick, Oxford: Oxford University Press, 1991.

——, *Confessions*, 2 vols, ed. and trans. William Watts, London: St Edmundsbury Press, 1912.

——, *De doctrina Christiana Libri Quattuor*, ed. William M. Green, Vindobonae: Hölding-Pichler-Tempsky, 1963.

——, *On Christian Doctrine*, trans. D. W. Robertson, Jr., New York: Liberal Arts Press, 1958.

Avianus, *Fables*, 667–749 in *Minor Latin Poets*, ed. and trans. J. Wight Duff and Arnold M. Duff, London: Heinemann, 1934.

Ayenbite of Inwyt or Remorse of Conscience, ed. Richard Morris, EETS o. s. 23 (1866).

Bakhtin, Mikhail, *Rabelais and his World*, trans. Hélène Iswolsky, Bloomington: Indiana University Press, 1984 [first trans. 1968; first pubd 1965].

Barron, Caroline, *London in the Later Middle Ages: Government and People, 1200–1500*, Oxford: Oxford University Press, 2004.

Beckwith, Sarah, 'Passionate Regulation: Enclosure, Ascesis, and the Feminist Imaginary', *South Atlantic Quarterly* 93 (1994), 803–24.

——, *Signifying God: Social Relation and Symbolic Act in the York Corpus Christi Plays*, Chicago: University of Chicago Press, 2001.

Bédier, Joseph, *Les Fabliaux*, 3rd edn, Paris: Champion, 1911.

Benjamin, Walter, 'The Work of Art in the Age of Mechanical Reproduction', 219–53 in *Illuminations*, ed. and intro. Hannah Arendt, trans. Harry Zohn, London: Cape, 1970.

Benson, Larry D., *Malory's Morte Darthur*, Cambridge, MA: Harvard University Press, 1976.

Bergson, Henri, *Laughter*, 61–190 in *Comedy: An Essay on Comedy by George Meredith, Laughter by Henri Bergson*, Baltimore: Johns Hopkins University Press, 1980 [first pubd 1956].

Berndt, Rolf, 'The Linguistic Situation in England from the Norman Conquest to the Loss of Normandy (1066–1204)', 369–91 in *Approaches to English Historical Linguistics: An Anthology*, ed. Roger Lass, New York: Holt, Rinehart & Winston, 1969.

——, 'The Period of the Final Decline of French in Medieval England (14th and 15th Centuries)', *Zeitschrift für Anglistik und Amerikanistik* 20 (1972), 341–69.

Black, Antony, *Guilds and Civil Society in European Political Thought from the Twelfth Century to the Present*, London: Methuen, 1984.

Blake, N. F., *Caxton and his World*, London: Deutsch, 1969.

——, 'Manuscript to Print', 403–32 in *Book Production and Publishing in Britain, 1375–1475*, ed. Jeremy Griffiths and Derek Pearsall, Cambridge: Cambridge University Press, 1989.

——, 'The Spread of Printing in English during the Fifteenth Century', 57–73 in his *William Caxton and English Literary Culture*, London: Hambledon Press, 1991 [first pubd in *Gutenberg-Jahrbuch* (1987), 26–36].

Bloomfield, Morton, 'Chaucer's Sense of History', *Journal of English and Germanic Philology* 51 (1952), 301–13.

Boethius, *The Consolation of Philosophy*, trans. V. E. Watts, Harmondsworth: Penguin, 1969.

——, *Philosophiae Consolationis Libri Quinque*, ed. Karl Büchner, Heidelberg: Carl Winter, 1977.

Bokenham, Osbern, *Legendys of Hooly Wummen*, ed. M. S. Serjeantson, EETS o. s. 206 (1938).

The Book of Curtesy, in *Caxton's Book of Curtesye*, ed. Frederick J. Furnivall, EETS e. s. 3 (1868).

A Book of London English, 1384–1425, ed. R. W. Chambers and Marjorie Daunt, Oxford: Clarendon Press, 1931.

A Book of Middle English, ed. J. A. Burrow and Thorlac Turville-Petre, 2nd edn, Oxford: Blackwell, 1996 [first pubd 1991].

Bowers, John, *The Politics of Pearl: Court Poetry in the Age of Richard II*, Cambridge: D. S. Brewer, 2001.

Bracton, Henry, *De Legibus et Consuetudinibus Angliae*, ed. George E. Woodbine, trans. and rev. Samuel E. Thorne, 4 vols, Cambridge, MA: Harvard University Press, 1968–.

Bradshaw, Henry, *The Life of Saint Werburge of Chester*, ed. Carl Horstmann, EETS o. s. 88 (1887).

Brehe, S. K., 'Reassembling the First Worcester Fragment', *Speculum* 65 (1990), 521–36.

Brentano, Robert, 'Western Civilization: The Middle Ages', 552–95 in *Propaganda and Communication in World History*, Vol. 1: *The Symbolic Instrument in Early Times*, ed. Harold D. Lasswell, Daniel Lerner and Hans Speier, Honolulu: University Press of Hawaii, 1979.

Brewer, D. S., '"The Hoole Book"', 41–63 in *Essays on Malory*, ed. J. A. W. Bennett, Oxford: Oxford University Press, 1963.

——, 'The Relationship of Chaucer to the English and European Traditions', 1–38 in *Chaucer and Chaucerians*, ed. D. S. Brewer, London: Thomas Nelson, 1966.

Brown, Carleton and R. H. Robbins, *The Index of Middle English Verse*, New York: Columbia University Press, 1943–65.

Bumke, Joachim, *The Concept of Knighthood in the Middle Ages*, trans. W. T. H. Jackson and Erika Jackson, New York: AMS Press, 1982 [originally pubd as *Studien zum Ritterbegriff im 12. und 13. Jahrhundert*, 1977].

Burrow, J. A., 'Autobiographical Poetry in the Middle Ages: The Case of Thomas Hoccleve', *Proceedings of the British Academy* 68 (1982), 389–412.

——, 'Honour and Shame in *Sir Gawain and the Green Knight*', 117–31 in his *Essays in Medieval Literature*, Oxford: Clarendon Press, 1984.

The Cambridge Companion to Chaucer, ed. Jill Mann and Piero Boitani, 2nd edn, Cambridge: Cambridge University Press, 2003 [1st edn 1986].

The Cambridge Companion to Medieval English Theatre, ed. Richard Beadle, Cambridge: Cambridge University Press, 1994.

The Cambridge Companion to Medieval Romance, ed. Roberta L. Krueger, Cambridge: Cambridge University Press, 2000.

The Cambridge Companion to Medieval Women's Writing, ed. Carolyn Dinshaw and David Wallace, Cambridge: Cambridge University Press, 2003.

Cannon, Christopher, *The Grounds of English Literature*, Oxford: Oxford University Press, 2004.

——, *The Making of Chaucer's English: A Study of Words*, Cambridge: Cambridge University Press, 1998.

——, 'Monastic Productions', 316–48 in *Cambridge History of Medieval English Literature*, ed. David Wallace, Cambridge: Cambridge University Press, 1999.

——, 'Malory's Crime: Chivalric Identity and the Evil Will', 159–83 in *Medieval Literature and Historical Inquiry: Essays in Honour of Derek Pearsall*, ed. David Aers, Cambridge: D. S. Brewer, 2000.

——, 'The Form of the Self: *Ancrene Wisse* and Romance', *Medium Ævum* 70 (2001), 47–65.

Capgrave, John, *Life of St Katharine of Alexandria*, ed. Carl Horstmann, EETS o. s. 100 (1893).

Carmen de Hastingae Proelio, ed. and trans. Frank Barlow, Oxford: Clarendon Press, 1999.

Carruthers, Mary, *The Search for St Truth: A Study of Meaning in Piers Plowman*, Evanston, IL: Northwestern University Press, 1973.

Cartlidge, Neil, 'The Linguistic Evidence for the Provenance of *The Owl and the Nightingale*', *Neuphilologische Mitteilungen* 99 (1998), 249–68.

Chadwick, Henry, *Boethius: The Consolations of Music, Logic, Theology, and Philosophy*, Oxford: Clarendon Press, 1981.

La Chanson de Roland, ed. Ian Short, Paris: Librairie Générale Française, 1990.

Charles d'Orléans, *Fortunes Stabilnes: Charles of Orleans's English Book of Love, a Critical Edition*, ed. Mary-Jo Arn, Binghamton, NY: Medieval and Renaissance Texts and Studies, 1994.

Chaucer's Dream Poetry: Sources and Analogues, ed. and trans. B. A. Windeatt, Cambridge: D. S. Brewer, 1982.

Chaucer's Poetry: An Anthology for the Modern Reader, ed. E. T. Donaldson, 2nd edn, New York: Ronald Press, 1975.

Chism, Christine, *Alliterative Revivals*, Philadelphia: University of Pennsylvania Press, 2002.

——, 'Robin Hood: Thinking Globally, Acting Locally', 12–39 in *The Letter of the Law: Legal Practice and Literary Production in Medieval England*, ed. Emily Steiner and Candace Barrington, Ithaca, NY: Cornell University Press, 2002.

Chrétien de Troyes, *Le Chevalier au Lion*, ed. David F. Hult, Paris: Librairie Générale Française, 1994.

——, *Yvain (The Knight with the Lion)*, 281–373 in *Arthurian Romances*, trans. D. D. R. Owen, London: J. M. Dent, 1987.

The Chronicle of Pierre de Langtoft, ed. Thomas Wright, 2 vols, Rolls Series 47 (1866–8).

Cipolla, Carlo M., *Clocks and Culture, 1300–1700*, London: Collins, 1967.

Clanchy, M. T., *From Memory to Written Record: England, 1066–1307*, 2nd edn, Oxford: Blackwell, 1993.

Claudian, ed. and trans. Maurice Platnauer, 2 vols, London: Heinemann, 1963.

Cleanness, 47–137 in *Sir Gawain and the Green Knight, Pearl, Cleanness, Patience*, ed. J. J. Anderson, London: J. M. Dent, 1996.

The Cloud of Unknowing, ed. Phyllis Hodgson, EETS o. s. 218 (1944).

Coleman, Janet, *English Literature in History, 1350–1400*, London: Hutchinson, 1981.

A Companion to the Book of Margery Kempe, ed. John H. Arnold and Katherine J. Lewis, Cambridge: D. S. Brewer, 2004.

A Companion to Chaucer, ed. Peter Brown, Oxford: Blackwell, 2002.

A Companion to the Gawain-poet, ed. Derek Brewer and Jonathan Gibson, Cambridge: D. S. Brewer, 1997.

A Companion to Malory, ed. Elizabeth Archibald and A. S. G. Edwards, Cambridge: D. S. Brewer, 1996.

A Companion to Middle English Literature and Culture, c. 1350–1500, ed. Peter Brown, Oxford: Blackwell, 2006.

A Companion to Piers Plowman, ed. John A. Alford, Berkeley: University of California Press, 1988.

A Concise Companion to Chaucer, ed. Corinne Saunders, Oxford: Blackwell, 2005.

Cooper, Helen, 'Counter-Romance: Civil Strife and Father-Killing in the Prose Romances', 141–62 in *The Long Fifteenth Century: Essays for Douglas Gray*, ed. Helen Cooper and Sally Mapstone, Oxford: Clarendon Press, 1977.

Copeland, Rita, *Pedagogy, Intellectuals, and Dissent in the Later Middle Ages: Lollardy and Ideas of Learning*, Cambridge: Cambridge University Press, 2001.

Crane, Susan, *Insular Romance: Politics, Faith, and Culture in Anglo-Norman and Middle English Literature*, Berkeley: University of California Press, 1986.

——, 'The Writing Lesson of 1381', 201–21 in *Chaucer's England*, ed. Barbara Hanawalt, Minneapolis: University of Minnesota Press, 1992.

Cursor Mundi, ed. R. Morris, 7 vols, EETS o. s. 57 (1874), 59 (1875), 62 (1876), 66 (1877), 68 (1878), 99 (1892), 101 (1893).

Curtius, Ernst Robert, *European Literature and the Latin Middle Ages*, trans. Willard R. Trask, Princeton, NJ: Princeton University Press, 1953.

Curye on Inglysch: English Culinary Manuscripts of the Fourteenth Century (Including the Forme of Cury), ed. Constance B. Hieatt and Sharon Butler, EETS s. s. 8 (1985).

Dame Sirith, 77–95 in *Early Middle English Verse and Prose*, ed. J. A. W. Bennett and G. V. Smithers, Oxford: Clarendon Press, 1968.

Dan Michel's Ayenbite of Inwyt or Remorse of Conscience, ed. Richard Morris, EETS o. s. 23 (1866).

D'Entrèves, Alexander Passerin, *The Notion of the State: An Introduction to Political Theory*, Oxford: Clarendon Press, 1967.

Dickinson, J. C., *The Origins of the Austin Canons and their Introduction into England*, London: SPCK, 1950.

Dicta Catonis, 585–639 in *Minor Latin Poets*, ed. and trans. J. Wight Duff and Arnold M. Duff, London: Heinemann, 1934.

The Dicts and Sayings of the Philosophers, ed. Curt F. Bühler, EETS o. s. 211 (1941).

Dimmick, Jeremy, ' "Reding of Romance" in Gower's *Confessio Amantis*', 125–37 in *Tradition and Transformation in Medieval Romance*, ed. Rosalind Field, Cambridge: D. S. Brewer, 1999.

Dinshaw, Carolyn, *Chaucer's Sexual Poetics*, Madison: University of Wisconsin Press, 1989.

——, *Getting Medieval: Sexualities and Communities, Pre- and Postmodern*, Durham, NC: Duke University Press, 1999.

Dobson, E. J., *The Origins of Ancrene Wisse*, Oxford: Clarendon Press, 1976.

Donaldson, E. T., 'Patristic Exegesis in the Criticism of Medieval Literature: The Opposition', 134–53 in *Speaking of Chaucer*, London: Athlone Press, 1970.

Duby, Georges, *The Three Orders: Feudal Society Imagined*, trans. Arthur Goldhammer, Chicago: University of Chicago Press, 1980.

Dyas, Dee, *Pilgrimage in Medieval English Literature, 700–1500*, Cambridge: D. S. Brewer, 2001.

Dyer, Christopher, *Standards of Living in the Later Middle Ages: Social Change in England c. 1200–1520*, Cambridge: Cambridge University Press, 1989.

Eagleton, Terry, *Criticism and Ideology: A Study in Marxist Literary Theory*, London: NLB, 1976.

——, *The Ideology of the Aesthetic*, Oxford: Blackwell, 1990.

——, 'The Ideology of the Aesthetic', 17–31 in *The Politics of Pleasure: Aesthetics and Cultural Theory*, ed. Stephen Regan, Buckingham: Open University Press, 1992.

The Early English Carols, ed. R. L. Greene, Oxford: Clarendon Press, 1935.

Early Middle English Texts, ed. Bruce Dickins and R. M. Wilson, Cambridge: Bowes & Bowes, 1951.

Early Middle English Verse and Prose, ed. J. A. W. Bennett and G. V. Smithers, 2nd edn, Oxford: Clarendon Press, 1968.

Early South-English Legendary, ed. Carl Horstmann, EETS o. s. 87 (1887).

Eisenstein, Elizabeth L., 'The Advent of Printing and the Problem of the Renaissance', *Past and Present* 45 (1969), 19–89.

——, *The Printing Press as an Agent of Change: Communications and Cultural Transformations in Early-Modern Europe*, 2 vols in 1, Cambridge: Cambridge University Press, 1979.

English Historical Documents, 2nd edn, gen. ed. David C. Douglas, London: Eyre Methuen, 1979–.

English Lyrics of the XIIIth Century, ed. Carleton Brown, Oxford: Clarendon Press, 1932.

English Mystery Plays: A Selection, ed. Peter Happé, London: Penguin, 1975.

The Execution of Simon Fraser, 14–23 in *Historical Poems of the XIVth and XVth Centuries*, ed. Rossell Hope Robbins, New York: Columbia University Press, 1959.

Farber, Lianna, *An Anatomy of Trade in Medieval Writing: Value, Consent, and Community*, Ithaca, NY: Cornell University Press, 2006.

Febvre, Lucien and Henri-Jean Martin, *The Coming of the Book: The Impact of Printing 1450–1800*, trans. David Gerard, ed. Geoffrey Nowell-Smith and David Wootton, London: NLB, 1976.

Ferster, Judith, *Fictions of Advice: The Literature and Politics of Counsel in Late Medieval England*, Philadelphia: University of Pennsylvania Press, 1996.

Field, P. J. C., *The Life and Times of Sir Thomas Malory*, Cambridge: D. S. Brewer, 1993.

'The First Shepherds' Play', 244–64 in *English Mystery Plays*, ed. Peter Happé, London: Penguin, 1975.

Fisher, John H., 'Chancery and the Emergence of Standard Written English in the Fifteenth Century', *Speculum* 52 (1977), 870–99.

The Five Dogs of London, 189–90 in *Historical Poems of the XIVth and XVth Centuries*, ed. Rossell Hope Robbins, New York: Columbia University Press, 1959.

The Flemish Insurrection, 9–13 in *Historical Poems of the XIVth and XVth Centuries*, ed. Rossell Hope Robbins, New York: Columbia University Press, 1959.

Floris and Blancheflour, 279–309 in *Middle English Verse Romances*, ed. Donald Sands, Exeter: University of Exeter Press, 1986.

The Floure and the Leafe, 85–102 in *The Floure and the Leafe and The Assembly of Ladies*, ed. D. A. Pearsall, Manchester: Manchester University Press, 1980.

Fortescue, John, *The Governance of England*, ed. Charles Plummer, Oxford: Clarendon Press, 1885.

Foucault, Michel, *The History of Sexuality*, Vol. 1: *An Introduction*, trans. Robert Hurley, New York: Vintage Books, 1980 [first pubd 1978].

——, *Technologies of the Self: Seminar with Michel Foucault*, ed. Luther H. Martin, Huck Gutman and Patrick H. Hutton, London: Tavistock, 1988.

Fourteenth-Century Verse and Prose, ed. Kenneth Sisam, Oxford: Clarendon Press, 1975.

'Fourth Lateran Council, Constitutions', 230–71 in *Decrees of the Ecumenical Councils*, Vol. 1: *Nicaea I to Lateran V*, ed. and trans. Norman P. Tanner, London: Sheed & Ward, 1990.

The Fox and the Wolf, 65–76 in *Early Middle English Verse and Prose*, ed. J. A. W. Bennett and G. V. Smithers, 2nd edn, Oxford: Clarendon Press, 1968.

Foxe, John, *Acts and Monuments*, 3 vols, New York: AMS Press, 1965.

Fradenburg, Louise, 'The Manciple's Servant Tongue: Politics and Poetry in The Canterbury Tales', *ELH* 52 (1985), 85–118.

Friar Daw's Reply, 145–200 in *Six Ecclesiastical Satires*, ed. James Dean, Kalamazoo, MI: Medieval Institute Publications, 1991.

Frugoni, Chiara, *Books, Banks, Buttons and Other Inventions from the Middle Ages*, trans. William McCuaig, New York: Columbia University Press, 2003 [originally pubd in Italian 2001].

Gamelyn, 154–81 in *Middle English Verse Romances*, ed. Donald Sands, Exeter: University of Exeter Press, 1986.

Geddes, Jane, 'Iron', 167–88 in *English Medieval Industries: Craftsmen, Techniques, Products*, ed. John Blair and Nigel Ramsay, London: Hambledon Press, 1991.

Georgianna, Linda, *The Solitary Self: Individuality in the Ancrene Wisse*, Cambridge, MA: Harvard University Press, 1981.

Die Gesetze der Angelsachsen, ed. F. Liebermann, 3 vols, Halle: Max Niemeyer, 1903.

A Gest of Robyn Hood, 80–168 in *Robin Hood and Other Outlaw Tales*, ed. Stephen Knight and Thomas Ohlgren, Kalamazoo, MI: Medieval Institute Publications, 2000.

Gesta Normannorum Ducum, of William of Jumièges, Orderic Vitalis, and Robert of Torigni, ed. Elisabeth M. C. Van Houts, 2 vols, Oxford: Clarendon Press, 1995.

Ghosh, Kantik, *The Wycliffite Heresy: Authority and the Interpretation of Texts*, Cambridge: Cambridge University Press, 2002.

Gimpel, Jean, *The Medieval Machine: The Industrial Revolution of the Middle Ages*, 2nd edn, London: Pimlico, 1992 [1st edn pubd 1976].

Gower, John, *Confessio Amantis*, 1: 1–456 and 2: 1–480 in *English Works of John Gower*, ed. G. C. Macaulay, EETS e. s. 81 (1900) and 82 (1901).

——, *In Praise of Peace*, 2: 481–94 in *English Works of John Gower*, ed. G. C. Macaulay, EETS e. s. 81 (1900) and 82 (1901).

Gray, Douglas, 'The Robin Hood Poems', 3–37 in *Robin Hood: An Anthology of Scholarship and Criticism*, ed. Stephen Knight, London: D. S. Brewer, 1999 [originally pubd in *Poetica* 18 (1984): 1–19].

'Great Cato', 562–609 in *Minor Poems from the Vernon MS, Part II*, ed. F. J. Furnivall, EETS o. s. 117 (1901).

Green, Richard Firth, 'John Ball's Letters: Literary History and Historical Literature', 176–200 in *Chaucer's England*, ed. Barbara Hanawalt, Minneapolis: University of Minnesota Press, 1992.

——, *Poets and Princepleasers: Literature and the English Court in the Late Middle Ages*, Toronto: University of Toronto Press, 1980.

Greenblatt, Stephen, *Renaissance Self-Fashioning: From More to Shakespeare*, Chicago: University of Chicago Press, 1980.

Guillaume de Lorris and Jean de Meun, *Le Roman de la rose*, ed. Daniel Poirion, Paris: Garnier-Flammarion, 1974.

——, *The Romance of the Rose*, trans. Charles Dahlberg, Hanover, NH: University Press of New England, 1971.

Hall, Donald J., *English Mediaeval Pilgrimage*, London: Routledge & Kegan Paul, 1966.

Hanna, Ralph, 'Alliterative Poetry', 488–512 in *The Cambridge History of Medieval English Literature*, ed. David Wallace, Cambridge: Cambridge University Press, 1999.

Hanning, Robert W., *The Individual in Twelfth-Century Romance*, New Haven, CT: Yale University Press, 1977.

Harriss, Gerald, *Shaping the Nation: England 1360–1461*, Oxford: Clarendon Press, 2005.

Harvey, Barbara, *Living and Dying in England, 1100–1500: The Monastic Experience*, Oxford: Clarendon Press, 1993.

Havelok the Dane, 55–129 in *Middle English Verse Romances*, ed. Donald Sands, Exeter: University of Exeter Press, 1986.

Hellinga, Lotte, *Caxton in Focus*, London: British Library, 1982.

——, 'Printing', 65–108 in *The Cambridge History of the Book in Britain*, Vol. 3: *1400–1557*, Cambridge: Cambridge University Press, 1999.

Herlihy, David, *Medieval Households*, Cambridge, MA: Harvard University Press, 1985.

Higden, Ranulph, *Polychronicon*, trans. John Trevisa and an unknown writer of the fifteenth century, ed. Joseph Rawson Lumby, 9 vols, Rolls Series 41, London, 1865–86.

Hilton, R. H., 'The Origins of Robin Hood', 197–210 in *Robin Hood: An Anthology of Scholarship and Criticism*, ed. Stephen Knight, Cambridge: D. S. Brewer, 1999 [first pubd in *Past and Present* 14 (1958), 30–44].

——, 'Towns in English Medieval Society', 19–28 in *The English Medieval Town: A Reader in English Urban History, 1200–1540*, ed. Richard Holt and Gervase Rosser, London: Longman, 1990 [first pubd in *Urban History Yearbook* 9 (1982), 19–28].

Hilton, Walter, *The Scale of Perfection*, ed. Thomas H. Bestul, Kalamazoo, MI: Medieval Institute Publications, 2000.

Hines, John, *The Fabliau in English*, London: Longman, 1993.

Historical Poems of the XIVth and XVth Centuries, ed. Rossell Hope Robbins, New York: Columbia University Press, 1959.

Hoccleve, Thomas, *Balade, After King Richard II's Bones Were Brought to Westminster*, 47–9 in *Hoccleve's Works: The Minor Poems*, ed. Frederick J. Furnivall and I. Gollancz, rev. Jerome Mitchell and A. I. Doyle, EETS o. s. 61 (1892).

——, *Dialogue with a Friend*, 110–39 in *Hoccleve's Works: The Minor Poems*, ed. Frederick J. Furnivall and I. Gollancz, rev. Jerome Mitchell and A. I. Doyle, EETS o. s. 61 (1892).

——, *The Regiment of Princes*, ed. Charles R. Blyth, Kalamazoo, MI: Medieval Institute Publications, 1999.

——, *Remonstrance to John Oldcastle*, 8–24 in *Hoccleve's Works: The Minor Poems*, ed. Frederick J. Furnivall and I. Gollancz, rev. Jerome Mitchell and A. I. Doyle, EETS o. s. 61 (1892).

——, *Thomas Hoccleve's Complaint*, 95–110 in *Hoccleve's Works: The Minor Poems*, ed. Frederick J. Furnivall and I. Gollancz, rev. Jerome Mitchell and A. I. Doyle, EETS o. s. 61 (1892).

Holsinger, Bruce, 'Vernacular Legality: The English Jurisdictions of *The Owl and the Nightingale*', 154–84 in *The Letter of the Law: Legal Practice and Literary Production in Medieval England*, ed. Emily Steiner and Candace Barrington, Ithaca, NY: Cornell University Press, 2002.

Holt, J. C., 'The Origins and Audience of the Ballads of Robin Hood', 211–32 in *Robin Hood: An Anthology of Scholarship and Criticism*, ed. Stephen Knight, Cambridge: D. S. Brewer, 1999 [first pubd in *Past and Present* 18 (1960), 89–110].

Homan, Richard L., 'Ritual Aspects of the York Cycle', *Theatre Journal* 33 (1981), 303–15.

Hopkins, Andrea, *The Sinful Knights: A Study of Middle English Romance*, Oxford: Clarendon Press, 1990.

How the Good Wife Taught her Daughter, 158–72 in *The Good Wife Taught her Daughter: The Good Wyfe Wolde a Pylgremage, The Thewis of Gud Women*, ed. Tauno F. Mustanoja, Helsinki: Academiae Scientiarum Fennicae, 1948.

Hudson, Anne, 'Lollard Book-Production', 125–42 in *Book Production and Publishing in Britain, 1375–1475*, ed. Jeremy Griffiths and Derek Pearsall, Cambridge: Cambridge University Press, 1989.

——, 'A Lollard Sect Vocabulary?', 15–30 in *So Meny People Longages and Tonges: Philological Essays in Scots and Medieval English presented to Angus McIntosh*, ed. Michael Benskin and M. L. Samuels, Edinburgh: Benskin & Samuels, 1981.

——, 'Lollardy: The English Heresy?', *Studies in Church History* 18 (1982), 261–83.

——, *The Premature Reformation: Wycliffite Texts and Lollard History*, Oxford: Oxford University Press, 1988.

——, 'Wyclif and the English Language', 85–103 in *Wyclif in his Times*, ed. Anthony Kenny, Oxford: Clarendon Press, 1986.

Hussey, S. S., 'Langland's Reading of Alliterative Poetry', *Modern Language Review* 60 (1965), 163–70.

Ingledew, Francis, 'The Book of Troy and the Genealogical Construction of History: The Case of Geoffrey of Monmouth's *Historia regum Britanniae*', *Speculum* 69 (1994), 665–704.

The Institutes of Justinian, ed. and trans. J. T. Abdy and Bryan Walker, Cambridge: Cambridge University Press, 1876.

The Insurrection and Earthquake, 57–60 in *Historical Poems of the XIVth and XVth Centuries*, ed. Rossell Hope Robbins, New York: Columbia University Press, 1959.

Interludium de Clerico et Puella, 196–200 in *Early Middle English Verse and Prose*, ed. J. A. W. Bennett and G. V. Smithers, 2nd edn, Oxford: Clarendon Press, 1968.

An Introduction to Middle English, ed. Simon Horobin and Jeremy Smith, Edinburgh: Edinburgh University Press, 2002.

Jack Upland, 119–44 in *Six Ecclesiastical Satires*, ed. James Dean, Kalamazoo, MI: Medieval Institute Publications, 1991.

James, Mervyn, 'Ritual, Drama and the Social Body in the late Medieval English Town', *Past and Present* 98 (1983), 3–29.

Jameson, Fredric, *The Political Unconscious: Narrative as a Socially Symbolic Act*, London: Methuen, 1981.

Julian of Norwich, *A Revelation of Love*, 121–381 in *The Writings of Julian of Norwich*, ed. Nicholas Watson and Jacqueline Jenkins, University Park: Pennsylvania State University Press, 2006.

Jusserand, J. J., *English Wayfaring Life in the Middle Ages*, trans. Lucy Toulmin Smith, London: Methuen, 1961 [first pubd 1889].

Justice, Alan D., 'Trade Symbolism in the York Cycle', *Theatre Journal* 31 (1979), 47–58.

Justice, Steven, *Writing and Rebellion: England in 1381*, Berkeley: University of California Press, 1994.

Kane, George, 'Some Fourteenth-Century "Political" Poems', 82–91 in *Medieval English Religious and Ethical Literature: Essays in Honour of G. H. Russell*, ed. Gregory Kratzmann and James Simpson, Cambridge: D. S. Brewer, 1986.

Kantorowicz, Ernst H., *The King's Two Bodies: A Study in Mediaeval Political Theology*, Princeton, NJ: Princeton University Press, 1957.

Kay, Sarah, *The* Chansons de geste *in the Age of Romance: Political Fictions*, Oxford: Clarendon Press, 1995.

Kean, P. M., *Chaucer and the Making of English Poetry*, 2 vols, London: Routledge & Kegan Paul, 1972.

Keen, Maurice, *Chivalry*, New Haven, CT: Yale University Press, 1984.

——, *England in the Later Middle Ages: A Political History*, London: Methuen, 1973.

——, *The Outlaws of Medieval Legend*, London: Routledge, 2000 [first pubd 1961].

Kempe, Margery, *The Book of Margery Kempe*, ed. Barry Windeatt, London: Pearson Education, 2000.

Ker, N. R., *Facsimile of British Museum MS. Harley 2253*, EETS o. s. 255 (1965).

Kerby-Fulton, Kathryn, *Books Under Suspicion: Censorship and Tolerance of Revelatory Writing in Late Medieval England*, Notre Dame, IN: University of Notre Dame Press, 2006.

——, 'Langland and the Bibliographic Ego', 67–143 in *Written Work: Langland, Labor, and Authorship*, ed. Steven Justice and Kathryn Kerby-Fulton, Philadelphia: University of Pennsylvania Press, 1997.

Kim, Margaret, 'Hunger, Need, and the Politics of Poverty in *Piers Plowman*', *Yearbook of Langland Studies* 16 (2002), 131–68.

King Horn, 15–54 in *Middle English Verse Romances*, ed. Donald Sands, Exeter: University of Exeter Press, 1986.

Kinney, Thomas L., 'The Temper of Fourteenth-Century English Verse of Complaint', *Annuale Mediaevale* 7 (1966), 74–89.

Kirk, Elizabeth D., 'Langland's Plowman and the Recreation of Fourteenth-Century Religious Metaphor', *Yearbook of Langland Studies* 2 (1988), 1–21.

Knapp, Ethan, *The Bureaucratic Muse: Thomas Hoccleve and the Literature of Late Medieval England*, University Park: Pennsylvania State University Press, 2001.

Knight, Stephen, *Robin Hood: A Complete Study of the English Outlaw*, Oxford: Blackwell, 1994.

Knighton's Chronicle, ed. and trans. G. H. Martin, Oxford: Clarendon Press, 1995.

Knowles, David, *The Monastic Order in England, 943–1216*, Cambridge: Cambridge University Press, 1940.

——, *The Religious Orders in England*, 3 vols, Cambridge: Cambridge University Press, 1948–59.

Kolve, V. A., *The Play Called Corpus Christi*, Stanford, CA: Stanford University Press, 1965.

Lagamon, *Brut or Hystoria Brutonum*, ed. and trans. W. R. J. Barron and S. C. Weinberg, Harlow: Longman, 1995.

Lambert, Mark, *Malory: Style and Vision in Le Morte Darthur*, New Haven, CT: Yale University Press, 1975.

The Land of Cokaygne, 136–44 in *Early Middle English Verse and Prose*, ed. J. A. W. Bennett and G. V. Smithers, 2nd edn, Oxford: Clarendon Press, 1968.

Langland, William, *Piers Plowman: An Edition of the C-text*, ed. Derek Pearsall, London: Edward Arnold, 1978.

——, *The Vision of Piers Plowman: A Complete Edition of the B-text*, ed. A. V. C. Schmidt, 2nd edn, London: J. M. Dent, 1995.

Lawton, David, 'Dullness and the Fifteenth Century', *ELH* 54 (1987), 761–99.

——, 'Gaytryge's Sermon, Dictamen and Middle English Alliterative Verse', *Modern Philology* 76 (1979), 329–43.

——, 'Lollardy and the *Piers Plowman* Tradition', *Modern Language Review* 76 (1981), 780–93.

The Lay Folks' Catechism, ed. Thomas Frederick Simmons and Henry Edward Nolloth, EETS o. s. 118 (1901).

The Lay Folks' Mass Book, ed. Thomas Frederick Simmons, EETS o. s. 71 (1879).

Lerer, Seth, 'Old English and its Afterlife', 7–34 in *Cambridge History of Medieval English Literature*, ed. David Wallace, Cambridge: Cambridge University Press, 1999.

Lewis, C. S., *The Allegory of Love: A Study in Medieval Tradition*, Oxford: Oxford University Press, 1936.

Lewis, Robert E. and Angus McIntosh, *A Descriptive Guide to the MSS of 'The Prick of Conscience'*, MÆ Monograph n. s. 12, Oxford: Society for the Study of Mediaeval Language and Literature, 1983.

The Libelle of Englyshe Polycye, ed. George Warner, Oxford: Clarendon Press, 1926.

'Little Cato', 553–62 in *Minor Poems from the Vernon MS, Part II*, ed. F. J. Furnivall, EETS o. s. 117 (1901).

'Lollard Disendowment Bill', 135–7 in *Selections from English Wycliffite Writings*, ed. Anne Hudson, Toronto: University of Toronto Press, 1997.

London Lickpenny, 222–5 in *Medieval English Political Writings*, ed. James M. Dean, Kalamazoo, MI: Medieval Institute Publications, 1996.

Loomis, Laura Hibbard, 'Chaucer and the Auchinleck MS', 111–28 in *Essays and Studies in Honor of Carleton Brown*, ed. P. W. Long, New York: New York University Press, 1940.

Love, Nicholas, *Mirror of the Blessed Life of Jesus Christ: A Reading Text*, ed. Michael G. Sargent, Exeter: University of Exeter Press, 2004.

Lukács, Georg, *The Meaning of Contemporary Realism*, trans. John Mander and Necke Mander, London: Merlin Press, 1962.

The Luve-Ron of Friar Thomas Hales, 352–57 in *Old and Middle English: An Anthology*, ed. Elaine Treharne, Oxford: Blackwell, 2000.

Lyall, R. J., 'Materials: The Paper Revolution', 11–29 in *Book Production and Publishing, 1375–1475*, ed. Jeremy Griffiths and Derek Pearsall, Cambridge: Cambridge University Press, 1989.

Lydgate, John, *The Churl and the Bird*, 468–85 in *Minor Poems, Part 2*, ed. Henry Noble MacCracken, EETS o. s. 192 (1934).

——, *The Complaint of the Black Knight*, 382–410 in *Minor Poems, Part 2*, ed. Henry Noble MacCracken, EETS o. s. 192 (1934).

——, *The Fall of Princes*, ed. Henry Bergen, EETS e. s. 121–4 (1918–19).

——, *Henry VI's Triumphal Entry into London*, 630–48 in *Minor Poems, Part 2*, ed. Henry Noble MacCracken, EETS o. s. 192 (1934).

——, *Isopes Fabulles*, 566–99 in *Minor Poems, Part 2*, ed. Henry Noble Mac-Cracken, EETS o. s. 192 (1934).

——, *The Life of Our Lady*, ed. J. Lauritis with R. Klinefelter and V. Gallagher, Pittsburgh: Duquesne University Press, 1961.

——, *The Minor Poems*, EETS o. s. 107 (1911).

——, *The Minor Poems, Part 2 (Secular Poems)*, ed. Henry Noble MacCracken, EETS o. s. 192 (1934).

——, *A Mumming at London*, 682–91 in *Minor Poems, Part 2*, ed. Henry Noble MacCracken, EETS o. s. 192 (1934).

——, *Reson and Sensuallyte*, 2 vols, ed. E. Sieper, EETS e. s. 84 (1901) and 89 (1903).

——, *St Edmund and Fremund*, 376–445 in *Altenglische Legenden*, ed. Carl Horstmann, Heilbron: Henninger, 1881.

——, *The Siege of Thebes*, 2 vols, ed. Axel Erdmann and Eilert Ekwall, EETS e. s. 108 (1911) and 125 (1930).

——, *The Temple of Glass*, 67–112 in *John Lydgate: Poems*, ed. John Norton-Smith, Oxford: Clarendon Press, 1966.

——, *Troy Book*, ed. Henry Bergen, 4 vols, EETS e. s. 97 (1906), 103 (1906), 106 (1910), 126 (1935).

MacFarlane, K. B., 'The Wars of the Roses', 231–61 in his *England in the Fifteenth Century: Collected Essays*, London: Hambledon Press, 1981.

Machan, Tim William, *English in the Middle Ages*, Oxford: Oxford University Press, 2003.

McKenzie, D. F., 'Printers of the Mind: Some Notes on Bibliographical Theories and Printing-House Practices', *Studies in Bibliography* 22 (1969): 1–75; repr. in *Making of Meaning: 'Printers of the Mind' and Other Essays*, ed. Peter D. McDonald and Michael F. Suarez, Amherst: University of Massachusetts Press, 2002, 13–85.

McKisack, May, *The Fourteenth Century, 1307–99*, Oxford: Clarendon Press, 1959.

McNamer, Sarah, 'Female Authors, Provincial Setting: The Re-Versing of Courtly Love in the Findern Manuscript', *Viator* 22 (1991), 279–310.

Malory, Thomas, *Works*, ed. Eugène Vinaver, rev. P. J. C. Field, 3 vols, Oxford: Oxford University Press, 1990 [1st edn 1967].

Mandeville's Travels, ed. M. C. Seymour, Oxford: Clarendon Press, 1967.

Manly, J. M., *Some New Light on Chaucer*, London: H. Holt, 1926.

Mann, Jill, 'Beast Epic and Fable', 556–61 in *Medieval Latin: An Introduction and Bibliographic Guide*, ed. F. A. C. Mantello and A. G. Rigg, Washington, DC: Catholic University of America Press, 1996.

——, *Chaucer and Medieval Estates Satire: The Literature of Social Classes and the General Prologue to the Canterbury Tales*, Cambridge: Cambridge University Press, 1973.

——, 'Chaucer and the Medieval Latin Poets: the Satiric Tradition', 172–83 in *Writers and their Background: Geoffrey Chaucer*, ed. Derek Brewer, London: Bell, 1974.

——, *Feminizing Chaucer*, Cambridge: D. S. Brewer, 2002 [1st edn pubd as *Geoffrey Chaucer* 1991].

——, ' "He Knew Nat Catoun": Medieval School-Texts and Middle English Literature', 41–74 in *The Text in the Community: Essays on Medieval Works, Manuscripts, Authors, and Readers*, ed. Jill Mann and Maura Nolan, Notre Dame, IN: University of Notre Dame Press, 2006.

——, *The Narrative of Distance, the Distance of Narrative in Malory's Morte Darthur*, London: Birkbeck College, University of London, 1991.

——, 'The Nature of Need Revisited', *Yearbook of Langland Studies* 18 (2004), 3–29.

Mannyng, Robert, *The Chronicle*, ed. Idelle Sullens, Binghamton, NY: Medieval & Renaissance Texts & Studies, Binghamton University, 1996.

——, *Handlyng Synne and its French Original*, ed. Frederick J. Furnivall, EETS o. s. 119 (1901) and 123 (1903).

——, *Handlyng Synne*, ed. Idelle Sullens, Binghamton, NY: Center for Medieval & Early Renaissance Studies, SUNY, 1983.

Map of Monastic Britain, 2nd edn, 2 sheets, Chessington: Ordnance Survey, 1954–6.

Markus, R. A., *Saeculum: History and Society in the Theology of St Augustine*, Cambridge: Cambridge University Press, 1970.

Marx, Karl, *Capital*, vol. 1, trans. Ben Fowkes, Harmondsworth: Penguin, 1976.

——, 'The Eighteenth Brumaire of Louis Bonaparte', 300–25 in *Selected Writings*, ed. David McLellan, Oxford: Oxford University Press, 1977.

——, *A Critique of Political Economy*, 388–92 in *Selected Writings*, ed. David McLellan, Oxford: Oxford University Press, 1977.

Matthews, David, *The Making of Middle English, 1765–1910*, Minneapolis: University of Minnesota Press, 1999.

Meale, Carol M., ' "The Hoole Book": Editing and the Creation of Meaning in Malory's Text', 3–17 in *A Companion to Malory*, ed. Elizabeth Archibald and A. S. G. Edwards, Cambridge: D. S. Brewer, 1996.

Meredith, Peter, 'The Towneley Cycle', 134–62 in *Cambridge Companion to Medieval English Theatre*, ed. Richard Beadle, Cambridge: Cambridge University Press, 1994.

Middle English Debate Poetry: A Critical Anthology, ed. John W. Conlee, East Lansing, MI: Colleagues Press, 1991.

Middle English Lyrics, ed. Maxwell S. Luria and Richard L. Hoffman, New York: W. W. Norton, 1974.

Middleton, Anne, 'Acts of Vagrancy: The C Version "Autobiography" and the Statute of 1388', 208–317 in *Written Work: Langland, Labor, and Authorship*, ed. Steven Justice and Kathryn Kerby-Fulton, Philadelphia: University of Pennsylvania Press, 1997.

——, 'William Langland's "Kynde Name": Authorial Signature and Social Identity in Late Fourteenth-Century England', 15–82 in *Literary Practice and Social Change in Britain, 1380–1530*, ed. Lee Patterson, Berkeley: University of California Press, 1990.

Miller, Mark, 'Displaced Souls, Idle Talk, Spectacular Scenes: *Handlyng Synne* and the Perspective of Agency', *Speculum* 71 (1996), 606–32.

——, *Philosophical Chaucer: Love, Sex and Agency in the Canterbury Tales*, Cambridge: Cambridge University Press, 2004.

Milroy, James, 'Middle English Dialectology', 156–206 in *The Cambridge History of the English Language*, vol. 2: *1066–1476*, ed. Norman Blake, Cambridge: Cambridge University Press, 1992.

Minor Latin Poets, ed. and trans. J. Wight Duff and Arnold M. Duff, London: Heinemann, 1934.

Mirk, John, *Festial*, ed. T. Erbe, EETS e. s. 96 (1905).

——, *Instructions for Parish Priests*, ed. E. Peacock, EETS o. s. 31 (1868; rev. 1902).

Moffat, Douglas, 'The Recovery of Worcester Cathedral MS F.174', *Notes and Queries* NS 32 (1985), 300–2.

Momen, Moojan, *An Introduction to Shi'i Islam: The History and Doctrines of Twelver Shi'ism*, New Haven, CT: Yale University Press, 1985.

Moore, Samuel, 'Lawrence Minot', *Modern Language Notes* 35 (1920), 78–81.

Mum and the Sothsegger, 137–202 in *The Piers Plowman Tradition*, ed. Helen Barr, London: J. M. Dent, 1993.

Murphy, James J., 'Roman Writing Instruction as Described by Quintilian', 19–76 in *A Short History of Writing Instruction: From Ancient Greece to Twentieth-Century America*, ed. James J. Murphy, Davis, CA: Hermagoras Press, 1990.

Muscatine, Charles, *Chaucer and the French Tradition: A Study in Style and Meaning*, Berkeley: University of California Press, 1957.

——, *Poetry and Crisis in the Age of Chaucer*, Notre Dame, IN: University of Notre Dame Press, 1972.

A New Index of Middle English Verse, ed. Julia Boffey and A. S. G. Edwards, London: British Library, 2005.

Newhauser, Richard, 'Historicity and Complaint in *Song of the Husbandman*', 203–17 in *Studies in the Harley Manuscript*, ed. Susanna Fein, Kalamazoo, MI: Medieval Institute Publications, 2000.

Nicholls, Jonathan, *The Matter of Courtesy: Medieval Courtesy Books and the Gawain-poet*, Woodbridge: D. S. Brewer, 1985.

Nietzsche, Friedrich, *On the Genealogy of Morals*, 449–599 in *Basic Writings of Nietzsche*, ed. and trans. Walter Kaufmann, New York: Random House, 1966.

Nightingale, Pamela, 'Capitalists, Crafts, and Constitutional Change', *Past and Present* 124 (1989), 3–35.

Nolan, Barbara, *Chaucer and the Tradition of the 'Roman Antique'*, Cambridge: Cambridge University Press, 1992.

Nolan, Maura, *John Lydgate and the Making of Public Culture*, Cambridge: Cambridge University Press, 2005.

The Norman Conquest of England: Sources and Documents, ed. R. Allen Brown, Woodbridge: Boydell, 1995 [first pubd 1984].

The Northern Homily Cycle, ed. Saara Nevanlinna, 3 parts, *Mémoires de la Société Néophilologique de Helsinki* 38 (1972), 41 (1973), 43 (1985).

The Northern Passion, ed. F. A. Foster, 2 vols, EETS o. s. 145 (1913) and 147 (1916).

An Old English Miscellany, ed. Richard Morris, EETS o. s. 49 (1872).

On the Recovery of the Throne by Edward IV, 2: 271–82 in *Political Poems and Songs Relating to English History from the Accession of Edw. III to that of Ric. III*, ed. Thomas Wright, 2 vols, Rolls Series 14, London, 1859.

Orme, Nicholas, *Medieval Schools from Roman Britain to Renaissance England*, New Haven, CT: Yale University Press, 2006.

The Owl and the Nightingale: Text and Translation, ed. Neil Cartlidge, Exeter: Exeter University Press, 2001.

The Owl and the Nightingale, ed. Eric Gerald Stanley, Manchester: Manchester University Press, 1960, rev. 1972.

The Oxford Dictionary of National Biography, 61 vols, ed. H. C. G. Matthew and Brian Howard Harrison, Oxford: Oxford University Press, 2004 [first pubd 1885–1901].

Paston Letters and Papers of the Fifteenth Century, 3 vols, ed. Norman Davis and (for vol. 3) Richard Beadle and Colin Richmond, EETS s. s. 20 (2004; first pubd 1971), 21 (2004; first pubd 1976), 22 (2005).

Patience, 139–65 in *Sir Gawain and the Green Knight, Pearl, Cleanness, Patience*, ed. J. J. Anderson, London: J. M. Dent and Sons, 1996.

Patterson, Annabel, *Censorship and Interpretation: The Conditions of Writing and Reading in Early Modern England*, Madison: University of Wisconsin Press, 1984.

Patterson, Lee, *Chaucer and the Subject of History*, Madison: University of Wisconsin Press, 1991.

——, 'Making Identities in Fifteenth-Century England: Henry V and John Lydgate', 69–105 in *New Historical Literary Studies*, ed. Jeffrey N. Cox and Larry T. Reynolds, Princeton, NJ: Princeton University Press, 1993.

——, '"What Man Artow?": Authorial Self-Definition in *The Tale of Sir Thopas* and *The Tale of Melibee*', *Studies in the Age of Chaucer* 11 (1989), 117–76.

Pearl, 3–47 in *Sir Gawain and the Green Knight, Pearl, Cleanness, Patience*, ed. J. J. Anderson, London: J. M. Dent and Sons, 1996.

Pearsall, Derek, *The Canterbury Tales*, London: George Allen & Unwin, 1985.

——, 'The English Romance in the Fifteenth Century', *Essays and Studies by Members of the English Association* 29 (1976), 56–83.

——, 'Hoccleve's *Regement of Princes*: The Poetics of Royal Self-Representation', *Speculum* 69 (1994), 386–410.

——, *John Lydgate*, Charlottesville: University of Virginia Press, 1970.

——, *Old English and Middle English Poetry*, London: Routledge & Kegan Paul, 1977.

——, 'The Origins of the Alliterative Revival', 1–24 in *The Alliterative Tradition in the Fourteenth Century*, ed. Bernard S. Levy and Paul E. Szarmach, Kent, OH: Kent State University Press, 1981.

——, 'Poverty and Poor People in *Piers Plowman*', 167–85 in *Medieval English Studies Presented to George Kane*, ed. Edward Donald Kennedy, Ronald Waldron and Joseph Wittig, Woodbridge: D. S. Brewer, 1988.

——, 'The Timelessness of *The Simonie*', 59–72 in *Individuality and Achievement in Middle English Poetry*, ed. O. S. Pickering, Cambridge: D. S. Brewer, 1997.

Pearsall, Derek and I. C. Cunningham, 'Introduction' to *The Auchinleck Manuscript, National Library of Scotland, Advocates' MS.19.2.1* (facsimile), London: Scolar Press, 1977.

The Peasants' Revolt of 1381, ed. R. B. Dobson, 2nd edn, London: Macmillan Press, 1983 [1st edn pubd 1970].

Perkins, Nicholas, *Hoccleve's Regiment of Princes: Counsel and Constraint*, Cambridge: D. S. Brewer, 2001.

Peterson, Clifford J., 'The *Pearl*-poet and John Massey of Cotton, Cheshire', *Review of English Studies*, n. s. 25 (1974), 257–66.

Pierce the Ploughman's Crede, 61–97 in *The Piers Plowman Tradition*, ed. Helen Barr, London: J. M. Dent, 1993.

Platt, Colin, *The English Medieval Town*, London: Secker & Warburg, 1976.

Plekhanov, Gyorgii, 'On Art for Art's Sake', 88–99 in *Marxism and Art: Writings in Aesthetics and Criticism*, ed. Berel Lang and Forrest Williams, New York: David McKay Company, 1972.

The Plowman's Tale, 51–114 in *Six Ecclesiastical Satires*, ed. James Dean, Kalamazoo, MI: Medieval Institute Publications, 1991.

The Poems of Laurence Minot, 1333–52, ed. Richard H. Osberg, Kalamazoo, MI: Medieval Institute Publications, 1996.

Poole, Austin Lane, *From Domesday Book to Magna Carta*, Oxford: Clarendon Press, 1955.

The Pricke of Conscience (Stimulus Conscientiae), ed. Richard Morris, Berlin: A. Asher, 1863.

'Prologue', 1–3 in *South English Legendary*, ed. Charlotte D'Evelyn and Anna J. Mill, 3 vols, EETS o. s. 235 (1956), 236 (1952), 244 (1959).

The Prologues and Epilogues of William Caxton, ed. W. J. B. Crotch, EETS o. s. 176 (1928).

The Proverbs of Alfred, ed. O. Arngart, Lund: C. W. K. Gleerup, 1955.

The Proverbs of Hendyng, 35–42 in *Specimens of Early English*, Part II, ed. R. Morris and W. W. Skeat, rev. edn, Oxford: Clarendon Press, 1872.

Punctuation Poem, II, 101 in *Secular Lyrics of the XIVth and XVth Centuries*, ed. Rossell Hope Robbins, Oxford: Clarendon Press, 1952.

Putter, Ad, *An Introduction to the Gawain-poet*, London: Longman, 1996.

Revard, Carter, 'Scribe and Provenance', 21–109 in *Studies in the Harley Manuscript*, ed. Susanna Fein, Kalamazoo, MI: Medieval Institute Publications, 2000.

Reynolds, Susan, *Fiefs and Vassals: The Medieval Evidence Reinterpreted*, Oxford: Oxford University Press, 1994.

——, *An Introduction to the History of English Medieval Towns*, Oxford: Clarendon Press, 1977.

Richard the Redeless, 101–33 in *The Piers Plowman Tradition*, ed. Helen Barr, London: J. M. Dent, 1993.

Riddy, Felicity, 'Contextualizing *Le Morte Darthur*: Empire and Civil War', 55–73 in *A Companion to Malory*, ed. Elizabeth Archibald and A. S. G. Edwards, Cambridge: D. S. Brewer, 1996.

The Riverside Chaucer, gen. ed. Larry D. Benson, Boston: Houghton Mifflin, 1987.

Robbins, Rossell Hope, 'On Dating a Middle English Moral Poem', *Modern Language Notes* 71 (1956), 473–6.

——, 'Dissent in Middle English Literature: The Spirit of (Thirteen) Seventy-Six', *Medievalia et Humanistica* 9 (1979), 25–51.

——, 'The Findern Anthology', *Publications of the Modern Language Association* 69 (1954), 610–42.

——, 'Middle English Poems of Protest', *Anglia* 78 (1960), 193–203.

Robert of Gloucester, *The Metrical Chronicle*, ed. William Aldis Wright, 2 vols, Rolls Series 86, London, 1857.

Robertson, D. W., Jr., 'Historical Criticism', 3–31 in *English Institute Essays, 1950*, ed. A. S. Downer, New York, 1951.

——, *A Preface to Chaucer: Studies in Medieval Perspectives*, Princeton, NJ: Princeton University Press, 1962.

Robin Hood and the Monk, 31–56 in *Robin Hood and Other Outlaw Tales*, ed. Stephen Knight and Thomas Ohlgren, Kalamazoo, MI: Medieval Institute Publications, 2000.

Robin Hood and the Potter, 57–79 in *Robin Hood and Other Outlaw Tales*, ed. Stephen Knight and Thomas Ohlgren, Kalamazoo, MI: Medieval Institute Publications, 2000.

Robinson, Neal, *Islam: A Concise Introduction*, London: Curzon, 1999.

Rolle, Richard, *Ego Dormio*, 60–72 in Rolle, *English Writings*, ed. Hope Emily Allen, Gloucester: Alan Sutton, 1988 [first pubd 1931].

——, *The Form of Living*, 82–119 in Rolle, *English Writings*, ed. Hope Emily Allen, Gloucester: Alan Sutton, 1988.

——, *Meditations on the Passion*, 17–36 in Rolle, *English Writings*, ed. Hope Emily Allen, Gloucester: Alan Sutton, 1988.

The Rule of Saint Benedict, ed. and trans. Justin McCann, London: Burns Oates, 1952.

'St Edmund the King', 2: 511–14 in *South English Legendary*, ed. Charlotte D'Evelyn and Anna J. Mill, 3 vols, EETS o. s. 235 (1956), 236 (1952), 244 (1959).

Saint Erkenwald, ed. Clifford Peterson, Philadelphia: University of Pennsylvania Press, 1977.

'St Kenelm', 1: 279–91 in *South English Legendary*, ed. Charlotte D'Evelyn and Anna J. Mill, 3 vols, EETS o. s. 235 (1956), 236 (1952), 244 (1959).

'St Thomas Becket', 2: 610–92 in *South English Legendary*, ed. Charlotte D'Evelyn and Anna J. Mill, 3 vols, EETS o. s. 235 (1956), 236 (1952), 244 (1959).

Salter, Elizabeth, 'Alliterative Modes and Affiliations in the Fourteenth Century', *Neuphilologische Mitteilungen* 79 (1978), 25–35.

——, *Fourteenth-Century English Poetry*, Oxford: Oxford University Press, 1983.

——, '*Piers Plowman* and *The Simonie*', *Archiv* 203 (1967), 241–54.

Samuels, M. L., 'Langland's Dialect', *Medium Ævum* 54 (1985), 232–47.

Satire on the Consistory Courts, 24–7 in *Historical Poems of the XIVth and XVth Centuries*, ed. Robbins.

Satire on the Retinues of the Great, 27–9 in *Historical Poems of the XIVth and XVth Centuries*, ed. Rossell Hope Robbins, New York: Columbia University Press, 1959.

Saul, Nigel, *Richard II*, New Haven, CT: Yale University Press, 1997.

Scase, Wendy, *Reginald Pecock*, Vol. 3 of *English Writers of the Late Middle Ages*, ed. M. C. Seymour, Aldershot: Variorum, 1996.

——, ' "Strange and Wonderful Bills": Bill-Casting and Political Discourse in Late Medieval England', *New Medieval Literatures* 8 (1998), 225–47.

Scattergood, V. J., *Politics and Poetry in the Fifteenth Century*, London: Blandford Press, 1971.

——, 'Authority and Resistance: The Political Verse', 163–201 in *Studies in the Harley Manuscript*, ed. Susanna Fein, Kalamazoo, MI: Medieval Institute Publications, 2000.

Schlauch, Margaret, *English Medieval Literature and its Social Foundations*, Warsaw: Państwowe Wydawnictwo Naukowe, 1956.

Schleusener, Jay, '*The Owl and the Nightingale*: A Matter of Judgment', *Modern Philology* 70 (1972–3), 185–9.

'The Second Shepherds' Play', 265–94 in *English Mystery Plays: A Selection*, ed. Peter Happé, London: Penguin, 1975.

Secretum Secretorum: Nine English Versions, ed. M. A. Manzalaoui, EETS o. s. 276 (1977).

Secular Lyrics of the XIVth and XVth Centuries, ed. Rossell Hope Robbins, Oxford: Clarendon Press, 1952.

Selections from English Wycliffite Writings, ed. Anne Hudson, Toronto: University of Toronto Press, 1997 [first pubd 1978].

Shepherd, Geoffrey, 'Poverty in *Piers Plowman*', 169–89 in *Social Relations and Ideas: Essays in Honour of R. H. Hilton*, ed. T. H. Aston, P. R. Coss, Christopher Dyer and Joan Thirsk, Cambridge: Cambridge University Press, 1983.

——, 'Early Middle English', 81–117 in *The Middle Ages*, ed. W. F. Bolton, London: Sphere, 1970.

The Simonie, 193–212 in *Medieval English Political Writings*, ed. James M. Dean, Kalamazoo, MI: Medieval Institute Publications, 1996.

Simpson, James, ' "After Craftes Conseil Clotheth Yow and Fede": Langland and London City Politics', 109–27 in *England in the Fourteenth Century*, ed. Nicholas Rogers, Stamford: Paul Watkins, 1993.

——, *Piers Plowman: An Introduction to the B-text*, London: Longman, 1990.

——, *Reform and Cultural Revolution: 1350–1547*, Oxford: Oxford University Press, 2002.

——, *Sciences and the Self in Medieval Poetry: Alan of Lille's* Anticlaudianus *and John Gower's* Confessio Amantis, Cambridge: Cambridge University Press, 1995.

——, 'The Constraints of Satire in *Piers Plowman* and *Mum and the Sothsegger*', 11–31 in *Langland, the Mystics, and the Medieval English Religious Tradition: Essays in Honour of S. S. Hussey*, ed. Helen Phillips, Cambridge: Cambridge University Press, 1990.

——, 'Ethics and Interpretation: Reading Wills in Chaucer's *Legend of Good Women*', *Studies in the Age of Chaucer* 20 (1998), 73–100.

Sir Gawain and the Green Knight, 167–277 in *Sir Gawain and the Green Knight, Pearl, Cleanness, Patience*, ed. J. J. Anderson, London: J. M. Dent and Sons, 1996.

Sir Orfeo, 185–200 in *Middle English Verse Romances*, ed. Donald Sands, Exeter: University of Exeter Press, 1986.

Skelton, John, *Collyn Clout*, 246–78 in *The Complete English Poems*, ed. John Scattergood, Harmondsworth: Penguin, 1983.

——, *Garlande or Chapelet of Laurell*, 312–58 in *The Complete English Poems*, ed. John Scattergood, Harmondsworth: Penguin, 1983.

——, *Magnyfycence*, 140–214 in *The Complete English Poems*, ed. John Scattergood, Harmondsworth: Penguin, 1983.

Smith, D. Vance, *The Arts of Possession: The Medieval Household Imaginary*, Minneapolis: University of Minnesota Press, 2003.

Song of the Husbandman, 251–3 in *Medieval English Political Writings*, ed. James M. Dean, Kalamazoo, MI: Medieval Institute Publications, 1996.

A Song of Lewes, 131–2 in *English Lyrics of the XIIIth Century*, ed. Carleton Brown, Oxford: Clarendon Press, 1932.

The South English Legendary, ed. Charlotte D'Evelyn and Anna J. Mill, 3 vols, EETS o. s. 235 (1956), 236 (1952), 244 (1959).

Southern, R. W., *The Making of the Middle Ages*, London: Random Century, 1987 [first pubd 1953].

The Southern Passion, ed. Beatrice Daw Brown, EETS o. s. 169 (1927).

Spearing, A. C., *Medieval to Renaissance in English Poetry*, Cambridge: Cambridge University Press, 1985.

Sponsler, Claire, *Drama and Resistance: Bodies, Goods and Theatricality in Late Medieval England*, Minneapolis: University of Minnesota Press, 1997.

The Stacions of Rome, 143–73 in *Political, Religious and Love Poems*, ed. F. J. Furnivall, EETS o. s. 15 (1866).

Stans Puer ad Mensam, 5–10 in Jonathan Nicholls, 'A Courtesy Poem from Magdalene College, Cambridge, Pepys MS 1236', *Notes and Queries* 227 (1982), 3–10.

Starkey, David, 'The Age of the Household: Politics, Society and the Arts', 225–90 in *The Later Middle Ages*, ed. Stephen Medcalf, London: Methuen, 1981.

Statius, ed. and trans. J. H. Mozley, London: Heinemann, 1961.

Statutes of the Realm, ed. T. E. Tolmins et al., 11 vols, London: Dawsons, 1810–28; repr. 1963.

Steiner, Emily, *Documentary Culture and the Making of Medieval English Literature*, Cambridge: Cambridge University Press, 2003.

Stephenson, Carl, *Mediaeval Feudalism*, Ithaca, NY: Cornell University Press, 1942.

Stevens, John, *Music and Poetry in the Early Tudor Court*, Cambridge: Cambridge University Press, 1979 [first pubd 1961].

Stevens, Martin, *Four Middle English Mystery Cycles: Textual, Contextual and Critical Interpretations*, Princeton, NJ: Princeton University Press, 1987.

Stock, Brian, 'Science, Technology, and Economic Progress in the Early Middle Ages', 1–51 in *Science in the Middle Ages*, ed. David C. Lindberg, Chicago: University of Chicago Press, 1978.

Strauss, Leo, *Persecution and the Art of Writing*, Chicago: University of Chicago Press, 1988 [first pubd 1952].

Strohm, Paul, *England's Empty Throne: Usurpation and the Language of Legitimation, 1399–1422*, New Haven, CT: Yale University Press, 1998.

——, 'The Origin and Meaning of Middle English *Romaunce*', *Genre* 10 (1977), 1–28.

——, *Politique: Languages of Statecraft between Chaucer and Shakespeare*, Notre Dame, IN: University of Notre Dame Press, 2005.

——, 'Politics and Poetics: Usk and Chaucer in the 1380s', 83–112 in *Literary Practice and Social Change in Britain, 1380–1530*, ed. Lee Patterson, Berkeley: University of California Press, 1990.

Ten Latin Schooltexts of the Later Middle Ages: Translated Selections, trans. Ian Thomson and Louis Perraud, Lewiston, NY: Mellen, 1990.

The Testimony of William Thorpe, 24–93 in *Two Wycliffite Texts*, ed. Anne Hudson, EETS o. s. 301 (1993).

Theophilus, *De Diversis Artibus* [*The Various Arts*], ed. and trans. C. R. Dodwell, Oxford: Clarendon Press, 1961.

Thompson, John J., *The Cursor Mundi: Poem, Texts and Contexts*, MÆ Monographs 19, Oxford: Society for the Study of Medieval Languages and Literature, 1998.

Thrupp, Sylvia, 'The City as the Idea of Social Order', 80–100 in *Society and History: Essays by Sylvia Thrupp*, ed. Raymond Grew and Nicholas H. Steneck, Ann Arbor: University of Michigan Press, 1977.

Tillyard, E. M. W., *Poetry Direct and Oblique*, rev. edn, London: Chatto & Windus, 1945 [first pubd 1934].

Tolkien, J. R. R., '*Ancrene Wisse* and *Hali Meiðhad*', *Essays and Studies* 14 (1929), 104–206.

Topsfield, Leslie T., *Troubadours and Love*, Cambridge: Cambridge University Press, 1975.

A Trade Policy, 168–73 in *Historical Poems of the XIVth and XVth Centuries*, ed. Rossell Hope Robbins, New York: Columbia University Press, 1959.

The Troubadours: An Introduction, ed. Simon Gaunt and Sarah Kay, Cambridge: Cambridge University Press, 1999.

Turville-Petre, Thorlac, *The Alliterative Revival*, Cambridge: D. S. Brewer, 1977.

——, 'Politics and Poetry in the Early Fourteenth Century', *Review of English Studies*, n. s. 39 (1988), 1–28.

Two Fifteenth-Century Cookery Books, ed. Thomas Austin, EETS o. s. 91 (1888).

Two of the Saxon Chronicles Parallel (with supplementary extracts from the others), ed. John Earle, rev. Charles Plummer, 2 vols, Oxford: Oxford University Press, 1892–9.

Two Wycliffite Texts, ed. Anne Hudson, EETS o. s. 301 (1993).

Twycross, Meg, 'The Theatricality of Medieval English Plays', 37–84 in *Cambridge Companion to Medieval English Theatre*, ed. Richard Beadle, Cambridge: Cambridge University Press, 1994.

Upland's Rejoinder, 204–15 in *Six Ecclesiastical Satires*, ed. James Dean, Kalamazoo, MI: Medieval Institute Publications, 1991.

Usk, Thomas, *The Testament of Love*, ed. R. Allen Shoaf, Kalamazoo, MI: Medieval Institute Publications, 1998.

——, *The Testament of Love*, 7: 1–145 in *The Complete Works of Geoffrey Chaucer*, ed. W. W. Skeat, Oxford: Clarendon Press, 1897–1926.

Virgil, *Aeneid*, 261–597 in *Eclogues, Georgics, Aeneid, 1–6*, ed. and trans. H. Ruston Fairclough, rev. G. P. Goold, Cambridge, MA: Harvard University Press, 1999 [first pubd 1916].

Volosinov, V. N., 'Concerning the Relationship of the Basis and Superstructures', 60–8 in *Marxist Literary Theory: A Reader*, ed. Terry Eagleton and Drew Milne, Oxford: Blackwell, 1996.

Wallace, David, *Chaucerian Polity: Absolutist Lineages and Associational Forms in England and Italy*, Stanford, CA: Stanford University Press, 1997.

——, 'Chaucer's Italian Inheritance', 36–57 in *Cambridge Companion to Chaucer*, ed. Jill Mann and Piero Boitani, 2nd edn, Cambridge: Cambridge University Press, 2003.

Walsingham, Thomas, *Historia Anglicana*, ed. Henry Thomas Riley, 2 vols, Rolls Series 28, London, 1863–4.

Watson, Nicholas, 'Censorship and Cultural Change in Late-Medieval England: Vernacular Theology, the Oxford Translation Debate, and Arundel's Constitutions of 1409', *Speculum* 70 (1995), 822–64.

——, 'Middle English Mystics', 539–65 in *Cambridge History of Medieval English Literature*, ed. David Wallace, Cambridge: Cambridge University Press, 1999.

Webb, Diana, *Pilgrimage in Medieval England*, London: Hambledon, 2000.

Weber, Max, 'The Profession and Vocation of Politics', 309–69 in *Political Writings*, ed. Peter Lassman and Ronald Speirs, Cambridge: Cambridge University Press, 1994.

Wenzel, Siegfried, *Preachers, Poets, and the Early English Lyric*, Princeton, NJ: Princeton University Press, 1986.

White, Lynn, Jr., 'Cultural Climates and Technological Advance', 217–53 in his *Medieval Religion and Technology: Collected Essays*, Berkeley: University of California Press, 1978.

——, 'Dynamo and Virgin Reconsidered', 57–73 in *Machina ex Deo: Essays in the Dynamism of Western Culture*, Cambridge, MA: MIT Press, 1968.

——, 'Eilmer of Malmesbury, an Eleventh Century Aviator', 59–73 in his *Medieval Religion and Technology: Collected Essays*, Berkeley: University of California Press, 1978.

——, 'The Iconography of *Temperantia* and the Virtuousness of Technology', 181–204 in his *Medieval Religion and Technology: Collected Essays*, Berkeley: University of California Press, 1978.

——, *Medieval Technology and Social Change*, Oxford: Oxford University Press, 1962.

William of Malmesbury, *Gesta Regum Anglorum*, 2 vols, ed. and trans. R. A. B. Mynors, completed R. M. Thomson and M. Winterbottom, Oxford: Clarendon Press, 1998–9.

William of Poitiers, *Histoire de Guillaume le Conquérant*, ed. Raymonde Foreville, Paris: Belles Lettres, 1952.

Williams, Raymond, 'Base and Superstructure in Marxist Cultural Theory', in his *Problems in Materialism and Culture*, London: Verso, 1997 [first pubd 1980].

——, *Culture and Society: Coleridge to Orwell*, London: Hogarth Press, 1993 [first pubd 1958].

——, *Keywords: A Vocabulary of Culture and Society*, London: Fontana Press, 1976.

——, *The Long Revolution*, London: Chatto & Windus, 1961.

——, *Marxism and Literature*, Oxford: Oxford University Press, 1977.

Windeatt, Barry, *Troilus and Criseyde*, Oxford: Oxford University Press, 1992.

Woolf, Rosemary, 'Chaucer as Satirist in the *General Prologue* to the *Canterbury Tales*', *Critical Quarterly* 1 (1959), 150–7.

——, 'The Theme of Christ the Lover-Knight in Medieval English Literature', *Review of English Studies*, n. s. 13 (1962), 1–16.

Women Defamed and Women Defended, ed. Alcuin Blamires, Oxford: Oxford University Press, 1992.

Wynnere and Wastoure, ed. Stephanie Trigg, EETS o. s. 297 (1990).

The Yale Companion to Chaucer, ed. Seth Lerer, New Haven, CT: Yale University Press, 2006.

The York Plays, ed. Richard Beadle, London: Edward Arnold, 1982.

Ywain and Gawain, ed. A. B. Friedman and N. T. Harrington, EETS o. s. 254 (1964).

Zacher, Christian, *Curiosity and Pilgrimage: The Literature of Discovery in Fourteenth-Century England*, Baltimore: Johns Hopkins University Press, 1976.

Index

Lightning Source UK Ltd.
Milton Keynes UK
UKHW022030041120
372787UK00007B/334